CLAIT 1

SUE PRICE

In easy steps is an imprint of Computer Step
Southfield Road . Southam
Warwickshire CV47 0FB . England

http://www.ineasysteps.com

Endorsed by OCR for use with the OCR Level 2 Certificate for IT Users (CLAIT Plus)

Copyright © 2003 by Computer Step. All rights reserved. No part of this book may be reproduced or transmitted in any form or by any means, electronic or mechanical, including photocopying, recording, or by any information storage or retrieval system, without prior written permission from the publisher.

Notice of Liability

Every effort has been made to ensure that this book contains accurate and current information. However, Computer Step and the author shall not be liable for any loss or damage suffered by readers as a result of any information contained herein.

Trademarks

Microsoft® and Windows® are registered trademarks of Microsoft Corporation. All other trademarks are acknowledged as belonging to their respective companies.

Printed and bound in the United Kingdom

ISBN 1-84078-252-8

Contents

1   Create, Manage and Integrate Files   9

The CLAIT suite	10
Unit One overview	12
View folders	14
Navigate the folders	16
Folder commands	17
Identify files	18
Manage files	20
Locate files	22
Print folder contents	23
Open and save	24
Headers and footers	25
Page numbers	27
Edit the document	28
Tables	29
Tabs	32
Bullets and numbering	33
Insert an image	34
Insert a chart	35
Insert a data file	36
Insert a symbol	37
Styles	38
Templates	40
Document management	41
Checklist	42

2   Spreadsheets   43

Spreadsheets	44
Open with, save as	45
Columns and rows	46
Text alignment	47
Cell references	48
Formula	52

Functions	54
Sort	60
Number format	61
Borders and shading	62
Document management	63
Headers and footers	64
Print	66
Checklist	68

3 Databases — 69

Databases	70
Create a database	71
Table design	72
Create a table	73
Save the table	75
Amend the design	76
Import data	77
Queries	82
Calculated field	84
Forms	85
Create labels	86
Report with summary	88
Report design	90
Report controls	92
Checklist	94

4 Desktop Publishing — 95

Desktop Publishing	96
Useful terms	97
Set the paper layout	98
The Master page	100
Create styles	102
Save, apply and modify styles	105
Save template	106
Text frame layout	107
Create a multipage layout	109

Link text boxes	110
Text box options	112
Text features	114
Tables	115
Image control	116
Copyfit	118
Printing	119
Checklist	122

5 Presentation Graphics — 123

Presentation Graphics	124
Getting started	125
The Slide Master	126
Create the slides	129
Organise the slides	130
Create a hyperlink	132
Tables	133
Charts	134
Organisation chart	136
Transitions	137
Animation effects	138
Timings	140
The Slide Show	141
Speaker notes	142
Print screen	143
Print	145
Checklist	146

6 Computer Art — 147

Computer Art	148
The software	149
Building the art work	151
Create the canvas	152
Insert images	153
Layer images	154
Working with layers	155

Edit and retouch tools	156
Tool and colour options	157
Coloured area selection	158
Text	159
Shapes	160
Deformation	161
Text effects	162
Print	163
Animation	165
Final frames	167
Animation Shop	168
Run the animation	169
Checklist	170

7 Web Pages 171

Web Pages	172
HTML	173
HTML code	174
Meta-variable tags	175
FrontPage	176
Download files	177
Create the web folder	178
Import the files	179
Create a template	180
Create Meta tags	182
Navigation table	183
Font formats and styles	185
Save the template	186
Insert text	188
Insert and format image	190
Tables	191
Forms	192
Feedback and hyperlinks	195
Checklist	196

8 Electronic Communications — 197

Electronic Communications	198
Microsoft Outlook	199
The Outlook window	200
Contacts	202
Distribution lists	204
The Calendar	206
Customise the Calendar	207
Create appointments	208
E-mail	210
Rules	212
Attachments	214
Create and send e-mail	215
Add a signature	216
Send options	217
Tasks	218
Notes and reminders	219
Print	220
Checklist	222

9 Graphs and Charts — 223

Graphs and Charts	224
Standard and Custom charts	225
The chart wizard	226
Chart elements	228
Chart toolbar	229
Bar/column chart	230
Format axes	231
Stacked vertical bar	232
XY scatter	233
Trend line	234
Exploded pie	235
XY scatter showing relationship	236
Line column	237
Update the data	238
Print	239
Checklist	240

10-16 CLAIT Plus Solutions — 241

Projects for Solutions	242
Spreadsheet Solutions	243
Database Solutions	245
Desktop Publishing Solutions	248
Presentation Graphics Solutions	251
Digital Imaging Solutions	253
Web Animation Solutions	256
Web Page Solutions	260

17-21 Microsoft Office Specialist — 263

OCR and Microsoft certification	264
Word Processing	266
Spreadsheets	269
Databases	272
Presentation Graphics	274
Electronic Communications	275
Exam practice	276

Appendix Support Material — 277

Selecting units	278
Practice e-mail	280
Downloadable exercises	281
Information sources	282

Index — 283

Create, Manage and Integrate Files

Unit One

This unit is mandatory if you wish to achieve the CLAIT Plus certificate. The unit covers file organisation and management, creating and using house styles, document editing and the integration of data from a variety of sources.

Covers

The CLAIT suite | 10

Unit One overview | 12

Folders | 14

Files | 18

Print folder contents | 23

Open and save | 24

Headers and footers | 25

Edit the document | 28

Tables | 29

Tabs | 32

Bullets and numbering | 33

Insert data files | 34

Styles | 38

Templates | 40

Document management | 41

Checklist | 42

The CLAIT suite

The CLAIT suite of courses has been developed by OCR to recognise and encourage the development of computing skills in the workplace.

New CLAIT

New CLAIT is the first level and requires a basic understanding of computer functions, applications and facilities. To gain certification for New CLAIT you must pass the core unit and at least four other units out of a choice of fourteen. However, for a solid grounding and understanding of basic functions, it is a good idea to have undertaken more of the New CLAIT units before progressing to the next level.

New CLAIT is the entry level course, and it is expected, but not required, that you will have completed a New CLAIT course before you start CLAIT Plus.

CLAIT Plus

The CLAIT Plus course is an intermediate or second level course and comparable to NVQs at Level 2 or GNVQs at Intermediate level. The syllabus covers a wide range of computing applications, as shown in the table below:

Unit 1	Create, Manage and Integrate files - Mandatory
Unit 2	Spreadsheets
Unit 3	Databases
Unit 4	Desktop Publishing
Unit 5	Presentation Graphics
Unit 6	Computer Art
Unit 7	Web Page Creation
Unit 8	Electronic Communication
Unit 9	Graphs and Charts
Unit 10	Spreadsheet Solutions
Unit 11	Database Solutions
Unit 12	Desktop Publishing Solutions
Unit 13	Presentations Graphics Solutions
Unit 14	Digital Imaging Solutions
Unit 15	Web Animation Solutions
Unit 16	Web Page Solutions
Unit 17	Word Processing - MOS Word Core
Unit 18	Spreadsheets - MOS Excel Core
Unit 19	Databases - MOS Access Core
Unit 20	Presentation Graphics - MOS PowerPoint Core/Comprehensive
Unit 21	Electronic Communications - MOS Outlook Core

MOS stands for Microsoft Office Specialist.

...cont'd

See page 12 for an overview of the Unit 1 content and objectives.

CLAIT Plus assessment

Unit 1, Create, Manage and Integrate Files is mandatory for the full award. You must take this core unit plus three others.

Unit 1-9 are assessed by OCR set assignments.

For Units 10 - 16, the Solution approach, assessment is by a locally set assignment which may take advantage of workplace experience. An Evidence Checklist must be completed for each of the Solutions. The checklist itemises the minimum standard that must be achieved by the submitted Solution.

Units 17-21 are Microsoft Office Specialist units and are assessed on-line.

See page 278 for a table showing how you can combine assignment, Solution and MOS units to achieve the CLAIT Plus Certificate.

All units are weighted the same, but you cannot take a combination of units which overlap. For example, you cannot combine Unit 2 Spreadsheets with Unit 10 Spreadsheet solutions.

CLAIT Advanced

CLAIT Advanced is a Level 3 course, and is comparable to an NVQ at Level 3, an Advanced Level VCE or an 'A' Level GCE. It is designed to develop and accredit those working at an advanced computing level: installing hardware and software, managing complex filing structures, designing and applying software solutions and supporting other computer users.

Is CLAIT Plus the right course for me?

CLAIT Plus is intended for those students who have undertaken a New CLAIT or equivalent course, or for those who work with computers on a regular basis and already possess basic IT skills.

Many CLAIT authorised centres offer advice and guidance if you are unsure of which course, or which level course to take.

The recommended learning time for each unit is 30 hours; full-time or part-time study is suitable. It would be helpful to have regular access to a computer, at home or work.

The units may also be taken and certificated individually, and in any order. This flexibility of approach would allow you to develop skills in areas which may be of interest or of value at work. You can choose units that will enhance and provide depth to your existing skills, or topics that will extend your abilities into other areas.

Unit One overview

This unit follows a complete integration exercise. The exercise and supporting data files can be downloaded from the In Easy Steps web site (see page 281).

Unit One - Create, Manage and Integrate Files - is the core unit of CLAIT Plus. It covers the following areas:

1 File management. You will be expected to use the operating system's facilities to access files; to create and manage folders; and to move, copy and delete files and folders.

2 Document management. You will learn how to create and apply a house style to format text consistently; and to manage document layout and presentation.

3 Document editing. You will be required to understand editing terms; to edit and amend a supplied document; to proof read and use tools such as a spell check facility; to insert special symbols; and to select and enter data from other sources.

Check the MOS Unit 17 for other word processing topics.

4 Integration. You will be provided with information in other file formats such as spreadsheet, graph or database file. You will learn how to import and present the data from these files.

5 Printed output. You will be required to provide screen prints to illustrate the file management requirements. You will also need to provide the required printouts of the integrated document.

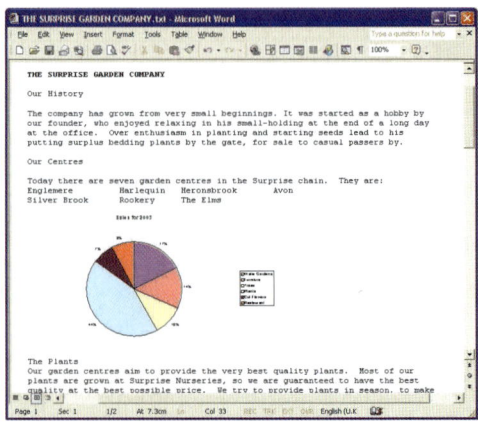

12 | CLAIT Plus in easy steps

...cont'd

In CLAIT Plus you will be presented with an exercise which requires you to demonstrate knowledge of all elements of the unit syllabus. The exercise is usually a 'workplace' scenario, with data files and documentation supplied. You will need to make sure that you have all the required documentation and access to the source files.

Exercise files and documentation

Before you start any exercise, take a moment to read through the documentation.

Use binders to organise your material, so that you don't lose any!

1. You will be given a text file which is the main draft document. You will use this file as the basis of the exercise.

2. You will also be given data and image files for integrating into the main document. These may be .xls, .csv and .gif file formats.

3. The supplied documents should include a house style sheet, which sets out in detail requirements such as font sizes, styles and alignment.

4. You will also be given an annotated copy of the draft document which indicates editing changes and where to insert images.

5. You should also receive some extra printed information, in the form of data sheets. You will be expected to select information from this data to include in the main document.

The software

In this unit we will be using Windows XP for the file management element of the exercise. Word 2002, part of Office XP, is used for editing the document and integration.

Any substantial differences between versions of the software used will be highlighted, and alternative methods suggested.

View folders

There are usually several ways to perform any activity using Microsoft Windows and Office. In this book we illustrate one of the ways, and include alternatives where appropriate.

At the start of Unit 1 you will be supplied with the files needed to complete an exercise. You will need to locate those files and follow the instructions to create a folder, and copy the files into the folder.

Windows Explorer is the program to use for managing folders and files on your PC. It shows the organisation of folders in a tree-like structure. It allows you to create, move and delete folders, and to copy, move and delete files.

1 To use Windows Explorer select Start, All Programs, Accessories, Windows Explorer.

2 The window that opens will be divided into two panes. The left pane shows the overall organisation of the drives and folders on the hard disk. The right pane shows folders and files stored within the location selected in the left pane, in this case the main C: drive.

Click on the + symbol next to a disk drive or folder to expand the list and see nested levels. Click on the – to contract the list.

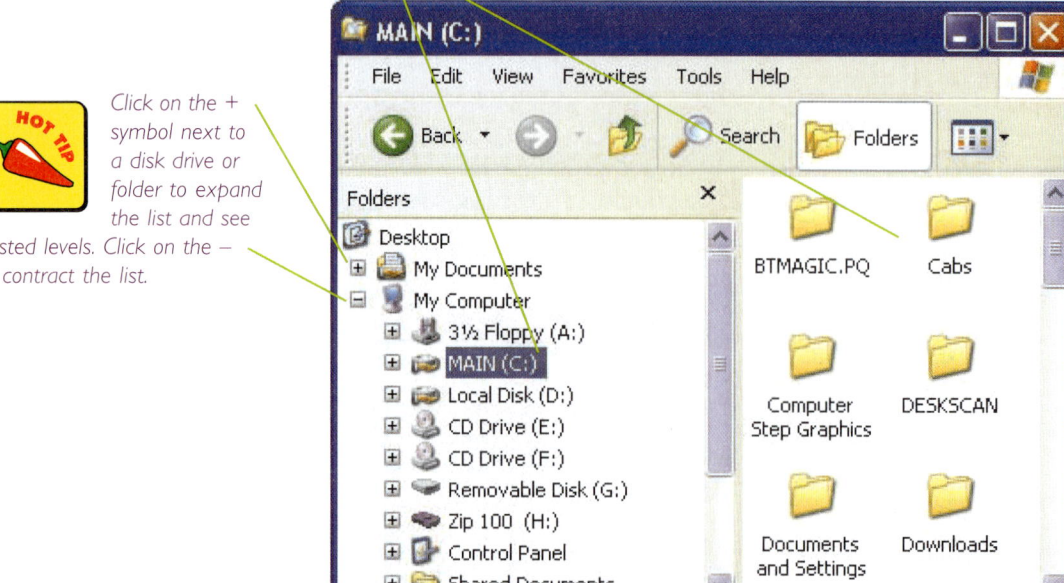

14 | CLAIT Plus in easy steps

...cont'd

The options offered in the Task pane are available through the Menu bar in previous versions of Windows.

As an alternative to using Explorer, you can double click My Computer on the Desktop.

1. The window will show the main drives and folders. The left pane shows the Task pane, a Windows XP feature. Double click the main C: drive to view the contents.

The Task pane changes according to context, and will only offer actions that are possible at that point.,

Click on the arrows to expand or contract the list of actions.

2. Click on the Folders icon to see the Folders pane. Click again, or select the close button to return to the System Tasks pane. When you select the Folders icon, the window will look the same as shown in the Explorer window on the opposite page.

1. Create, Manage and Integrate Files | 15

Navigate the folders

In Explorer it is easy to move from one folder to another and to view the contents of each. Select the drive or folder in the left pane, and its contents will be displayed in the right pane.

 *It is possible to move (drag and drop) folders in Explorer inadvertently, so be careful with the mouse.*

You can also navigate the folders by using the Standard toolbar.

 *Select View, Standard toolbar (if it is not already enabled).*

1 The Back and Forward buttons allow you to retrace your steps quickly. You can also select from a list of previous folders.

2 The Up button opens the parent folder.

3 History shows the activities of the last two weeks and lists sites visited, local and Internet.

16 | CLAIT Plus in easy steps

Folder commands

Folders, with their contents, can be copied and moved using the same commands and in the same way as files. See page 20-21 for more details.

1. To create a folder, open Windows Explorer. Select the drive and folder in which to make your new folder. Note that the Title bar shows the name of the selected folder.

2. From the Menu, select File, New, Folder.

3. The folder will appear with the New Folder name, highlighted in blue. Simply type the required folder name and press Enter.

4. To rename the folder, make sure it is selected. Then click with the right mouse button and select Rename.

You can delete a folder using the Delete key on the keyboard.

5. To delete the folder, select Delete. The folder and its contents will be removed to the Recycle Bin.

1. Create, Manage and Integrate Files | 17

Identify files

You will be given source or data files for the units you decide to take for the course. The files will be different types, appropriate to the data they contain, and to the application in which you are working. Windows provides various ways to identify the type.

furniture.doc	Word
sg company.txt	Text
centre sales.xls	Excel
shrubs.csv	Excel/ Access
Attic Book List.mdb	Access
Surprise Gardens.pub	Publisher
Demo.ppt	PowerPoint
sample.htm	FrontPage
SC pic2.jpg	Image
boat.gif	Image
pc.bmp	Paint

1 On the left are the standard file icons that would be shown in the right hand pane of the Explorer window. In most cases the icon identifies the file type.

2 For applications such as Word, Excel, PowerPoint etc. the data file type is associated with the particular application. When you double click the file, it will open in that program. Plain text and image files will open in different programs, according to the way your software is installed.

3 In the examples illustrated, the three letter file extension, which also identifies the file type, is shown. To reveal the three letter file extension on your own system, in the Explorer window select Tools, Folder Options.

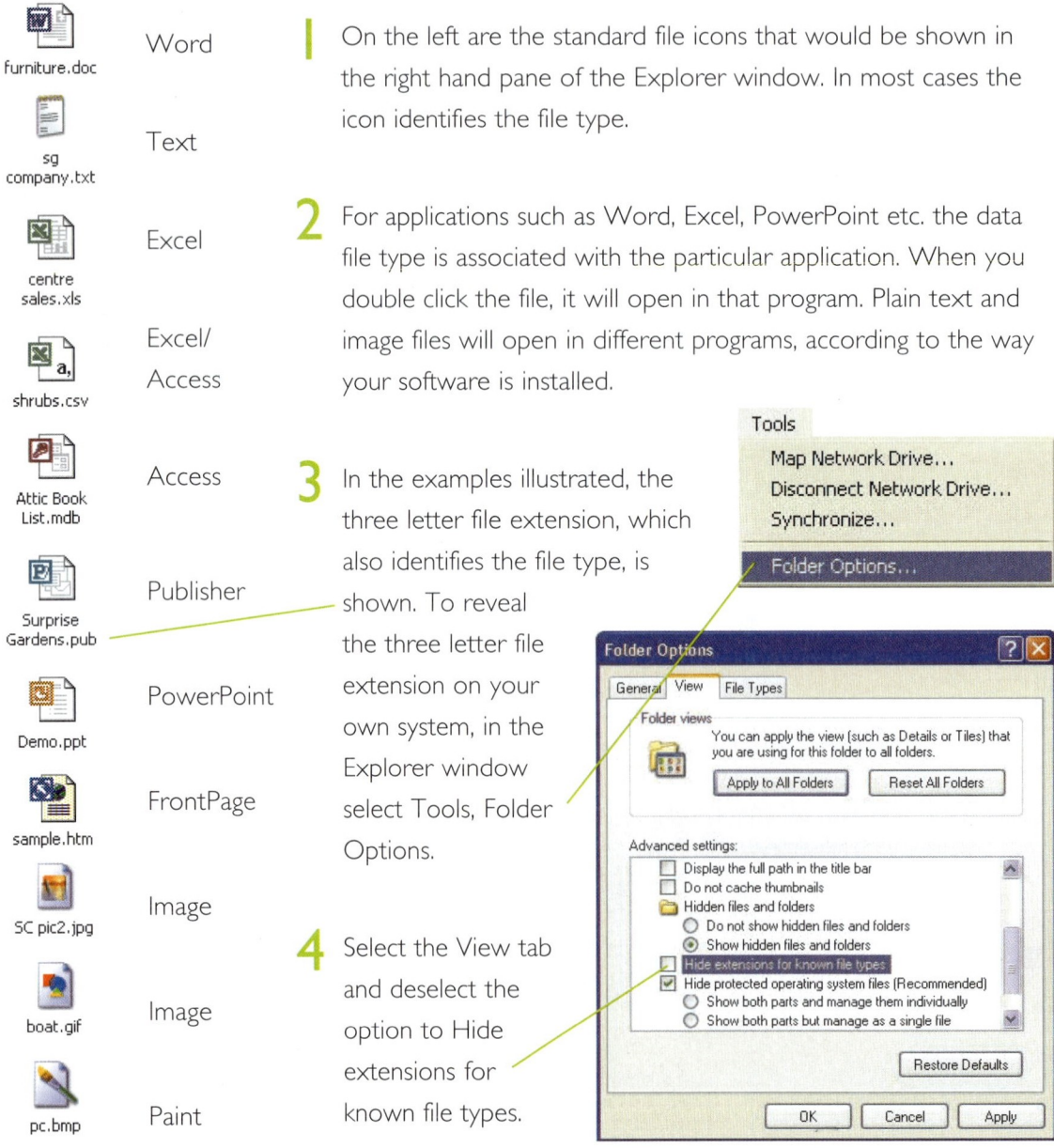

4 Select the View tab and deselect the option to Hide extensions for known file types.

...cont'd

Revealing file extensions and changing the Explorer view can be very useful but are not required by CLAIT Plus. You may only be given the first part of the file name for the required source files.

You can change the way files are shown in the Explorer window, to give more information about the files.

1 Select View from the Menu bar, or click the down arrow on the Views button.
Thumbnails will show miniature versions of any image files in the folder, very useful for folders containing photographs.

2 Select List to display the contents of folders that contain a large number of files. This lets you see the maximum possible.

3 Select Details to see the file size, type, date and time of modification. You can widen the columns to display truncated details, the same way as in spreadsheets. Move the mouse arrow to the line between the column headings and drag sideways.

Initially the files will be shown in alphabetical order, with any nested folders listed first. Click on Name in the column heading to reverse the order. Click on Type in the column heading to group like files together. Click on Date Modified to arrange by date.

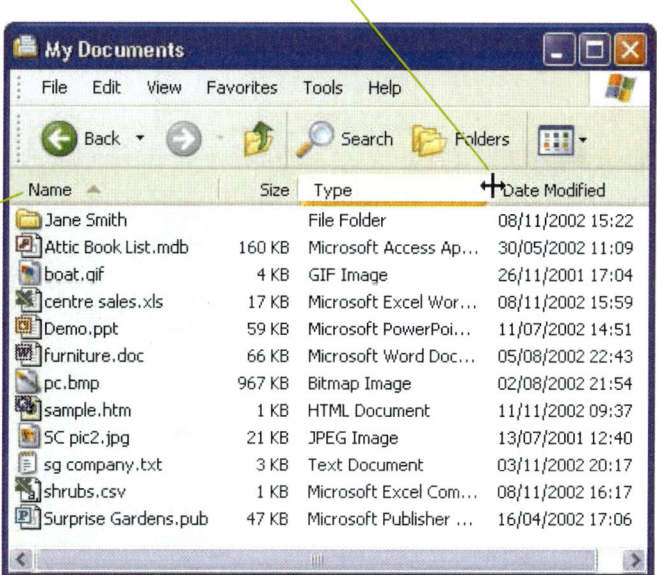

1. Create, Manage and Integrate Files | 19

Manage files

Selecting files

For multiple files it's a good idea to switch to the List or Details view in Explorer, as this allows you to see more files at one time.

1 Open Windows Explorer. In the left pane select, and open if necessary, the folder that contains the required file or files.

2 For a single file, just click on the file in the right pane. You may need to scroll the window to see the file.

3 For a list of adjacent files, select the first in the list, hold down the Shift key and select the last in the list. For randomly spaced files, hold down the Ctrl key as you select, click again to deselect.

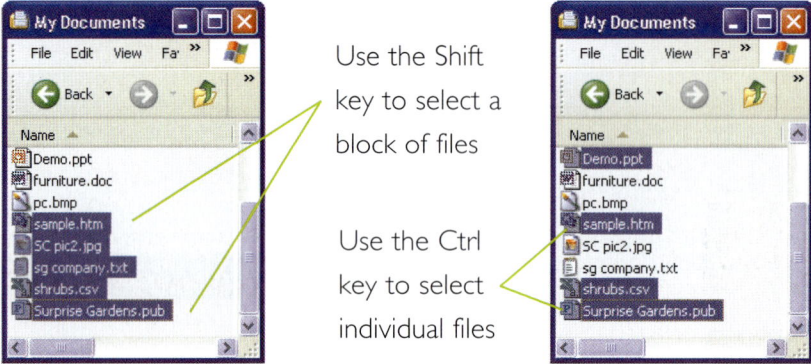

Use the Shift key to select a block of files

Use the Ctrl key to select individual files

Select View, Toolbars, Customise to add the Cut, Copy and Paste buttons to the Explorer toolbar. You can then use these shortcuts instead of the menu.

Copying files

Windows offers various ways to copy files. Each method has its advantages, but for copying multiple files it is easiest to use the method below.

1 With the file(s) selected, click on Edit, Copy from the Menu.

2 In the left pane of the Explorer window, locate and select the destination folder and select Edit Paste.

...cont'd

If you drag and drop files or folders on the same drive, they will be moved, not copied.

To copy files between different drives, for example A: drive to C: drive, you can use drag and drop. This method is best used for copying one object such as a single file or a complete folder.

If you make a mistake, or something unexpected happens, you can select Edit, Undo move/copy.

3 Select the file in the right pane. Move the cursor with the attached file until the desired location is highlighted in the left (folder) pane. Then release the mouse button. Always check to see that the action has completed successfully.

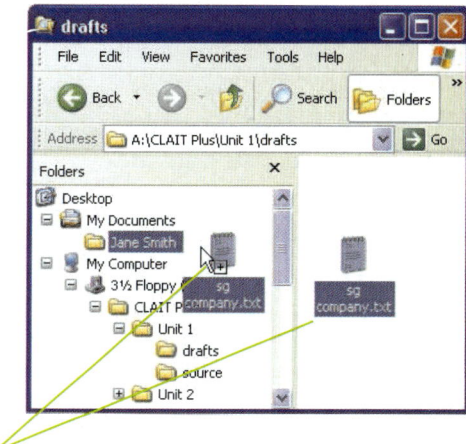

Moving files

Use the drag and drop method to move files between folders on the same drive.

1 With the files selected, click on Edit, Cut. The files will remain but the icons will appear lighter.

2 In the left pane of the Explorer window, select the destination folder and click on Edit, Paste.

Deleting files

If you decide to delete files on the A: drive, they will be deleted completely, not passed to the Recycle Bin.

1 With the files selected, just press the Delete key on the keyboard. You will get a message confirming that you wish to delete the file. Files on the C: drive or other hard drive will be moved to the Recycle Bin.

Locate files

You may be told where to find the source files that you will need for each unit, or you may have to find the files for yourself.

On the previous pages, you have seen how to browse through the drives and folders using Windows Explorer. The Windows Search function will help you locate specific files quickly.

1 Select Start, Search. This opens the Search Results window. In the left panel, the Search Companion suggests search categories.

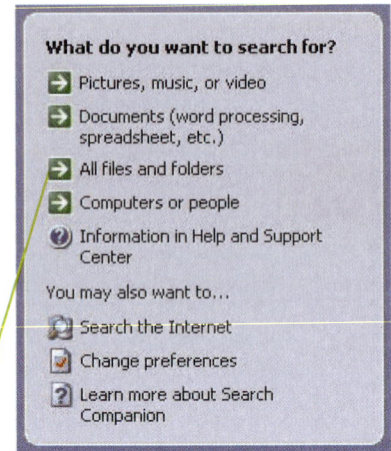

Earlier versions of Windows use Find on the Start menu, rather than Search.

2 As Unit 1 source files are a variety of types, (txt, csv, xls, and gif), you need to select the All files and folders option.

3 You can type in part of the file name, all of it or several names separated by commas. The search will be limited to the specified drives, but you can change it if you wish.

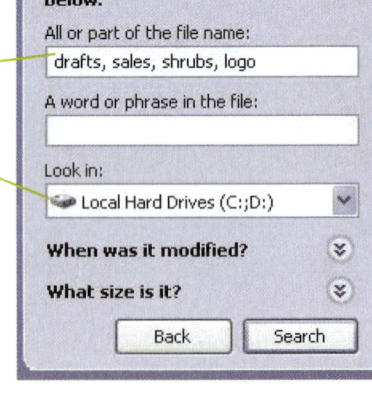

As a quick way to move to the required folder, select the file in the Search result, then from the Menu click on File, Open Containing Folder.

4 The Search results will list any folders or files that match, and display the folder hierarchy. If you double click a data file in the Search result it will open the file in the associated application.

22 | CLAIT Plus in easy steps

Print folder contents

A requirement of the CLAIT Plus course is to demonstrate that you have created, copied and deleted files and folders.

Windows Explorer does not offer a specific print function to enable you to print the contents of the drives and folders as lists, or show the organisation of nested folders and their content. To achieve a print of your folder structure and contents:

1. Open the Explorer window, and select and open the folder in the left pane so that the files are shown on the right. Shrink the window to a reasonable size if necessary.

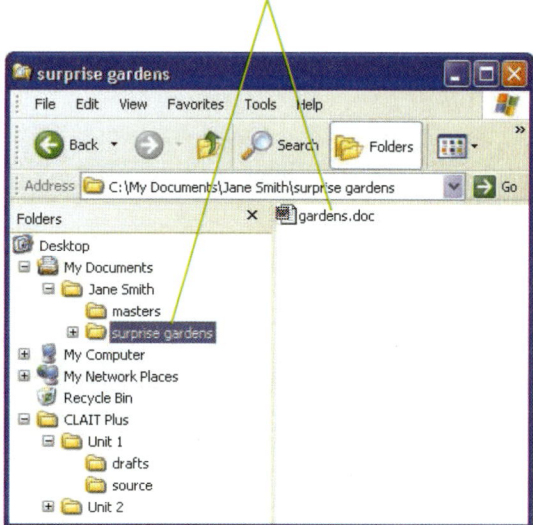

The working folder could have the student's name, such as Jane Smith. This makes the folder easily identified, and confirms the student name added to the printout.

2. Using the keyboard, press Alt and Print Screen together. This will place a copy of the active window into the Clipboard.

3. Open Word, and use the Edit, Paste facility. The copied screen will be pasted into the Word document.
Repeat the process for each folder, to add a screen copy of each to the Word document.

4. You can then add your name, and other required details, and print the Word document.

1. Create, Manage and Integrate Files | 23

Open and save

See page 18 for more details on file types.

Double clicking on most files in the Explorer window will open the file in its associated application. Some file types, however, may be associated with a different application than the one you want to use. Text files (.txt) may fall into this category as they are usually associated with NotePad or WordPad. To open a .txt file in Word, from the Explorer window:

The file icon or file extension indicates the application. The icon for a plain text file is a small notepad.

sg draft.txt

1. Select the .txt file. With the mouse still on the file, click with the right mouse button and select Open with. You'll see the recommended options listed. In this instance, select Word.

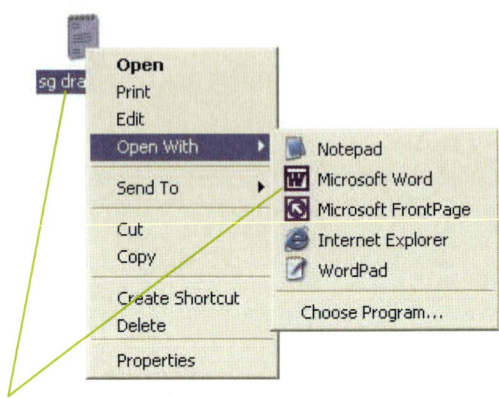

With an image file selected, using Open with will provide a different list of applications.

2. With the file now open in Word, select File, Save as from the Menu. Check that the file is in the correct folder, change the file name if necessary, and then select Word Document (*.doc) from the Save as type box. Click Save when finished.

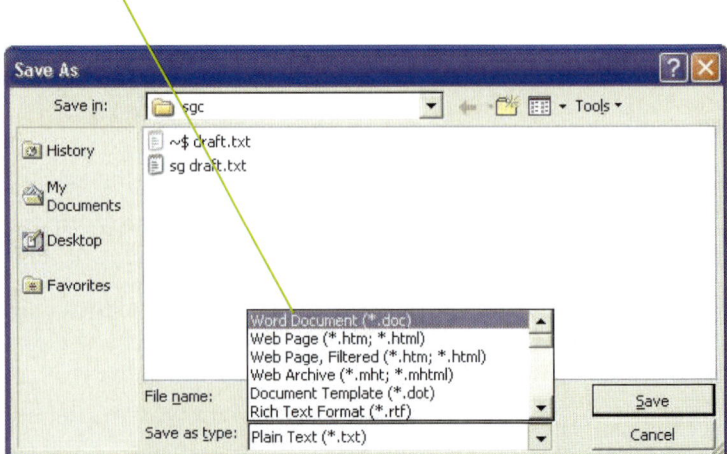

24 | CLAIT Plus in easy steps

Headers and footers

It's a good idea to set your margins first (refer to the House style sheet for details). All amendments and integrated data should then conform.

Create

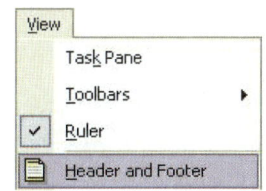

1. Select View, Header and Footer. The cursor will be visible in the Header area, and the toolbar displayed.

2. You can type into the Header or Footer area, or use Autotext to create entries that will be updated.

Once you have created a header or footer, you can double click in the header or footer area and skip the Menu.

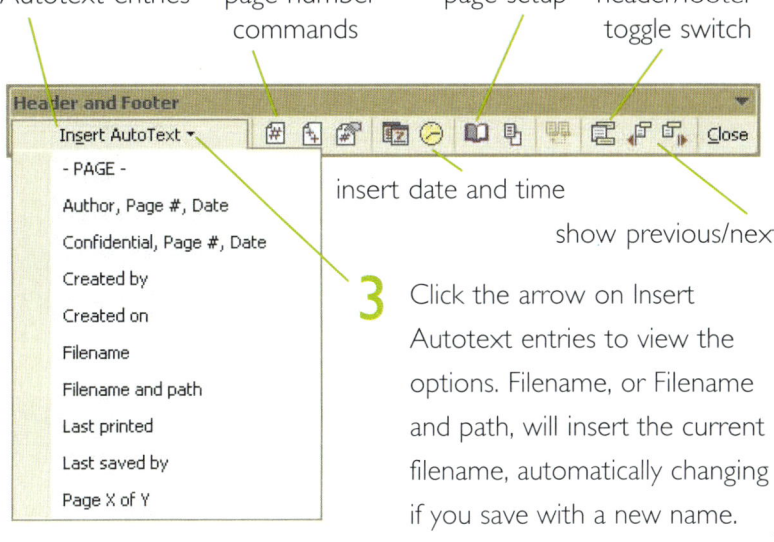

3. Click the arrow on Insert Autotext entries to view the options. Filename, or Filename and path, will insert the current filename, automatically changing if you save with a new name.

Creating matching margins for Header/Footer and the main document is not a CLAIT Plus requirement, but the document does look a lot better if you can achieve it.

4. The Header and Footer areas have different tab settings from the main body of the document. You may find that you need to set a new right aligned tab manually to prevent text extending into the margin area. See page 32 for setting tabs.

5. You will need to refer to the House Style sheets to see what information is required and its particular location. Click the Close button to return to the main document when you have finished.

...cont'd

Different first page

Headers or Footers are usually identical throughout the document, but occasionally you may need to set a different first page, for example a title page. To set a different first page in Word:

Press Ctrl+Home to go straight to the beginning of the document.

1. Make sure that you have at least two pages in your document. See page 41 for details on creating Page breaks. Position the cursor at the start of the document and select View, Header and Footer.

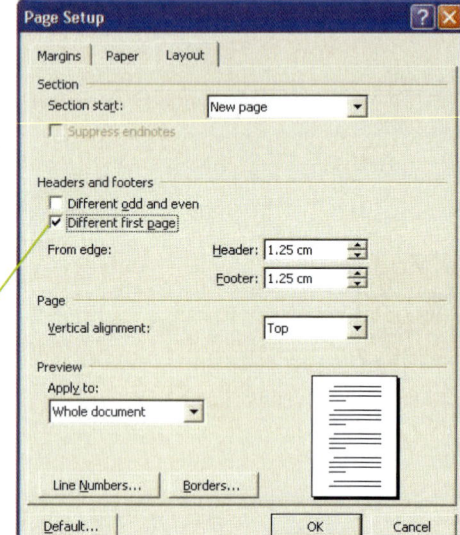

2. First select the Page Setup button on the toolbar, then in the dialog box, select Different first page and click on OK.

3. You will see that the Header now indicates First Page. Create your Header or Footer for Page 1 as required in the House Style sheet.

4. On the Header/Footer toolbar select the Show Next button. This will move you to Page 2. Now set up the header and footer as required for the rest of the document.

5. If either the Header or the Footer is the same on all the pages, select it on the first page, copy and paste it to the second page.

Page numbers

Page numbers can be inserted using the Header and Footer facility.

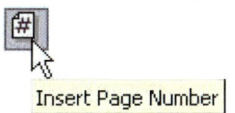

1. With the Header and Footer toolbar displayed, position the cursor where required and click on Insert Page Number.

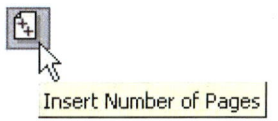

2. You can choose to insert the total number of pages in the document, but you will need to add your own separator between the numbers, a slash or hyphen, for example 1/3.

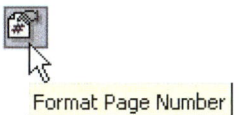

3. Select the Format button to view further options. You can choose your numbering style - Roman, numeric or alphabetic.

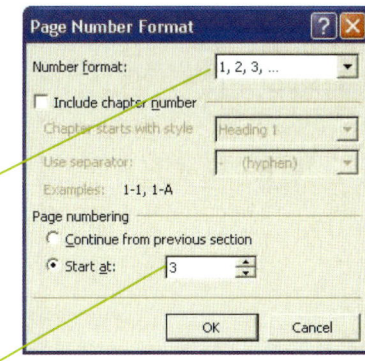

4. The Format window allows you to specify a chapter number, and the starting page number.

To create page numbers when no other Header or Footer information is required:

1. Select Insert, Page Numbers, from the Menu.

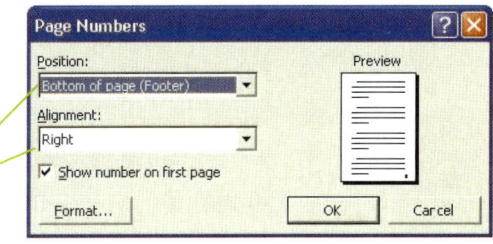

2. This dialogue box allows you to select the position and the alignment. You also have the option to Show on first page. Select the Format button to open the Page Number Format window (as shown above).

1. Create, Manage and Integrate Files | 27

Edit the document

Many of the editing tools, such as insert, delete, find and replace, and the spell checking facility were covered in the New CLAIT syllabus.

In CLAIT Plus you are required you to know some of the standard editing marks. The table below illustrates the most often used.

Paste Special and Autocorrect in Word are covered in the MOS section on pages 266-267.

Symbol	Meaning	Example
◡	close up	print as o ne word
∧ or ⋏	caret	insert here ⌐ something
stet	let stand	let original ~~text~~ stay
tr	transpose	change ⌒order⌒ the
np or new para //	begin a new paragraph	
sp	spell out	change 3ins to 3 inches
cap	set in CAPITALS	change usa to USA
lc	set in lowercase	change North to north
ital	set in *italic*	
Run on	Join two paragraphs	office job. ⌒ The first SG C

Always proof read your document carefully. The spell checker may not be set to check word in capitals. It will not check numbers or encoded data for you.

Check your document

- English (UK) dictionary used for automatic spell checking
- English date format - 15-08-03, 15/8/03, 15 Aug 03
- Correct capitalisation - follow the capitalisation shown
- Data selected and encoded as specified in the exercise

Tables

Create

Tables allow you to manage lists or columns of text easily. You can apply formatting and alignment styles to a selected cell, a column or row. For CLAIT Plus they are the preferred method of text alignment, but you could also use Tabs. See page 32.

1 Position the cursor where you want the table. On the Menu bar select Table, Insert, Table.

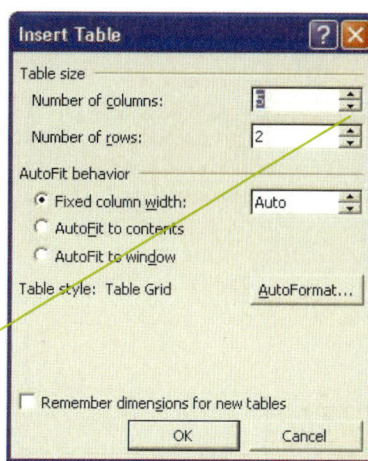

2 Use the arrows to increase or decrease the number of columns and rows. Click on OK when finished.

Initially the Insert Table button only offers a table size of 5 columns by 4 rows. Continue dragging past the boundary shown and the number of each will be increased.

3 As an alternative, you can use the Insert Table button on the toolbar. Press the left mouse button and drag the mouse pointer across the cells until you have the required numbers. Then release the button.

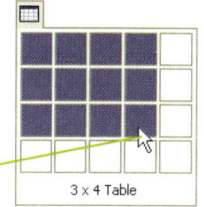

4 You can select the whole table, columns or rows, or individual cells.

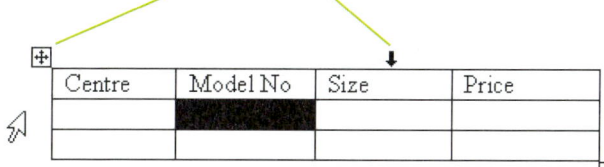

To access the table functions, such as insert columns and rows, the cursor must be within the table.

5 To insert rows and columns, position the cursor in the table next to where you wish to insert. Select Table, Insert, Columns or Rows as appropriate.

6 To add more rows as you fill the table, press the Tab key in the bottom right cell. To move from cell to cell press the Tab key.

1. Create, Manage and Integrate Files | **29**

...cont'd

Make sure that your columns are wide enough to display the data in full, and that words are not split. This is a CLAIT Plus requirement. Be careful if you choose one of the Autofit options as this leaves Word in control of the column widths.

Adjusting column width

Word will automatically adjust the cell depth to accommodate the contents as you type, using spaces between words to wrap the text onto a new line within the cell. To manually adjust the columns width to allow for varying quantities of content:

Centre	Model No	Size

The Ruler is a very useful facility when you are working with tables. If it is not already enabled, select View, Ruler.

1. Position the cursor within the table. The table is created to fit within the set margin and the Ruler will indicate the column boundaries. Make a note of the current position of the right hand marker. In CLAIT Plus the table must not extend into the margin.

2. Move the mouse pointer until it is over one of the column markers. It will change to a double headed arrow, indicating that you can drag in either direction.

Centre	Model No	Size	Price

If a cell is selected, i.e. shown in black, the width of just that cell will be altered.

3. Adjust the column widths appropriately, to conform with the exercise requirements. Be careful, however, when increasing any column width, as the whole table will be affected and it may extend into the margin.

Delete

1. Press the delete key to delete the contents of any selected area of the table. To delete the columns, rows or whole table itself, select the area and use the Table functions on the Menu.

...cont'd

Table grid lines will always show when you are working in Normal or Print layout view in Word. They may, however, not actually print, it depends on how Word has been set up. To check if they will print, select Print Preview.

Grid lines
To enable borders and lines:

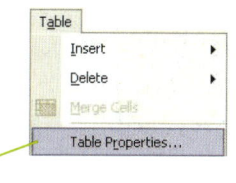

1. Position the cursor inside the table and select Table, Table Properties.

2. With the Table tab selected, click on the Borders and Shading button. Now choose from the preset options on the left, such as None or All, or select individually and preview on the right.

Select the Shading tab to apply shading and effects to the table.

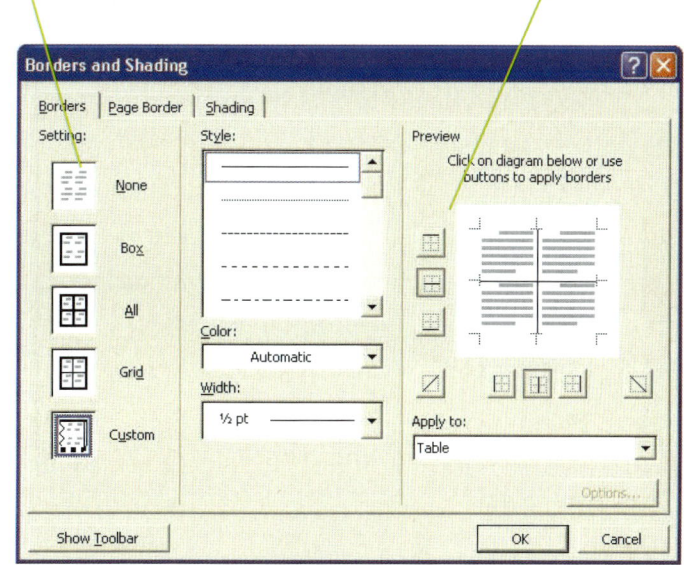

The Borders button icon will change to reflect the most recently chosen option.

3. The Borders button provides a useful shortcut. You can choose one or more of the options. In the example shown, internal grid lines only are selected.

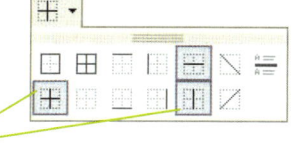

4. Use Print Preview to check the effect.

1. Create, Manage and Integrate Files | 31

Tabs

Fonts, today, are proportional. Some letters are

wider than others. When you press the space bar Word creates a variable space making it very difficult to line up columns of text using the space bar. Tabs move the cursor a defined amount that is consistent.

Tabs are a quick and easy way to line up text in columns. Default tab stops are set at every 1.27 cms, as shown on the Ruler. To define your own settings:

1. Position the cursor before the text where you want the new tab settings to start. Select Format, Tabs.

2. Type the required tab position into the Tab stop box, and choose the alignment, left, centred etc.

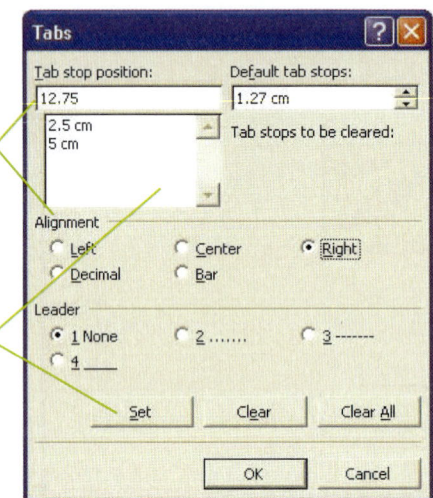

Tables let you format a column, and wrap text in the same column. With tabs you can only format the row, and text wraps to the left margin.

3. Click the Set button and the tab setting will be moved to the lower pane. Repeat the process for each tab position, selecting the alignment for each tab. When finished, click OK.

4. To delete or change a setting, select the stop position in the left pane, and change the alignment, or select Clear.

You can also use the Ruler to set tabs, although it is not as easy to be accurate with the position.

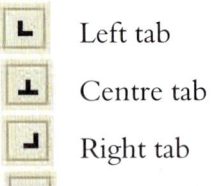

Left tab
Centre tab
Right tab
Decimal tab

5. Cycle through the tab types at the left of the Ruler. When you see the one you want, click on the Ruler in the desired position.

Bullets and numbering

Bullets and numbering work in the same way so the techniques that you learn for one can be applied to the other.

 *You can apply bullets to the text as you type, but it is generally easier to apply bullets after the text has been created.*

1 Select the text to be bulleted or numbered, then click the Bullets or Numbering button on the toolbar.

2 To add more items to the bulleted list, just press Enter at the end of the last item. A new bullet point is automatically created.

3 To revert to normal text, press Enter twice, or move to a new line and click on the selected button to turn the facility off.

Using the Menu to apply bullets or numbering allows you to change the bullet point or the numbering style and the indentation.

 *On the Bullets and Numbering window, select None to turn Bullets off.*

4 Select the text and click Format, Bullets and Numbering. Select a new style from the options or click on the Customise button to change the bullet point style and indentation.

 *To amend the indentation of Bullets and Numbering quickly, select the bulleted text and click on the Increase or Decrease Indent button on the Tool bar.*

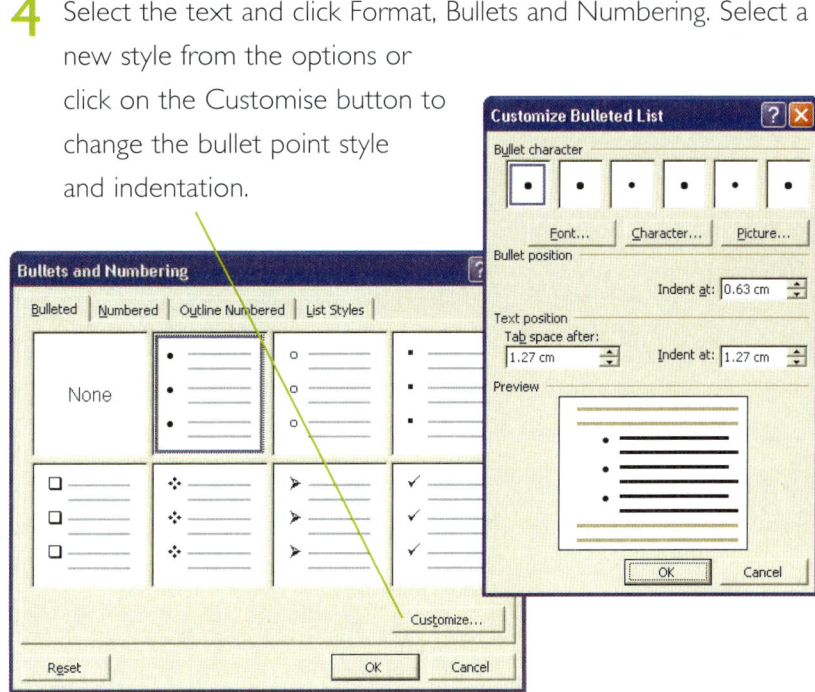

1. Create, Manage and Integrate Files | 33

Insert an image

Inserting an image was covered in New CLAIT in Desktop Publishing, Computer Art, Presentation Graphics and Web Pages.

1 Position the cursor at the insertion point, and select Insert, Picture, From File.

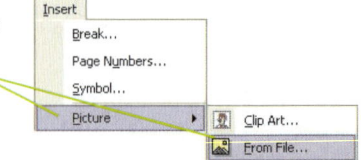

2 Word will open the My Pictures folder. You will need to look in your named working folder to locate the image file.

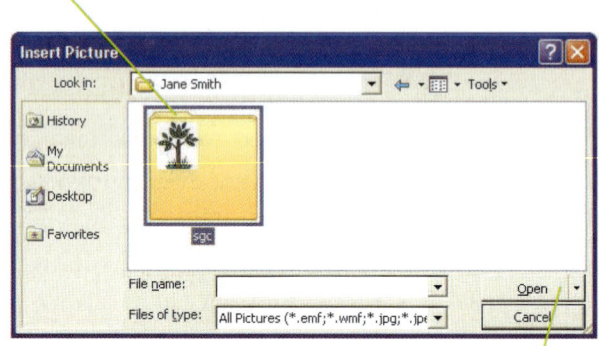

Word shows thumbnail pictures of the images that are stored within the folders to help you locate the file.

3 When you open the folder and select a file the button will change from Open to Insert. Click Insert or double click the icon.

To wrap text on all sides, you may need to select Format Picture, the Layout tab, and the Advanced button. The Text Wrapping tab allows you to select one or all sides.

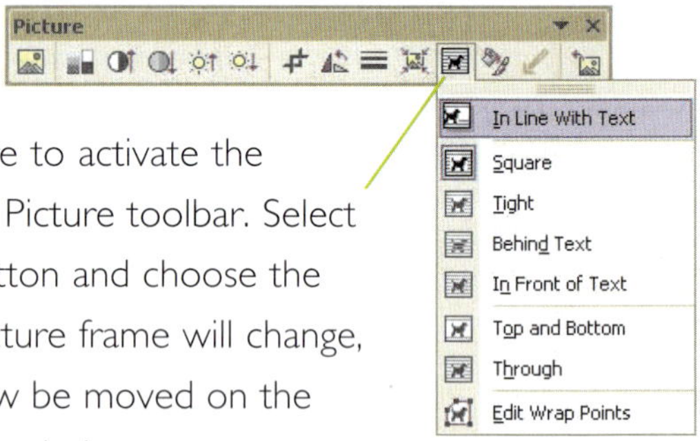

4 Click within the picture to activate the picture frame and the Picture toolbar. Select the Text wrapping button and choose the required style. The picture frame will change, and the image can now be moved on the page, using the four-headed arrow.

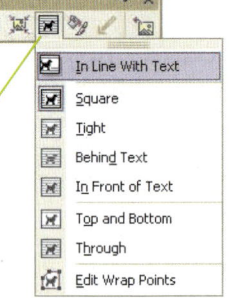

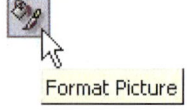

5 If you need to resize the image, drag the corner handle, as this maintains the correct proportions. Alternatively, select Format Picture and the Size tab. You can type in the required size, but check that the Lock aspect ratio box is ticked.

34 | CLAIT Plus in easy steps

Insert a chart

 *Office XP handles copying and pasting charts between applications very successfully. If you are using a previous version of Office, it is a good idea to shrink the chart before you copy it. In Excel, change its location to 'an object in' the spreadsheet, and it will be made smaller for you.*

1 Open your Word document, then open the chart in Excel. Note the Taskbar at the bottom of the screen shows both applications active. You can use the Taskbar to switch between them.

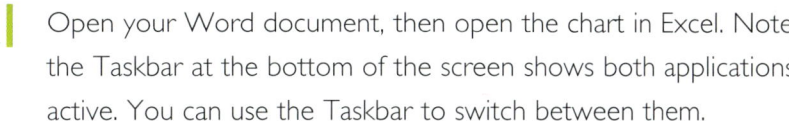

2 The House Style sheet, supplied with the exercise, will specify a font style for the chart. It is easiest to check and modify the font, if necessary, before you insert it into your Word document.

 *It's a good idea to set the correct page margins before you copy and paste the chart, as in Word 2002, it will honour the margins set.*

3 When you have checked the font, click inside the chart area to activate the frame, you will see the frame handles. Select Copy, or Edit, Copy from the menu.

4 Switch to your Word document and position the cursor at the correct insertion point. Click on Paste, or Edit, Paste. The chart will appear and should fit correctly between the margins.

 *You must ensure that all the text in the chart is legible.*

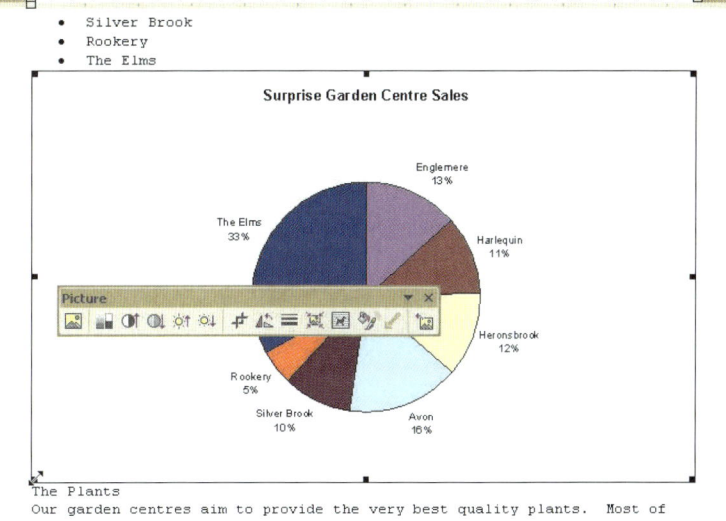

 *If you need to resize the chart, use only the corner handles to maintain the correct proportions.*

1. Create, Manage and Integrate Files | 35

Insert a data file

You will be given a .csv (comma separated variable) data file to insert into the integrated document. These are plain text files and are composed of lists of data, such as you would use in a spreadsheet or database. Each field is separated by a comma, each new row is created by a Carriage Return. The files can be read by NotePad, Word, Excel or Access. The simplest way to work with them for the CLAIT Plus course is to use Excel.

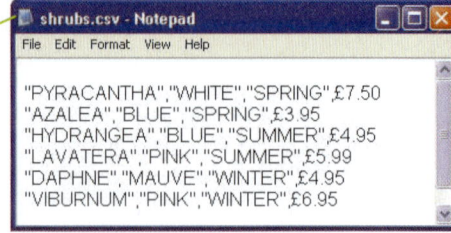

 *Double click on the file in Windows Explorer, and it should open in Excel automatically.*

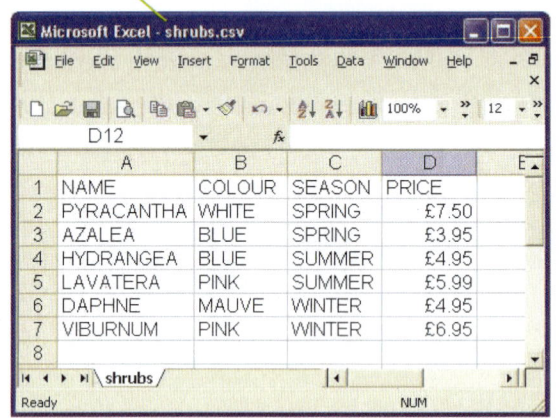

 *Use the Taskbar to switch applications, as described on the previous page.*

1 Open the file with Excel. It looks just like a normal spreadsheet file with columns of text and numbers.

You could insert the file straight into Word, using Insert, File in Word. You would then need to select the text and use the Convert Text to Table facility. However, you may find that the table still contains inverted commas and does not convert easily.

2 Select the data area, and click on Copy. Switch to the integrated Word document and position the cursor at the insertion point. Click on Paste.

3 Check that the columns are wide enough to display all the data. You will also need to consult the House Style sheet to make the required amendments, e.g. centre headings.

Insert a symbol

The term symbol refers to unusual characters, such as an accented or foreign letter, copyright, registered trademark, or the Yen or Euro sign. To insert a symbol:

1 Position the cursor in the text where you want the symbol. From the Menu select Insert, Symbol.

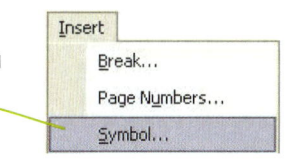

2 The window, which can be scrolled to reveal further examples, shows symbols available in the current font. It also displays recently used symbols, and details of the selected symbol.

> **HOT TIP**
> *The symbols shown are from the Symbol font. Click the down arrow to find fonts such as Wingdings and Webdings.*

> **HOT TIP**
> *A shortcut key combination is shown at the bottom of the window. If you need the symbol frequently, it would be worth remembering. You can also assign your own shortcut key combination.*

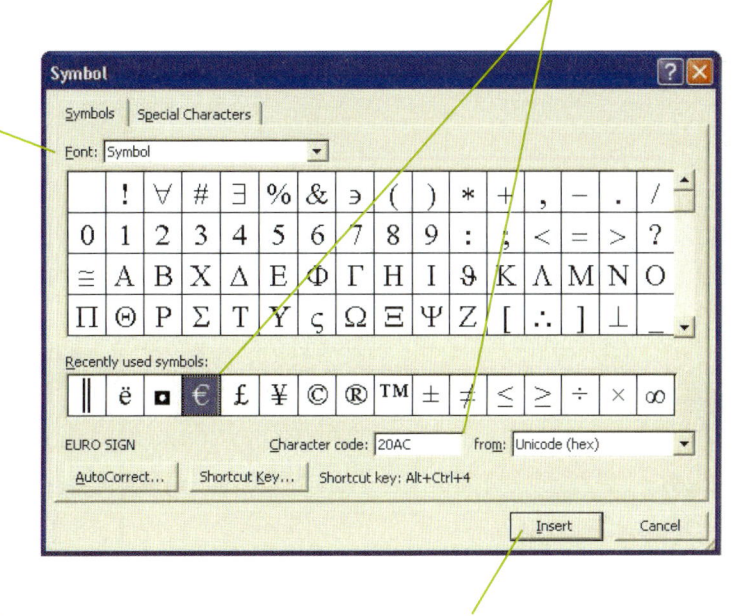

3 Select the required symbol and click Insert. Then click Close.

4 As an alternative to using the Insert symbol facility, in Word you can compose symbols with key combinations. For example, press **Ctrl+Comma c** to get a ç cedilla, press **Ctrl+Single quote e** to get an accented letter é, press **Ctrl+Colon o** to get an ö umlaut.

1. Create, Manage and Integrate Files | 37

Styles

In previous versions of Word, you would need to select Format Styles from the Menu. The options then would be the same.

Create

1. Office XP makes creating and using standard styles very easy. Click on the down arrow and select Styles and Formatting from the Task pane list.

2. Word provides three heading levels and a normal text style. When you hover the mouse over a selected style, you will see the default style and formatting.

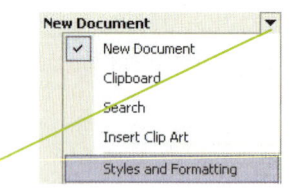

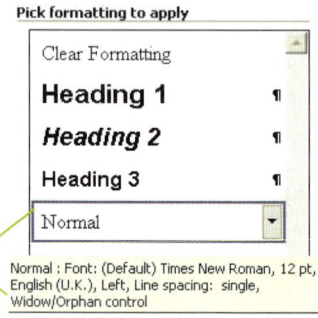

3. For CLAIT Plus you will probably need to make changes to each of the styles. Select the style and click on the down arrow, and choose Modify.

When choosing font styles, the standard Serif font is Times New Roman. The standard Sans Serif font is Arial.

4. You will see the name of the style you are modifying, together with the standard components, such as font style, size and alignment that you can amend. Note the Format button, which is used in Step 5 on the next page.

Only tick the Add to Template button if you wish to make the change a permanent one for all future documents.

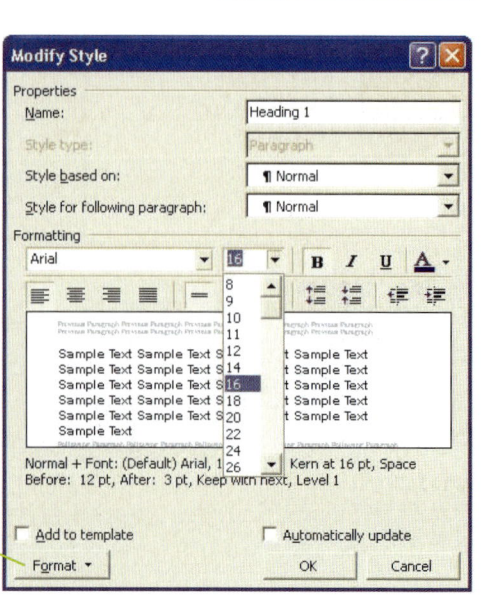

...cont'd

Spacing in the document must be consistent. Use the Style feature to set spacing. You may wish to use the default settings, but exercises could require different settings in order to fill the text area.

5. In some circumstances in the CLAIT Plus exercises, you may need to modify the spacing between headings and the main text of the document. To do this, select the Format button, and choose Paragraph.

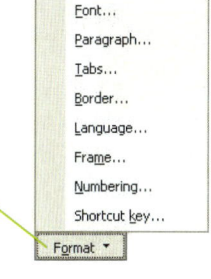

6. The Before and After buttons on the Indents and Spacing tab let you refine the spacing in the document.

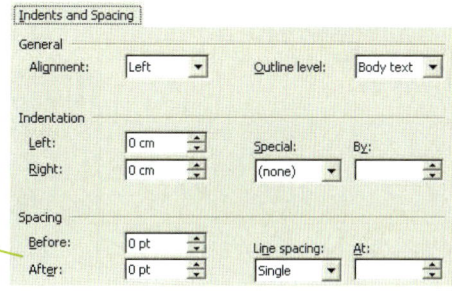

Widows and Orphans means a single line at the bottom of the document on its own (a widow), or a single line on the top of the next page (orphan). See page 267, in the MOS Word Processing section for more information on this topic.

7. Select the Line and Page Breaks tab to enable Widows and Orphans control.

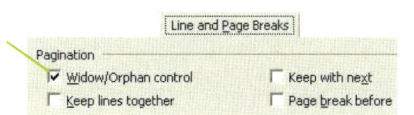

Apply Styles

With previous versions of Word, or if you do not wish to use the Task pane, you can select the style from the Style bar at the top left of the window. Click the down arrow and select as appropriate.

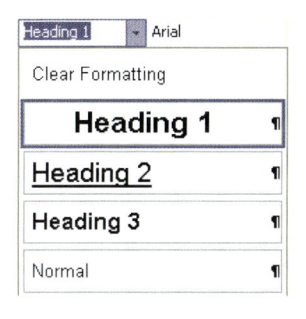

1. When you return to the document, you will see that the styles in the Task pane have changed to reflect the amendments. To apply the styles, click in the appropriate text, for example the Heading and select the style from the Task pane.

Templates

You are not required to create and use a Template in this CLAIT Plus unit, but it is a really useful facility in a business environment.

Using Styles, as shown on the previous page, changes the settings for just that document. If you were to create a style or document layout that you wanted to use on a regular basis, the most efficient approach is to set up a Template.

1. Select File, New. From the Task pane click on General Templates.

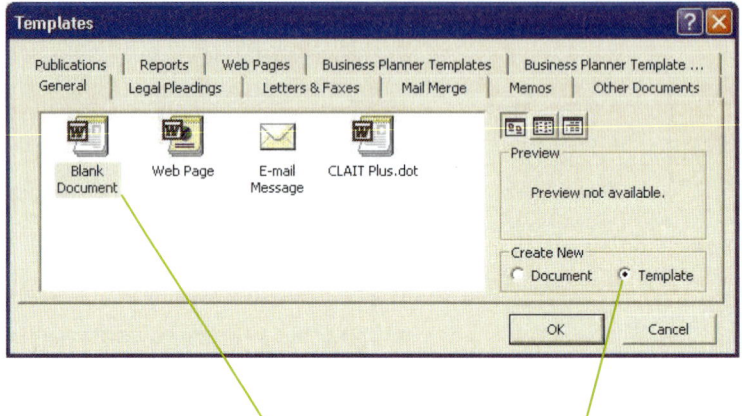

2. Select the Blank Document icon, and click the Template button. Then click on OK.

You can change almost any element, for example fonts, styles, page size, margins and orientation. You could insert an image or company logo into the Template. You can also create letterheads, forms or invoices.

3. The title bar will indicate that you are working on a template. Modify the layout as required, then save and name the template.

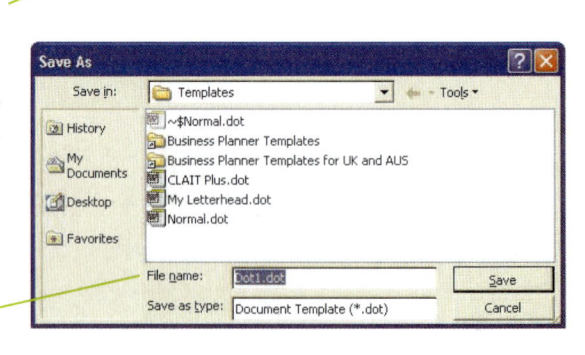

4. To use the template, select from the Task pane, as in Steps 1 and 2 above, but this time be sure to click Create New Document.

40 | CLAIT Plus in easy steps

Document management

Page breaks

Setting margins sizes was covered in the New CLAIT syllabus. It's a good idea to set your margins before editing the document or importing data and images.

1. Automatic page breaks will occur when the page is full. In Normal view they are shown as a dotted line across the page. In Print Layout view, you will see background space between the pages. You cannot delete an automatic page break, but it will adjust automatically when you insert a manual break.

2. When you are required to insert a page break, select Insert, Break, and choose Page break. Alternatively, press Ctrl+Enter together.

The automatic page break just shows as a dotted line across the page. The required page break displays the words Page Break.

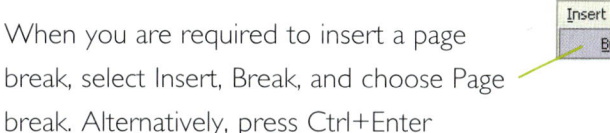

3. To delete a manual page break, in Normal view position the cursor on the Break line and press the delete key. In Print Layout view just press delete after the text above the break.

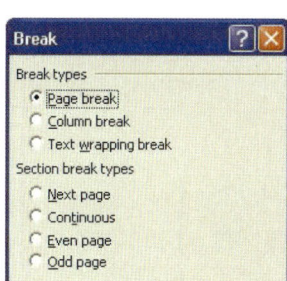

Page borders and shading are covered in the MOS unit on page 268.

Page orientation

To change from portrait to landscape at some point in the document:

1. Position the cursor in the page where you wish to start the new layout. Select File, Page Setup. Select the new orientation, and choose Apply to: This point forward.

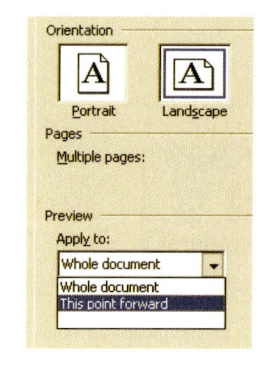

Section breaks occur when you change an element of the document layout, for example page orientation, borders or margins.

2. When you return to the document, you will see a Section break inserted. Check the effect using Print Preview.

1. Create, Manage and Integrate Files | 41

Checklist

It's a good idea to check the document completely before moving or deleting any files.

When you have completed the exercise, run through a final check to ensure that the fine details meet the specifications. Have you:

- used the correct file and folder names

- provided screen prints showing folders, contents and your name, centre number and date

You are allowed three hours to complete the OCR CLAIT Plus assessment.

- created headers and footers that include the correct details in the specified positions

- set margins and ensured integrated files honour the margins

- ensured that images and text are not superimposed

- created page breaks where specified, and ensured imported data is not spread across two pages

- checked for consistent linespacing throughout

- avoided widows and orphans

If you have used the downloadable exercises, you can check your work against the files in the Worked Copy folder.

- applied House Style throughout the document, including tables and imported data

- replaced specified text, including text in imported data

- spell checked the document using an English dictionary

- used English format for dates

- encoded the required data

- proofread the final printed document

Marking

This should not be taken as an exhaustive list of critical errors. You are allowed three accuracy errors, which could be a spelling mistake, or failure to complete a task, such as justify text. Critical and accuracy errors are different in each unit.

You are not allowed any critical errors. The following are considered critical errors:

- a specified data file is missing or incomplete

- a specified image is missing or incomplete

- a specified chart is missing or incomplete

- an incomplete printout

Spreadsheets

In this unit you will learn how to enter and manipulate data, use functions and formulae, and format and present data. You will learn how to link spreadsheets and use them to project results.

Covers

Spreadsheets | 44

Open with, save as | 45

Columns and rows | 46

Text alignment | 47

Cell references | 48

Formula | 52

Functions | 54

Sort | 60

Number format | 61

Borders and shading | 62

Document management | 63

Headers and footers | 64

Print | 66

Checklist | 68

Unit Two

Spreadsheets

In this unit we will be using Excel 2002, part of Office XP. Any substantial differences between software releases will be highlighted and alternative methods suggested.

Unit Two overview
This unit covers the following areas:

1. Opening a generic data file, a .csv (comma separated variable) file and saving it in the standard file format for the application used.

2. Entering, amending and manipulating text and data, and projecting results. You will be required to sort and hide ranges.

This unit follows a complete spreadsheet exercise. The data files and exercise can be downloaded from the In Easy Steps web site (see page 281).

3. Using standard spreadsheet formulae and functions to perform calculations. These include: SUM, MAX, MIN, AVERAGE, SQRT, IF and COUNT or equivalents.

4. Using a variety of cell references. These include: relative, absolute, mixed references, named cells, and references to cells in other spreadsheets.

5. Presenting the data. You will be required to widen columns, enhance text, use lines and borders, and present numeric data in a variety of ways.

Spreadsheets are also covered in the Solutions and Mos units later in the book.

6. Printing reports. You will need to print ranges of data, include where required column and row headings, fit to pages and include personal details. You will also need to print formulae.

Exercise files and documentation
You should have the following items:
- two .csv files
- the exercise
- a House Style sheet
- a Formulae sheet

Open with, save as

A .csv file is a plain text file. The data that it contains is organised into lines of text, each line containing data separated by commas. These files are used because they can be read by many applications including NotePad, WordPad, Word, Excel and Access.

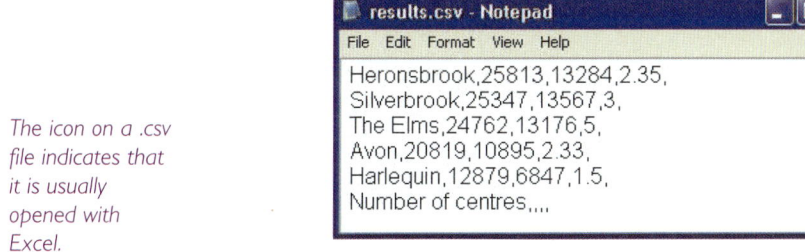

The icon on a .csv file indicates that it is usually opened with Excel.

1 You can open the .csv file in Excel by double clicking on the file icon in the Folder view. Alternatively, with it selected, click with the right mouse button and select the program to use.

2 To open the file with Excel already running, select File, Open. You will need to select from the Files of type box, and choose Text files or All files to see the file name.

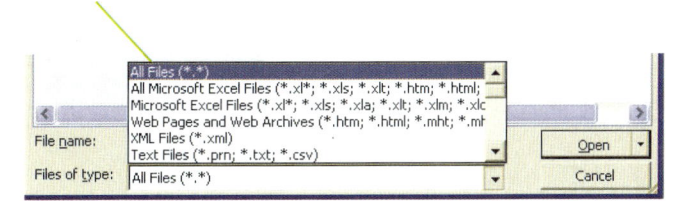

3 To save the file, select File, Save As. Supply the required name in the File name box, but make sure to change the Save as type from .csv to the standard Excel format of .xls.

2. Spreadsheets | 45

Columns and rows

You can set column and row labels to remain visible when you scroll the window. Position the cursor below and to the right of the labels, and select Window, Freeze panes (see page 269).

Set column width

1. Position the cursor in the column, or you can select the whole column. Click on Format, Column, Width.

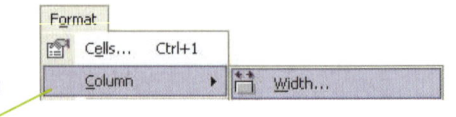

Use a similar series of commands to adjust the row height. Select the row and click Format, Row, Height. Type the amount and click OK.

2. Type in the required number. This represents the number of characters that will be displayed using the normal font. If you set the column width to zero, you will hide the column.

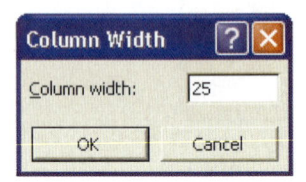

Delete columns or rows

Hiding columns and rows is covered in printing. See page 66.

1. Select the whole column or row by clicking on the column or row heading (ABC, or 123 etc). Select Edit, Delete. The entire column or row, with its contents, will be removed.

When you insert and delete whole columns or rows, remember that data currently not displayed may also be affected.

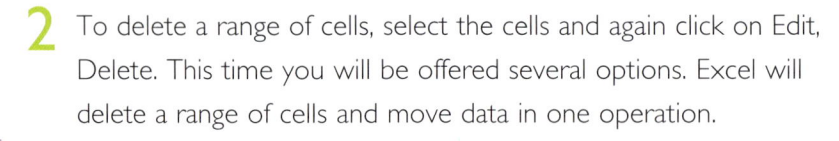

2. To delete a range of cells, select the cells and again click on Edit, Delete. This time you will be offered several options. Excel will delete a range of cells and move data in one operation.

This is especially useful if data is misaligned with its data labels, or if you wish to remove a space between headings and data without affecting other areas of the spreadsheet.

46 | CLAIT Plus in easy steps

Text alignment

Don't forget: *Text is left aligned and numbers are right aligned by default.*

1. For simple text alignment within cells, you can use the standard alignment buttons on the Formatting toolbar. Select the cells or range of cells and click as required.

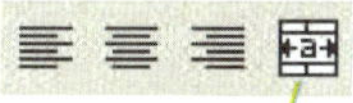

2. Excel provides a Merge and Centre button on the Formatting toolbar to allow you to centre a title across columns. Select the range of cells to use and click the button.

Hot tip: *The Merge and Centre button is a toggle switch. Both it and the Centre buttons show as selected on the Formatting toolbar. To edit this text, double click on it, or amend it in the Formula bar.*

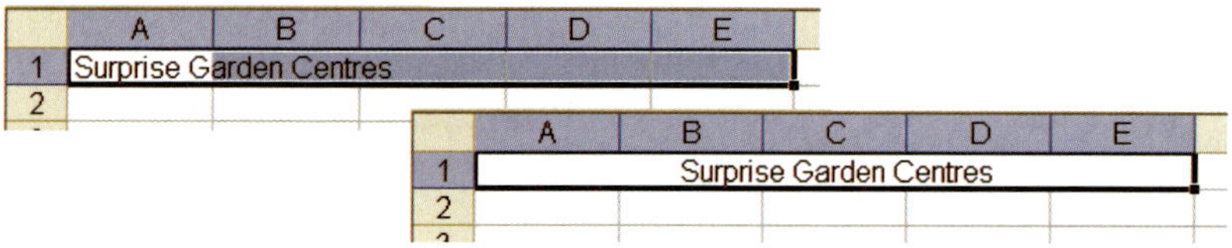

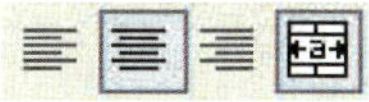

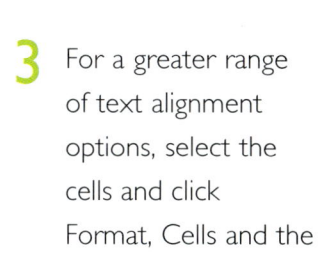

3. For a greater range of text alignment options, select the cells and click Format, Cells and the Alignment tab.

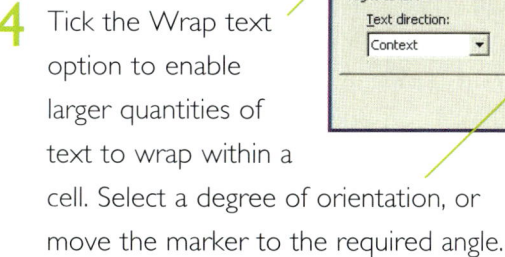

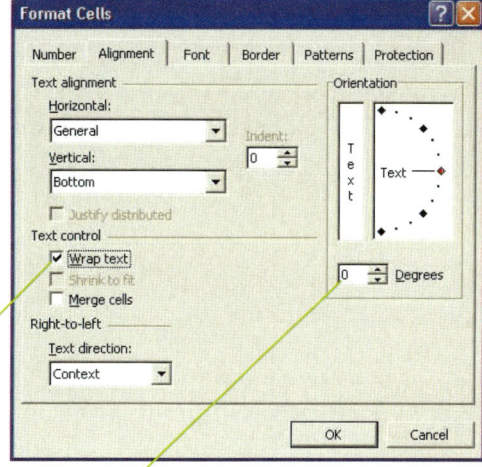

Don't forget: *Refer to the supplied House Style sheet for alignment and formatting.*

4. Tick the Wrap text option to enable larger quantities of text to wrap within a cell. Select a degree of orientation, or move the marker to the required angle.

Hot tip: *Centre Across Selection is Merge and Centre.*

5. Text alignment, Horizontal (as shown), or Vertical, offers further options, including Centre across Selection, described above.

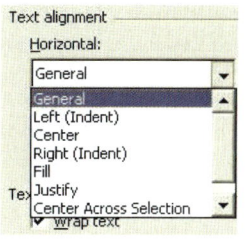

2. Spreadsheets | 47

Cell references

A cell reference is simply the address of a cell e.g. A1, or G7 or range of cells, e.g. G7:H12. You will be familiar with using cell references from the New CLAIT course.

There are three types of cell references:

Relative cell references
This is the usual type of reference and is where the formula is positioned relative to the cell references. In the example shown, the formula is adding the contents of the cell positioned two to the left to the cell located one to the left. This formula can be copied down the spreadsheet as it is using cells in the same relative position and so will automatically adjust.

		TOTAL
24	15	=F6+G6
22	23	
10	16	

Absolute cell references

Hot Tip: The F4 function key can be used to create absolute and mixed cell references. Create the reference and press F4. It will cycle through full absolute, row, column or none: H9, H$9, $H9, H9.

These are references that refer to cells in a specific location. To make the reference absolute the $ symbol is used. In the example shown, the formula is multiplying the contents of the cell located one cell to the left, by the VAT figure of 17.5% which is in a fixed or absolute position. As the 17.5% (H9) cell reference is an absolute reference, the formula can be copied successfully. The relative reference will adjust, (H7, H8, etc.) but the absolute reference remains the same.

	TOTAL	VAT
	15	39	=H6*H9
	23	45
	16	26
VAT		17.5%

TOTAL	VAT
=F6+G6	=H6*H9
=F7+G7	=H7*H9
=F8+G8	=H8*H9
0.175	=H9*H9

Mixed cell references

Hot Tip: In this example the Retail values are multiplied by each discount rate in turn. When the formula is copied across, the column reference for the Discount is incremented, the row reference remains the same. When the formula is copied down, the row reference for the Retail value is incremented, the column stays the same.

These references are a combination of mixed and absolute, for example $J9, or K$8. In $J9 the column ($J) reference is absolute. With K$8 the row ($8) reference is absolute.

RETAIL	DISCOUNT @ 0.2	DISCOUNT @ 0.5
35	=$J9*K$8	=$J9*L$8
50	=$J10*K$8	=$J10*L$8
27	=$J11*K$8	=$J11*L$8
10	=$J12*K$8	=$J12*L$8

RETAIL	DISCOUNT @ 20%	DISCOUNT @ 50%
£ 35.00	£ 7.00	£ 17.50
£ 50.00	£ 10.00	£ 25.00
£ 27.00	£ 5.40	£ 13.50
£ 10.00	£ 2.00	£ 5.00

...cont'd

Named references

Individual cells or ranges of cells can be given names. The names can then be used in formulae instead of the regular letter-number reference. Using names is efficient and helpful and reduces the opportunity for errors. To name a cell:

1 Select the cell to name. From the Menu choose Insert, Name, Define.

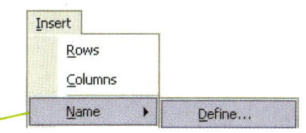

2 Type the name in the Names in Workbook. Type the reference in the Refers to: box, or use the Collapse Dialog button to minimise the window and select the reference from the sheet.

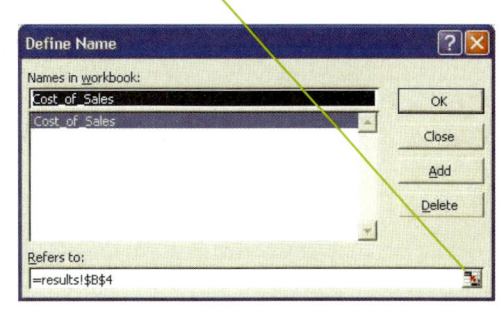

When you create a name you will need to type underscores between words, as Excel will not accept spaces in names.

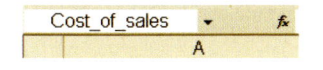

3 If you need to create several names, select Add to add it to the list. Otherwise just click on OK. The name will appear in the cell address area on the Formula bar.

4 Alternatively, you can create a named reference by taking advantage of the spreadsheet layout. In the example shown, the cell label is adjacent to the cell to be named.

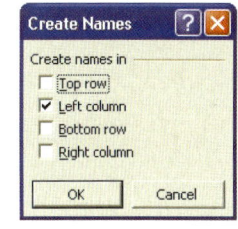

5 Select the two cells, and from the Menu, choose Insert, Name, Create. Select Left column and click OK.

2. Spreadsheets | 49

...cont'd

> **For CLAIT Plus you must create a link to another workbook. However, in many situations it would be better to link to another worksheet within the same workbook.**

Linked references

You can create and use a reference to a cell or range of cells in another spreadsheet. This is known as a linked reference. The spreadsheet file that contains the data you wish to link to is known as the 'source'. The file that contains the link is called the 'destination' or 'target'. To create a linked reference:

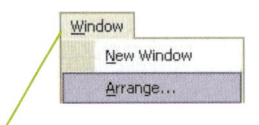

1. Open both of the workbooks. Select Window, Arrange. Click on Tiled, and then click OK.

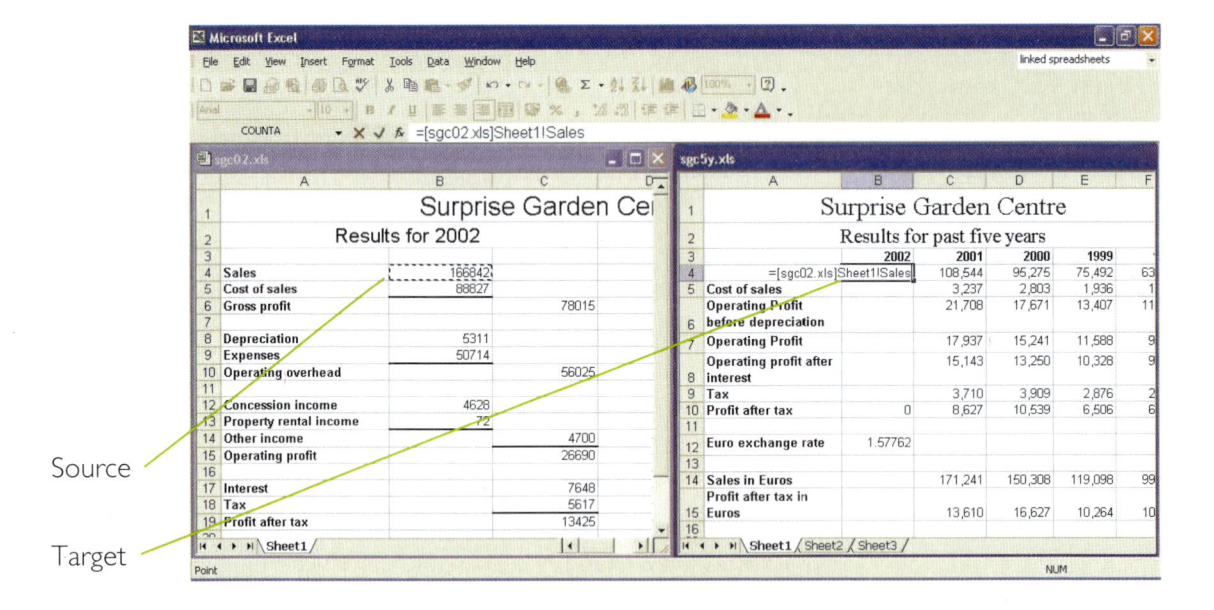

Source

Target

2. Click in the target worksheet where you wish to create the link. Press = (the equals symbol). Click twice in the source worksheet, in the cell containing the required data. (The first click just activates the worksheet).

50 | CLAIT Plus in easy steps

...cont'd

HOT TIP: *The advantage of linked references is that you can work with each file independently and update if and when required. The main disadvantage is that links can break or become corrupted, if for example a file is moved.*

3 The cell now contains both filename and cell reference, in this case a named reference, Sales.

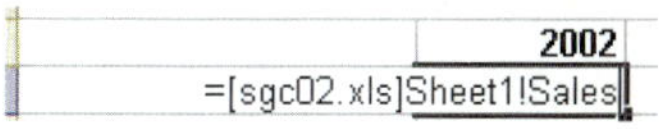

	2002
	=[sgc02.xls]Sheet1!Sales

4 You can use linked or remote cell references in any formulae. This formula adds the contents of B7 in the current workbook to the cell named Depreciation in the file sgc02.xls.

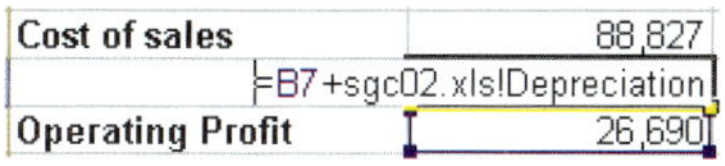

Cost of sales	88,827
	=B7+sgc02.xls!Depreciation
Operating Profit	26,690

5 When you work with both files open, the link is dynamic. If you move or edit data in the source file, the target file is immediately updated. This applies to all types of cell references: relative, absolute and named.

6 If you work with only the source file open, and make amendments to the data, Excel will remember. When you open the target file with the links, Excel will ask if you wish to update.

BEWARE: *If cells are moved, by insert or delete of columns for example, in the source file, then Named references will remain valid. Other references, even absolute references, will no longer point to the correct data.*

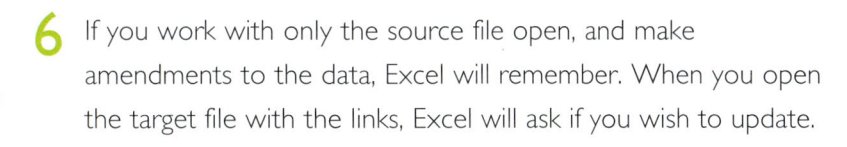

Microsoft Excel

This workbook contains links to other data sources.
- If you update the links, Excel attempts to retrieve the latest data.
- If you don't update, Excel uses the previous information.

[Update] [Don't Update] [Help]

DON'T FORGET: *This is not a CLAIT Plus requirement, but could be useful in a work situation.*

7 Click Update to refresh the data, click Don't Update to ignore any changes to the source file. If you wish to keep a snapshot of the target file at a point in time, then select Don't Update. Open the file and save it with another name. You can then open the original again and this time select Update.

Formula

*Creating formulae using the standard operators of + (plus), - (minus), * (multiply) and / (divide) was covered in New CLAIT.*

Simple formulae

1. To create a simple formula, position the cursor where you want the answer. Type = then click on the first cell, type the operator and click on the second cell, type the operator and click on the third, etc. Press Enter when finished.

2. Excel displays the formula in the formula bar, and also indicates the reference for the current cell, in this instance a named reference, Profit.

	A	C
5	Cost of sales	
6	Gross profit	78015
10	Operating overhead	56025
14	Other income	4700
15	Operating profit	26690

Profit   =C6-C10+C14

3. With named cells in a formula, the names replace cell references.

C10   =Depreciation+Expenses

4. Excel applies the normal rules of mathematical precedence, commonly known as BODMAS or BEDMAS.

*Calculators use what is known as Reverse Polish Notation (RPN). This means that formulae are calculated in the order they are entered. This means that on a calculator 2+2*4=16. Don't rely on your calculator to confirm the answer Excel gives.*

B   Brackets
O/E   (power)Of or Exponential
D   Division
M   Multiplication
A   Addition
S   Subtraction

For example, if you enter the expression
=2+2*4   Excel calculates 10   - multiply first
=(2+2)*4   Excel calculates 16   - brackets first

...cont'd

Percentages

1 To calculate a simple percentage, multiply by the percentage factor and include the % symbol in the formula.

TOTAL	10% Surcharge
£ 39.00	=C14*10%

2 To calculate a figure including the percentage factor, multiply the percentage factor plus 100. Again include the % symbol in the formula.

TOTAL	Including 10% Surcharge
£ 39.00	=C14*110%

3 To calculate one figure as a percentage of another, first calculate the ratio. In the example shown, we divide Gross Profit by Sales. No percentage symbol is used in the formula.

	A	B	C	D
3				Profit %
4	Sales	166842		
5	Cost of sales	88827		
6	Gross profit		78015	=C6/Sales

4 The result of the calculation is displayed as a decimal.

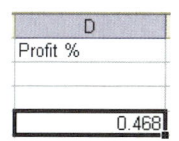

D
Profit %
0.468

You must not use both the Percent Style format and the percentage symbol on the same formula. Your resulting figure will be either 100 times larger or 100 times smaller than it should be, depending on the actual calculation.

5 To convert the decimal to a percentage, select Format, Cells, and the Number tab. Select Percentage, and the number of decimal places.

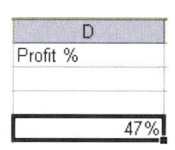

D
Profit %
47%

6 Alternatively, select the cell and click the Percent Style button on the toolbar.

%

Functions

Excel recommends that you use functions from the AutoSum button for calculations with a single range of cells, and the Insert Function facility for more complex functions or multiple ranges.

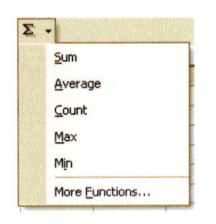

Functions are predefined formulae that compute standard values, such as sum, average or count. Functions allow you to work with a range of cells in a calculation, rather than referencing cells individually. Excel provides a Function Wizard to help you select and use the most appropriate function.

1 To view the list of Functions, select the Insert Function button on the Formula bar.

2 As a first approach you could type in a description of the calculation you wish to make, such as calculate the interest on a payment, and then select Go. The Wizard will return a selection of appropriate functions for you to choose.

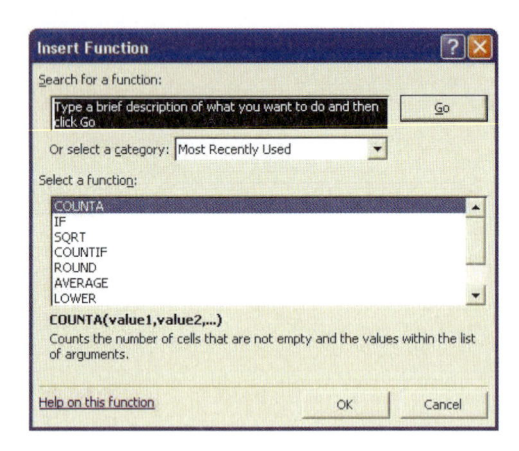

The lower part of the Insert function window describes how the function works. You may find that this description is not very helpful, so there is a further option for Help on this function which opens the Help facility.

With all formulae and functions, it is worth practising on an empty spreadsheet until you are confident. Use simple numbers so that you can verify the outcome.

3 Alternatively, you could select from a list of categories: the Most Recently Used category is currently selected and those functions are displayed in the lower pane.

4 Click in the category box to see a full list of categories. Select All to see the list of over 200 functions arranged alphabetically.

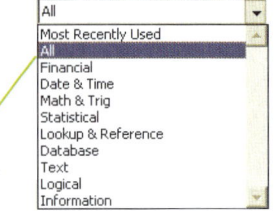

5 When you have selected the function, click on OK and the Function Arguments window will open, see page 56.

...cont'd

AutoSum

The AutoSum Function is the most frequently used function. You will probably be familiar with it from the New CLAIT course. You can type the formula yourself, or you can use the AutoSum button.

> **HOT TIP**: In CLAIT Plus you are expected to create formulae using non-consecutive ranges, or non-adjacent cells. You will need to check carefully which cells AutoSum selects in its formulae.

1 Position the cursor in the cell where you want the answer. Click on the AutoSum button.

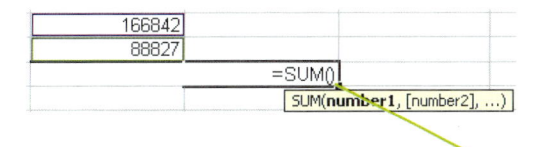

```
166842
 88827
        =SUM()
        SUM(number1, [number2], ...)
```

2 AutoSum will normally add figures above itself. In this instance the figures required are to the left and the cells directly above are empty. In the cell showing SUM, the brackets are empty as Excel does not know which figures to use.

3 You can type in the cell or range references, but it is easier to select them with the mouse. The AutoSum formula shows the cell range.

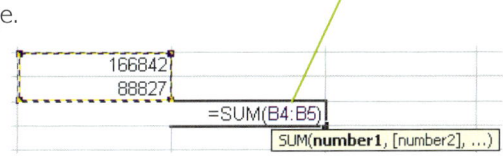

```
166842
 88827
        =SUM(B4:B5)
        SUM(number1, [number2], ...)
```

4 When the correct cells have been selected, press Enter, or click on the tick in the Formula bar.

> **HOT TIP**: When you have clicked AutoSum, select the first range of cells, press and hold Ctrl and select the second range. Excel inserts the comma into the formula for you.

5 To add non-adjacent cells or ranges, separate the references with commas.

TOTAL	Inc VAT	GRAND TOTAL
39	6.825	
45	7.875	
26	4.55	
		=SUM(E10:E12,G10:G12)
		SUM(number1, [number2], ...)

...cont'd

Average function

> In Office 2000, the Average function must be selected from the Insert Function button.

1. The spreadsheet Average function syntax is similar to the Sum function, =average(cell reference:cell reference). You can type it yourself, select it from the AutoSum button, or access it from the Insert Function button.

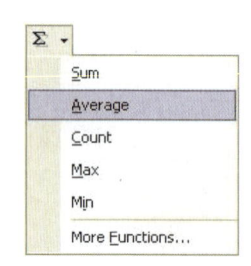

> The Insert Function button provides access to the full list of functions, and it is worth using it for a simple formula such as average, to see how it works.

2. To use the Insert Function method, position the cursor in the correct cell. Click the Insert Function button (see page 54) and select the required function, in this instance Average, and then click OK.

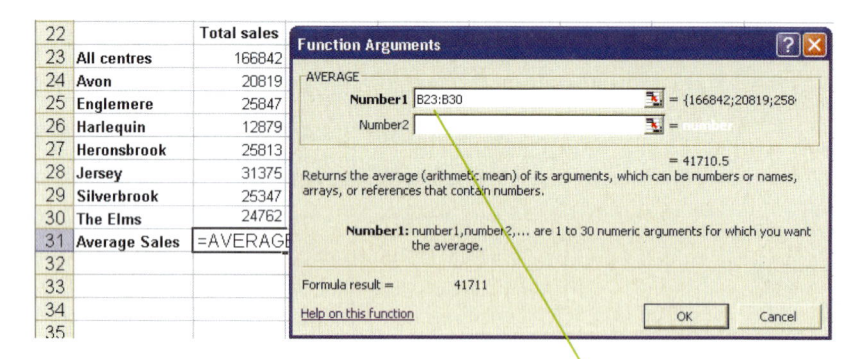

> You could calculate an average without using the spreadsheet function. Calculate a total and divide by the number of constituents, for example =sum(B10:B16)/7. However, if you add another entry, you would manually have to change the divide by 7 to divide by 8.

3. Check that the function has selected the correct range of cells. In this example it has incorrectly included the All Centres figure. Click the Collapse Dialog button to minimise the window and reselect the range. The new range is displayed in the Number box. Click again to restore the window. You could select a second range for the Number 2 box. Click OK when finished.

...cont'd

Max and Min functions are accessed through the Insert Function button, and also on the AutoSum button in Office XP.

Maximum and Minimum functions

To find the largest and smallest numbers in a range of cells use the Max and Min functions. Once again, you can type the formula or let Excel create it for you.

1. Position the cursor in the correct cell and click on the arrow on the AutoSum button to display other standard functions.

The Max and Min functions can be found in the Statistical category, if they are not currently listed in the Most Recently Used.

2. Click on the required function, in this instance Max, and Excel will display the function with the selected range highlighted. Reselect if necessary, and press Enter.

22		Total sales
23	All centres	166842
24	Avon	20819
25	Englemere	25847
26	Harlequin	12879
27	Heronsbrook	25813
28	Jersey	31375
29	Silverbrook	25347
30	The Elms	24762
31	Maximum	=MAX(B24:B30)
32		MAX(**number1**, [number2], ...)

Square root function

The square root function can be found in the Math and Trig category. The syntax for this function is: =sqrt(cell reference).

8	16
9	=SQRT(A8)
10	SQRT(**number**)

Using a Date function is not required by CLAIT Plus, but can be very useful in a working environment.

Date functions

Excel allocates each date a number, starting with 1 for 1st January 1900. As each date has a value it can be used in calculations, such as how many days to Christmas.

Christmas	37980
Today	=TODAY()
How many days to Christmas?	=G4-G5

Christmas	25/12/2003
Today	02/12/2003
How many days to Christmas?	23

To see a date as a number, type in any date and select Format, Cells, click the Number tab and select Number with zero decimal places.

Date and time functions have their own category. To insert today's date into the spreadsheet the syntax is: =today()

Date functions such as =today() and =now() are volatile, which means that they will update automatically each time the spreadsheet is opened.

2. Spreadsheets | 57

...cont'd

> **Hot Tip:** The logical test normally compares two values using: < less than, > greater than, = equal to. The logical test could be an expression with calculated values, such as: IF(A1+B1=C1,..)

If function

The If function will evaluate a logical expression and test if it is true or false. The function syntax is:
=IF(logical_test,value_if_true,value_if_false).
The easiest way to create the function is to use Insert Function.

1 Position the cursor in the correct cell, and click the Insert Function button. Select the If function from the Logical category.

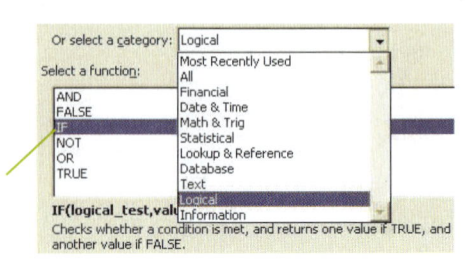

2 In the Function Arguments window, first create the logical test. In this example, we are checking if E24 is greater than E23.

> **Hot Tip:** The cell reference E24 is an absolute reference in this instance as we will need to copy the formula to other cells.

> **Hot Tip:** The text in the 'Value_if_true' box and the 'Value_if_false' box is known as a text string. If you wish to type the whole IF function yourself, you must remember to include any text strings in inverted commas.

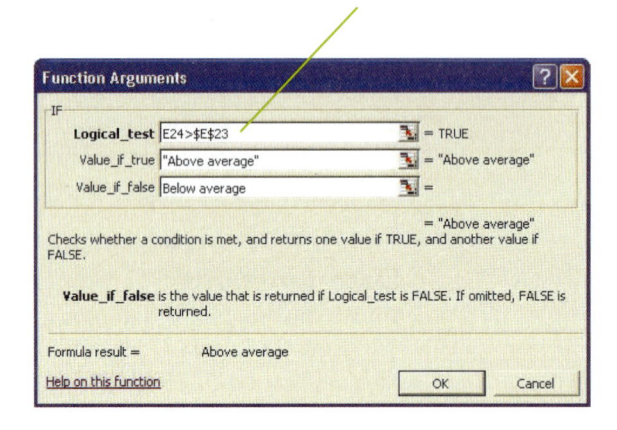

3 In the Value_if_true box type the required text, and again for the Value_if_false. The Function Arguments window is updated to include more helpful information as you complete each field. Note that Excel inserts the inverted commas around the text automatically. Click OK when finished.

...cont'd

The Count functions are found in the Statistical category.

Count functions

Count counts entries within a selected range that contain numbers.
Counta counts the number of text entries in a selected range.
Countif counts the number of entries that match a given criteria.
Countblank counts the number of empty cells in a range.

For simple functions like Count and Counta, it may be faster to type them in.

1 For the Count or Counta functions, use the Insert Function button and choose the required function. Select the range of cells to be counted and click OK.

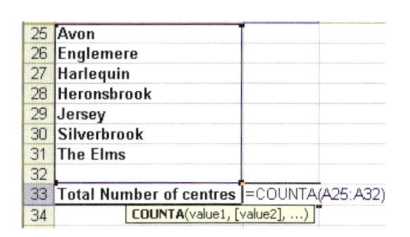

	A	B
25	Avon	
26	Englemere	
27	Harlequin	
28	Heronsbrook	
29	Jersey	
30	Silverbrook	
31	The Elms	
32		
33	Total Number of centres	=COUNTA(A25:A32)
34		COUNTA(value1, [value2], …)

	A	B
25	Avon	20819
26	Englemere	25847
27	Harlequin	12879
28	Heronsbrook	25813
29	Jersey	31375
30	Silverbrook	25347
31	The Elms	24762
32		
33	Total Number of centres	=COUNT(B25:B32)
34		COUNT(value1, [value2], …)

Familiarity with the If function will help when using Countif.

2 The Countif function will count entries that meet a condition. The condition could be an expression that uses a comparison (=,>,<), a number, or a text string.

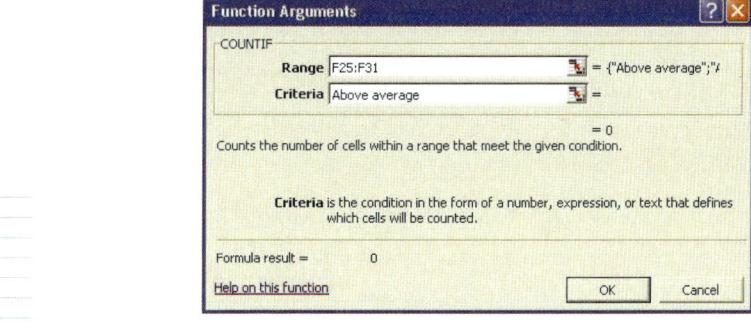

```
Function Arguments
COUNTIF
   Range    F25:F31          = {"Above average";"/
   Criteria Above average    =
                             = 0
Counts the number of cells within a range that meet the given condition.

   Criteria is the condition in the form of a number, expression, or text that defines
            which cells will be counted.

Formula result =         0
Help on this function                          OK        Cancel
```

Above average
Above average
Below average
Above average
Above average
Below average
Below average

=COUNTIF(F25:F32,"Above average")
COUNTIF(range, criteria)

3 Enter the range of cells to count and in the Criteria box enter the condition. In the example shown, Countif will count those cells that contain the text 'Above average'. Click OK when finished.

Sort

For CLAIT Plus you are only required to use the Sort feature.

See page 270 in Spreadsheet Solutions for other database functions in the spreadsheet.

Excel has an extensive database facility. It allows you to sort data, by one or several keys. It can apply filters, search for data and let you create complex queries.

When using the database facilities in Excel, you can specify the data range to use. However, it is often worth separating data ranges with blank lines as Excel recognises and works within a data range if it is separate. To use the Sort facility:

1. If you have a separate data area, just position the cursor within the data range. Otherwise, select the required data area. From the Menu choose Data, Sort.

2. When the Sort window opens you should see the selected data range highlighted in the background. Check that it is correct.

3. The Sort window allows you to sort by three levels, and at each level in ascending or descending order. Excel will usually recognise if the columns have a header row, and if so offer the headings in the Sort by box.

4. Select the Options button for further sorting options, if for example you wished to sort left to right, rather than the more normal top to bottom. Click OK when finished, and check the result on the spreadsheet.

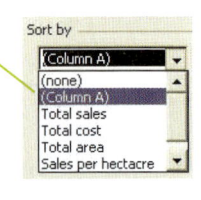

The Undo button will undo an incorrect Sort, which could be very useful if headings were sorted as well in error.

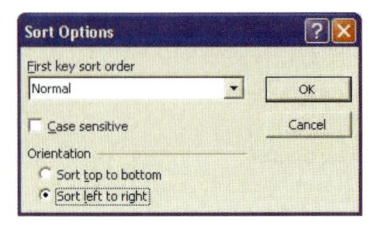

60 | CLAIT Plus in easy steps

Number format

You will be given a House Style sheet to use with the exercise. This will dictate the various number formats you will be required to use.

Excel uses the General format for all text and numbers when you open a new spreadsheet. This means that numbers will be displayed as typed, except for trailing zeros which will be dropped. So for example 1.50 will display as 1.5.

1 You can use the Increase and Decrease decimal buttons on the toolbar. If your numbers display a variety of decimals places, then the first click of the button will consolidate the number of decimals. Continue the clicking until the correct number shows.

Select Currency or Accounting to be able to select the Euro symbol from the Symbol box.

2 Use Format, Cells and the Number tab for a greater choice of formats. In this window you can select number of decimal places, to use a comma separator in thousands or show negative numbers in red or in brackets.

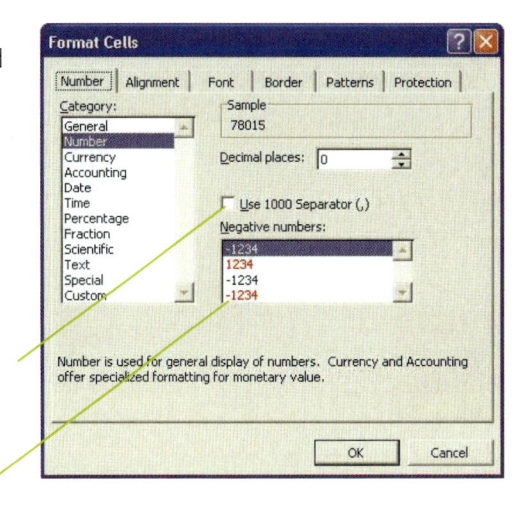

3 Select Currency to display the £ symbol, or Accounting to display the £ symbols left aligned.

Total sales
£20,819.00
£25,847.00
£12,879.00

Total sales	
£	20,819.00
£	25,847.00
£	12,879.00

For dates within the Header and Footer, see page 65.

4 For displaying dates within the spreadsheet, select Date in the Category box, and the format in the Type box. Note that the Locale must be English (UK).

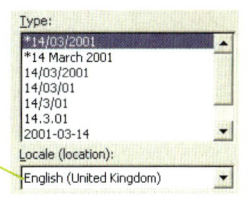

2. Spreadsheets | 61

Borders and shading

HOT TIP: *The Borders button on the toolbar allows you to draw a border. When you select it the Borders toolbar opens and the mouse becomes a pen. Click the Close button on the Borders toolbar when finished.*

1. To create a border around a cell or range of cells, first select the cells.

2. The Borders button on the toolbar gives quick access to the range of border options. You can select one or several sides, an outside border, or a full grid. The toolbar button displays the latest selection used.

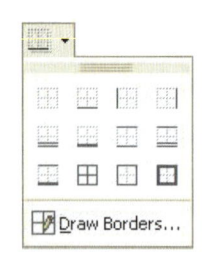

DON'T FORGET: *Gridlines, as opposed to Borders, are available from Page Setup, see page 67.*

3. For the full range of options, including selecting line thickness, you must use the Menu and select Format, Cells, Borders tab.

4. First select the Line Style. You can then choose from the Presets of None, or Outline and/or Inside. Alternatively, select a side or sides by clicking inside the Preview pane, or by using the buttons around it. The buttons are toggles, click to select, click to deselect. Click OK to return to the spreadsheet.

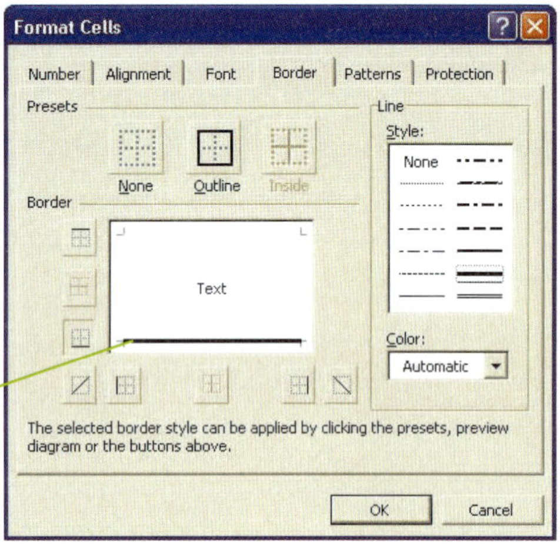

HOT TIP: *From this window you can select a colour for your border, or even to have diagonal lines, in effect crossing out each cell.*

HOT TIP: *To remove a border, select the range and choose None.*

HOT TIP: *Shading areas of the spreadsheet can be a very effective way of highlighting specific elements such as totals.*

5. Select the Patterns tab to choose an option to fill the cells with colour or pattern. If you do shade the cells, it's a good idea to stay with paler colours, to avoid obscuring the contents.

Document management

Margins

1. To set the margins for the spreadsheet, select File, Page Setup.

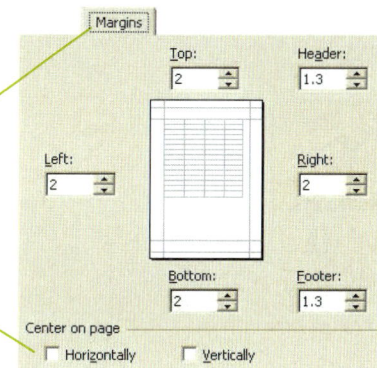

2. Select the Margins tab and adjust the settings as required.

You should check the House Style sheet in the CLAIT Plus exercise and make sure to follow its specifications.

3. This window provides the option to centre the printed area on the page.

4. To see how the margins will affect the page layout, select the Print Preview button. The Print Preview window provides another, but different, Margins button. Click on it to display the margins that have been set. Click again to remove the lines.

Always use the Print Preview window. It will save much time, ink and paper.

Orientation

1. The page orientation will be specified by the exercise. The Excel default is Portrait. Select File, Page Setup, or choose Print Preview and Setup.

2. Click in the required orientation.

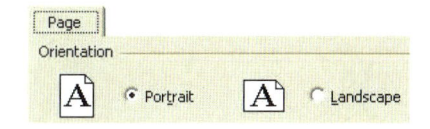

3. The spreadsheet will maintain the selected orientation for any future prints. New files will revert to Portrait.

2. Spreadsheets | 63

Headers and footers

You can access the Headers and Footers window by selecting Print Preview and Setup.

Headers and Footers that have been created previously can be viewed and selected by clicking on the drop down arrow on the Header or Footer bar.

1. To create Headers and Footers to your document, select File, Page Setup and the Headers and Footers tab.

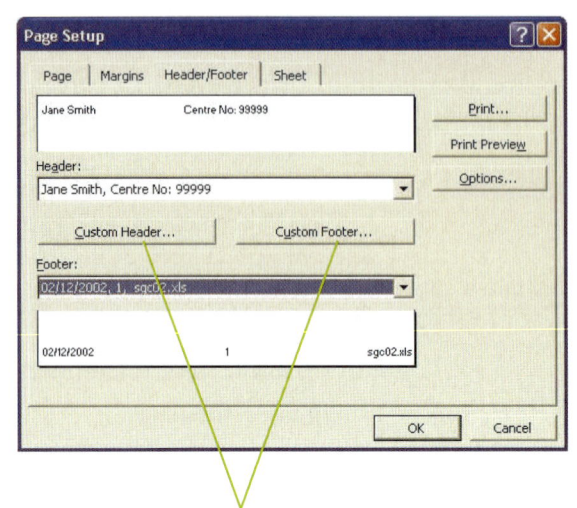

2. Click on the Custom Header or Custom Footer button.

Use the format font button to change your text style to conform with the House style.

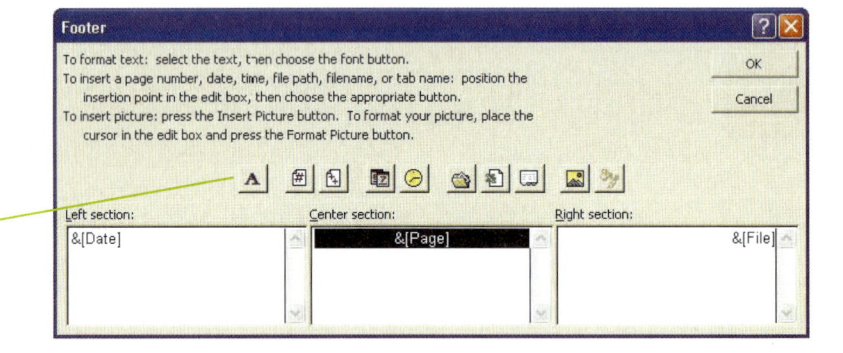

3. The Header or Footer area is divided into three sections and each section or edit box is treated independently.

4. For plain text, such as your name or centre number, you can just click in a box and type.

...cont'd

Using Autotext means that file names, dates and page numbers get automatically updated.

Autotext

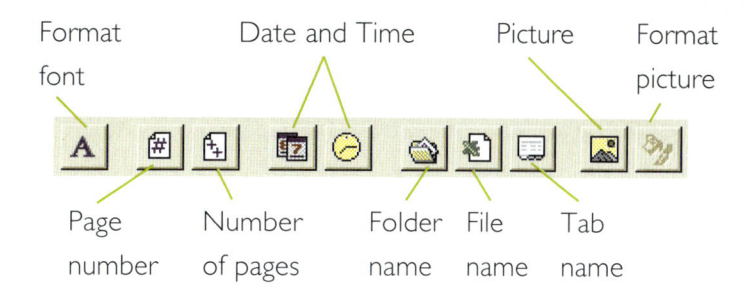

Format font — Date and Time — Picture — Format picture

Page number — Number of pages — Folder name — File name — Tab name

For CLAIT Plus you will only need to be able to insert filename, page number and date. Check that the date format is English - dd/mm/yyyy.

5 The Header and Footer toolbar provides autotext buttons. Click in each section of the Header or Footer in turn and select the required item. You will only see symbols, such as &[File] or &[Page].

6 Format font can be used with the text you type, or for the autotext fields. Select the autotext entry and then click the Format font button.

7 Select the Folder name to identify where the file is saved. If you have several drives, or a complex folder structure this option can be very useful.

To rename the sheet from Sheet 1, go to the normal spreadsheet window, double click on the tab at the bottom of the screen. The name will be selected and you can type a new name.

8 Selecting the Tab name will include the Sheet number or name.

9 When you are using several sheets in your workbook, you can create Headers and Footers that apply to all sheets. Click on the first Sheet tab at the bottom of the screen, press the Shift key and click on the last Sheet tab. Now when you create your Header or Footer, it will apply to all.

2. Spreadsheets | 65

Print

In Excel 2000, you will need to select Tools, Options, and on the View tab, click the Formula option. In any version of Excel use Ctrl+` (the key above the tab key) as a shortcut.

Print formulae

1. To display formulae on the spreadsheet, select Tools, Formula Auditing and Formula Auditing Mode.

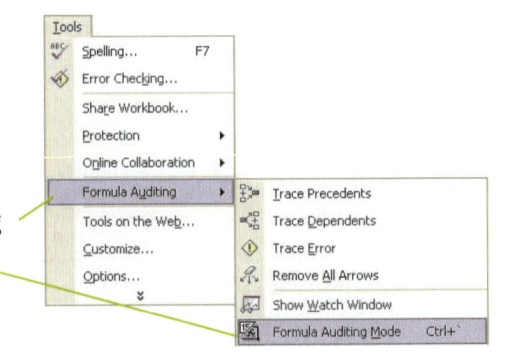

Check the final printout to make sure that no data or ends of formulae are missing.

2. With formulae displayed, text and numbers will lose special formatting, such as number of decimal places and alignment. Columns will widen automatically, but not necessarily enough to display the complete formulae. You may need to manually adjust the columns.

Print selection or hide columns and rows

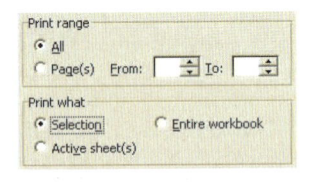

1. To print an area of the spreadsheet, you can select the area, and select File, Print, and click in the Print selection box. Check in the Print Preview window before printing.

This can be a useful way of working with a large spreadsheet. The data remains, and can be used in calculations. See page 269 for Freezing Panes in a large spreadsheet.

To print non-consecutive columns or rows, you can hide the intervening range.

2. Select the columns or rows that are not required and click on Format, Columns/Rows and Hide. See page 271 for further information.

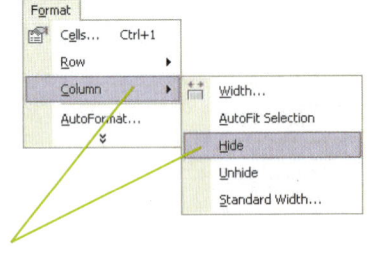

3. To restore the hidden area, select the columns or rows either side of the hidden area, and click Format, Columns/Rows, Unhide.

...cont'd

Print headings and gridlines

Printing column and row headings lets you check formulae in hard copy.

1 Select File, Page Setup and the Sheet tab to access special features for printing. You can select a Print area, Print titles, Gridlines and Row and column headings - ABC, 123. You can also select the Page order.

If you select Setup from the Print Preview menu, you will be unable to set a Print area, or Print titles. These options are only available when you use File, Page Setup.

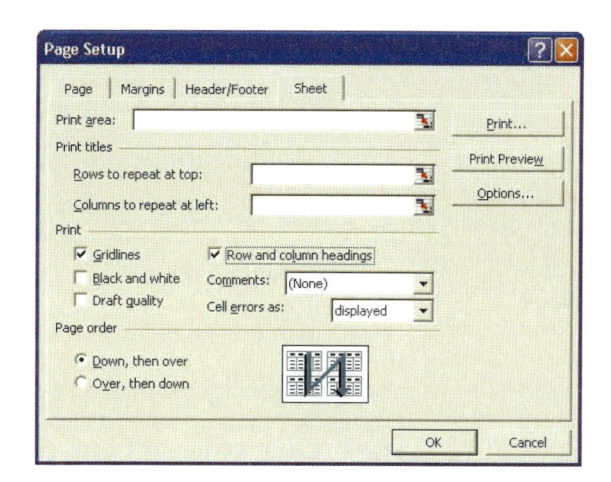

2 Be sure to use Print Preview before actually printing to confirm you have the required details and everything displays correctly.

Fit to page

You will be required to fit a document to a specified number of pages. However, using Fit to page this way will shrink the text size. You should try to make the document fit by narrowing columns or rows.

1 In the Page Setup window, select the Page tab, and view the Scaling options. You can click the Adjust box and choose your scaling percentage, larger or smaller.

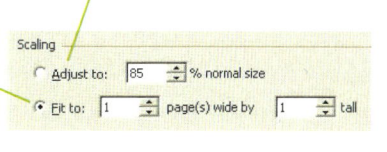

Use Print Preview to check the effect of the degree of scaling chosen.

2 Select the Fit to: box and set the number of pages. Excel will adjust the scaling for you.

2. Spreadsheets | 67

Checklist

You are allowed three hours to complete the OCR CLAIT Plus assessment.

When you have completed the exercise, run through a final check to ensure that you meet the specifications. Have you:

- used the correct file names
- input new data accurately
- created correct formulae
- created relative, absolute, named and linked references
- followed the House Style sheet for text and number formats
- set the correct margins, headers and footers
- used English date format
- included your name, Centre number and date on all prints
- produced the required number of prints
- printed the formulae used
- checked your prints to ensure all data is displayed
- proofread your prints
- saved the spreadsheets

If you have used the downloadable exercises, you can check your work against the files in the Worked Copy folder.

Marking

You are not allowed any critical errors. The following are considered critical errors:

- error in entering numeric data that could be used in calculations
- failure to link data from one spreadsheet to another
- formulae or functions that produce incorrect results
- failure to display data in full
- project incorrect results
- incorrect sort results

You should consult your tutor for full details of critical and accuracy errors.

Databases

In this unit you will learn how to create a database and input data. It includes importing and manipulating data, and creating queries and reports.

Covers

Databases | 70

Create a database | 71

Table design | 72

Create a table | 73

Save the table | 75

Amend the design | 76

Import data | 77

Queries | 82

Calculated field | 84

Forms | 85

Create labels | 86

Report with summary | 88

Report design | 90

Report controls | 92

Checklist | 94

Unit Three

Databases

This unit follows a complete database exercise. The exercise and data files can be downloaded from the In Easy Steps web site (see page 281).

More database topics are covered in the Solutions Units 10-16, pages 245-247, and the MOS units 17-21 pages 272-273.

Use Find and Replace, as covered in New CLAIT, to swiftly encode data.

In this unit we will be using Access 2002, part of Office XP. Any substantial differences between software releases will be highlighted and alternative methods suggested.

Unit Three overview

This unit covers the following areas:

1. Creating a database. You will create fields, select data types and set field lengths and formats.

2. Selecting the relevant data from a supplied data source, entering data into tables and using codes.

3. Importing data from an external source to create a database. You will be given a .csv (comma separated variable) file to use.

4. Managing the database table by inserting, deleting and moving fields, and inserting, deleting and replacing data.

5. Creating and saving complex queries. You will use multiple search criteria and learn to use a variety of logical and mathematical operators.

6. Creating and saving various reports. This includes creating labels, tabular reports and grouped or summary reports.

Exercise files and documentation

You should have the following items:

- a .csv file
- the exercise, including some data records
- a House Style sheet

Create a database

HOT TIP: *Using a database to manage data and create queries was covered in New CLAIT. If you did not cover this unit, or are unfamiliar with database, it would be a good idea to explore the New CLAIT unit before you start.*

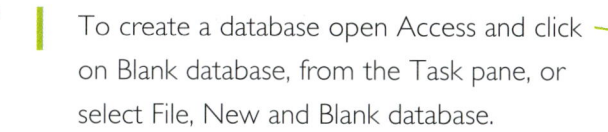

1 To create a database open Access and click on Blank database, from the Task pane, or select File, New and Blank database.

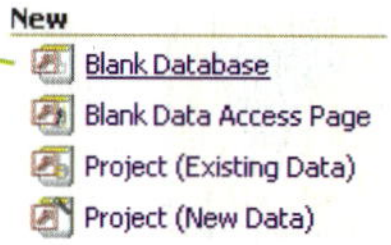

2 Access saves data directly to the hard disk. To do this it needs a file name and location, so first name the file and click on Create.

Navigation panel

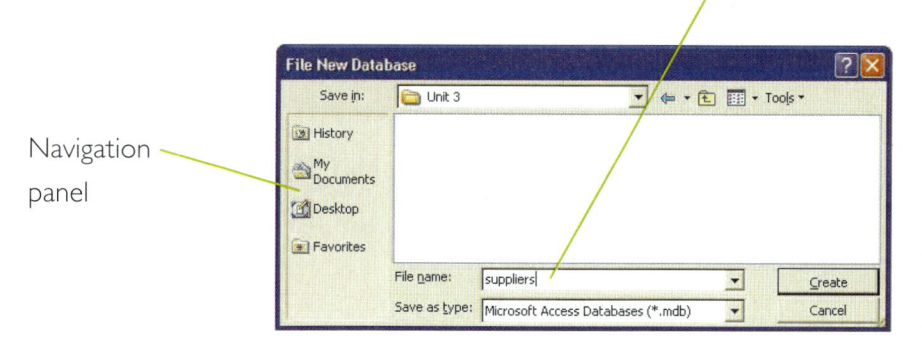

3 The Title bar of the main database window indicates the database name, and the file format. This window provides access to database objects such as Queries, Forms and Reports through the navigation panel.

HOT TIP: *Access 2002 (the XP version) is able to save databases in the Access 2000 file format.*

DON'T FORGET: *In the CLAIT Plus course, you will be working with Tables, Queries and Reports.*

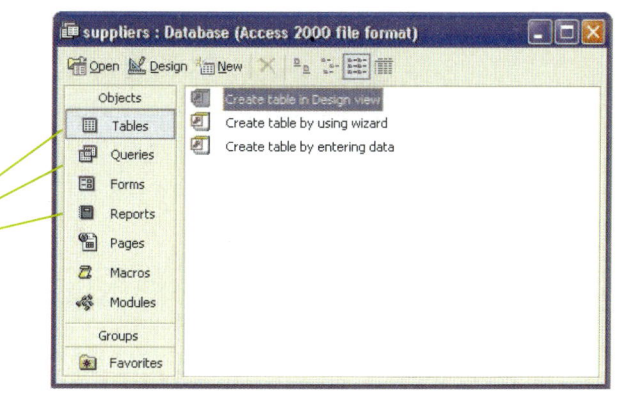

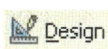

4 Select Create table in design view, or click on the Design icon.

3. Databases | 71

Table design

Even if you have taken the New CLAIT database unit, you may not have created a table from scratch.

A database table has a defined structure. It is composed of a series of records where each record is all the information about one item or entry in the table.

Each record is divided into fields, and each field has a type of content or characteristic such as text, number, date etc.

Field names
These are used to identify the contents, and are given in the CLAIT exercise.

Data type
Text - for text and alphanumeric, such as telephone numbers

For CLAIT Plus you will be expected to use text, number, date/time, currency, autonumber and logical field types.

Memo - for larger amounts of general text

Number - for numbers that may be used in calculations

Date/Time - with selected formats

Currency - with £ or Euro

Autonumber - a unique identifying number, system generated

Yes/No - logical, true/false

OLE - linked to an object elsewhere on the computer

See Relationships between Tables on pages 245-247.

Hyperlink - linked to an object on a network

Lookup Wizard - link to another table

Description

You are not required to use a description when you create the table.

The Description is used to tell other users of the database what is required in that field. Any description you create will be displayed in the Status bar when you enter data into or amend that field.

Field Properties
These are used to set the Field size or to select a format for the data display. For example, you can select a date to display as 25/09/03 or 25 September 2003. With the logical data type, you can select Yes/no, True/false or On/off. In this section you can also set default values and validate entries, by only allowing entries between a set of values.

Create a table

1 The Table Design window is divided into two sections. The top part is for Field Names, Data Type and any Description. The lower part is for Field Properties for the selected Field Name.

2 Type in the first Field Name, retaining the capitalisation as presented in the exercise. Press Enter or Tab to move to the Data Type column.

BEWARE: You cannot use Name as the name for a field as it is known as a reserved term. Using it causes conflict in some database activities.

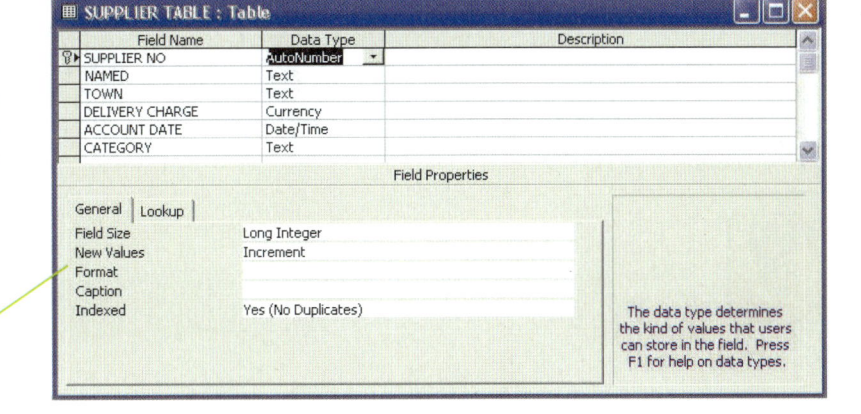

Field properties

HOT TIP: For fields such as Supplier No or Customer No you would normally select Autonumber. See page 75.

3 Click on the down arrow in the Data Type column to see the list of data types and select as appropriate. You will need to look at the exercise data forms to decide on the data type.

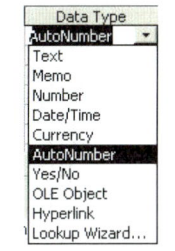

HOT TIP: See page 74 for setting the field size for numbers.

4 In the Field Properties section, set the Field Size as appropriate. For Text the default field size is 50, but you may have up to 255 characters. For encoded fields you may wish to reduce the size substantially. Changing the Field Size does not affect the column widths on the datasheet, just how many characters can be entered.

3. Databases | 73

...cont'd

HOT TIP
Single and Double will handle 7 and 15 digits respectively.

5 In the Field Properties panel, Number fields are by default set to Integer (whole numbers). To enter decimals, first select Single or Double from the Field Size drop down list.

6 You will also need to select General or Fixed for decimals from the Field Format options.

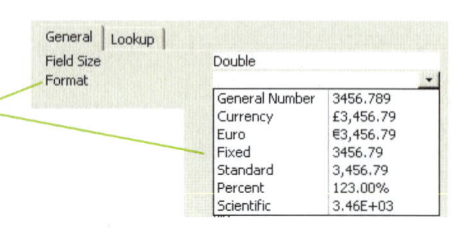

DON'T FORGET
Including the £ sign in the datasheet can make the numbers less clear, so you could put the symbol in the field heading. You must however, follow the exercise instructions.

7 If you choose a General format for the numbers you can also set number of decimal places.

8 When the Data Type is set to Currency, the £ symbol will display on the datasheet and the number of decimal places will be set to Auto. You could also choose Euro •, or choose Fixed to show two decimal places and no currency sign.

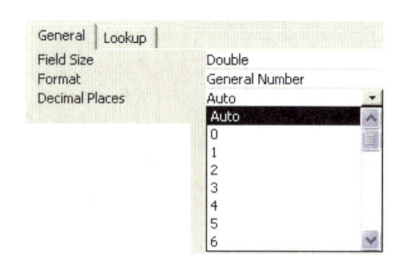

HOT TIP
If you select the Long or Medium date you can still type in just numbers, such as 25/12/03. Access will convert it automatically. Note however, that it is often easier to accommodate the Short Date format in a report.

9 For a Date field, the date must display an English format, day/month/year, set by Regional Settings in the Control Panel.

74 | CLAIT Plus in easy steps

Save the table

When you have created all the field headings and specified the data types and formats, you can switch to the datasheet to enter data.

You can save the table by clicking on the Close button on the Table Title bar. You will be prompted to save the design and asked for a name. You will also be prompted for a Primary Key, as in Step 3.

1. Click on the Datasheet view button on the toolbar. The button alternates between Datasheet and Design view according to your current view.

2. You will be prompted to save the table. Click Yes to save the table and supply a name. Click OK to finish.

3. Access will now recommend that you create a primary key. Setting a primary key allows you to link tables together and is good database practice. Access will normally use Autonumber as the primary key as this is a unique identifying number.

Access is a full relational database. You can create and use several tables within the same database and link them using the primary key.

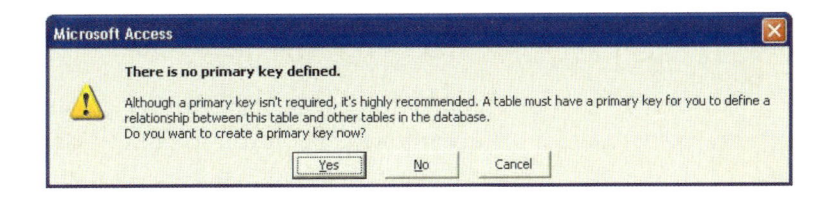

4. Click Yes to agree to a primary key and the datasheet view will open. As Supplier No was set to the Autonumber data type, it is used as the primary key.

The autonumber data type field will increment automatically. You cannot type in the field, just press Enter or Tab to skip it.

5. Press Enter to skip the first field. As you type the next field, the autonumber changes to a 1.

Amend the design

1 You can change or create field headings by simply switching to Design view and editing as normal.

It's a good idea to create a copy of the main table using the standard Copy and Paste icons in the main database window. You can always delete the second table when you are sure everything is correct.

2 If you need to amend the data type, you must make sure that you have selected the correct field. Changing the data type may change the field contents permanently. You will not be warned of the problems that may occur, or be able to revert to the original data once you save the table.

Amending the design or deleting fields cannot be undone. Make sure that you are selecting the correct fields.

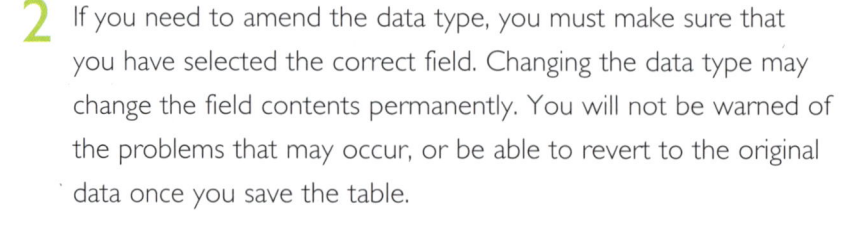

3 To delete a complete field and its contents in Design view, simply select the row in the side bar and press the delete key on the keyboard. You will get a warning message and need to confirm the deletion.

4 To insert a new field in between existing fields, position the cursor in the row below where you want it. Click on the Insert Rows button on the toolbar, or Insert, Rows on the Menu.

You can move a column in either Datasheet or Design view. For consistency however, changes should be applied in Design view.

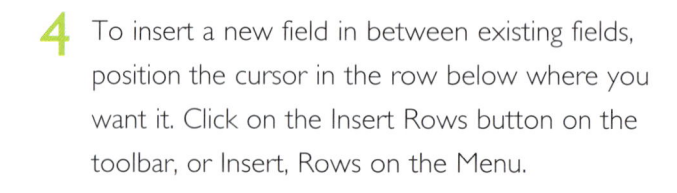

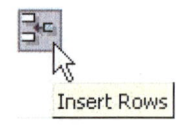

You can also move a column in Datasheet view. Select the column, press the mouse again, and drag the column to its new location.

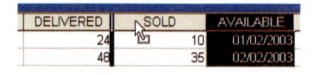

The table layout does change, but the fields will still be listed in the original order in Design view.

5 In Design view, click in the side bar to select the row to move and release the mouse button. The mouse will now become an arrow when it is on the selected row. Press the mouse button again and drag the row to its new position. As you move up or down the rows, you will see a thicker black band. Release the mouse button when ready.

76 | CLAIT Plus in easy steps

Import data

An Access table, an Excel spreadsheet and a Word table all have a similar structure. This means that data can be transferred between them quite easily.

Access and Excel are both database applications and each uses its own coding to manage the structure of records and fields. However, it is possible to create a generic file format that can be shared by both. A .csv (comma separated values file) can be read by Excel and Access, just as a plain .txt file can be read by WordPad and Word.

For the CLAIT Plus exercise you will be given a database, supplied as a .csv file. If you open the file in NotePad, you can see the structure.

When you import data, the original file remains intact so that if you need to, you can start again.

You can import data into an existing or a new database. The CLAIT Plus exercise will usually require a new database.

Create the database file, then import the data as the table.

1 Create a new database file, as described on page 71, Steps 1 and 2. Use the name given in the CLAIT Plus exercise.

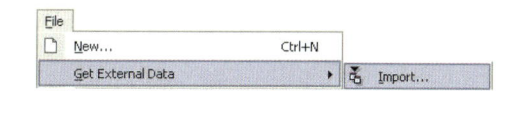

You can use the Windows Search/Find facility to locate the file before you start.

2 Click on File, Get External Data and Import.

3 In the Import window change the Files of type box to look for Text Files, and navigate the folders, if necessary, to the data file location.

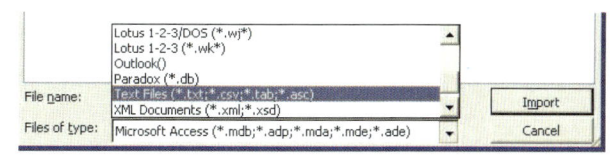

3. Databases | 77

...cont'd

4 Select the file and click on Import.

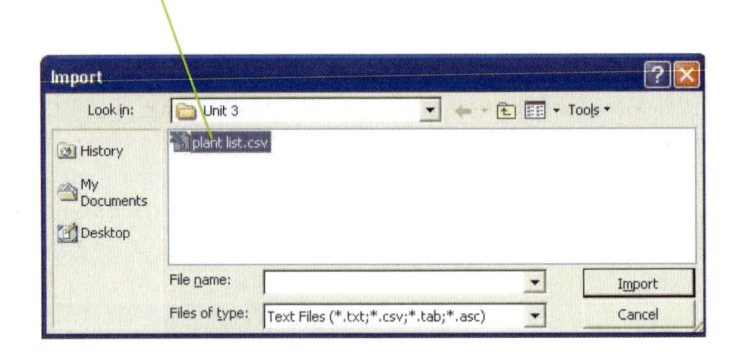

The Import Text wizard

The Wizard will take you a step at a time through the process of converting a .csv file to a database table. It assesses the format of the data and shows sample data from the file in a preview pane. You'll see that Access treats each line as a separate entry or record.

Access has recognised that the fields are delimited (separated) by commas.

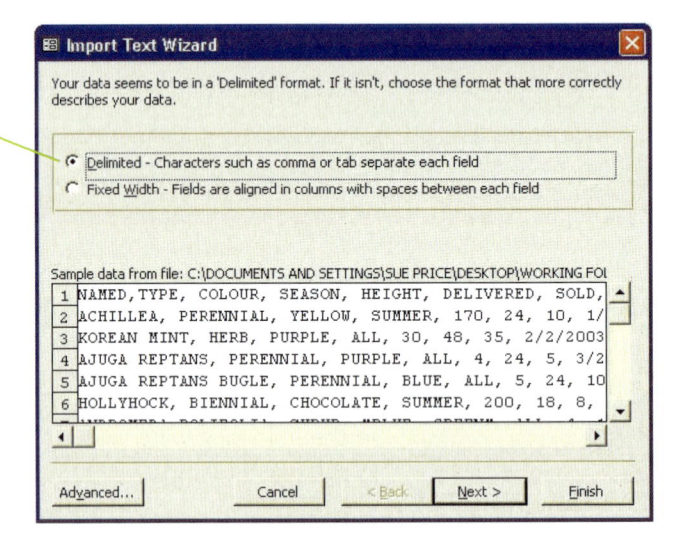

Click Next to move to the next step of the Wizard, where you will be able to select a greater degree of formatting for the data table.

...cont'd

> **Hot Tip:** *Access has correctly chosen Comma as the separator but you can try other options for yourself to see the effect.*

> **Hot Tip:** *A text qualifier keeps a text field together. For example, in the Colour field a plant is described as having two attributes - blue, green. The words are separated by a comma. To keep this as one field, the words "blue, green" are in inverted commas. You should select a text qualifier, even if you cannot see any potential problems.*

> **Beware:** *If you reverse steps 3 and 4, you will get an error message indicating that the field headings are incorrect. Click OK to proceed and Access will resolve the problem.*

2 With the Comma separator already selected by the Wizard, the data table begins to take shape.

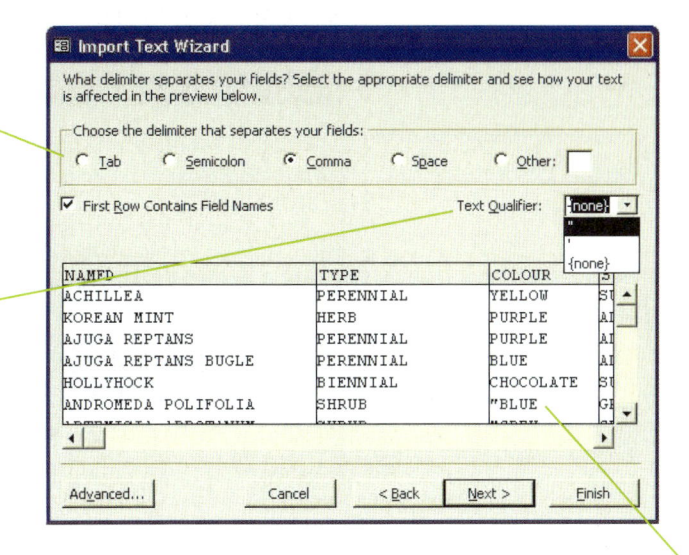

3 The first step on this window is to select a Text Qualifier. In the sample data shown you can see inverted commas before the word Blue. Select the Inverted Commas Text Qualifier and Blue, Green will be treated as one field.

4 Then tick the box to confirm that First Row Contains Field Names. Click the Next button.

5 In the following window choose to store the data In a New Table. You could type a name or select from a drop down list if you wanted to use an existing table. Click Next.

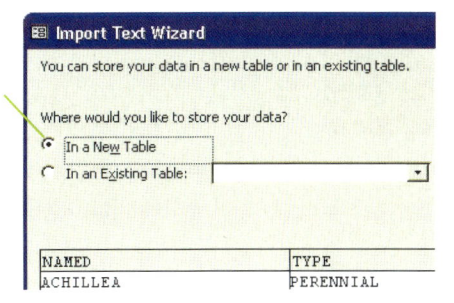

3. Databases | 79

...cont'd

6 In this step you can check each field individually to see the field name and data type assigned and modify them if necessary. Click Next when finished.

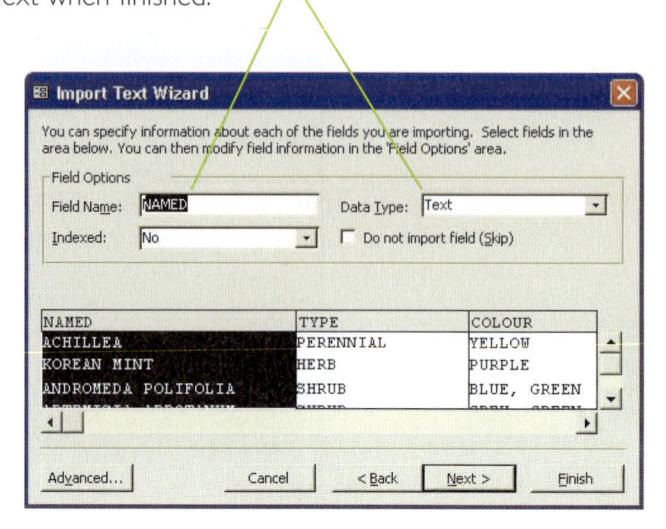

Use the scroll bars to view the other fields.

See page 75 for more information on the Primary key.

7 Next Access will recommend that you use a primary key, and will insert an ID field. Accept the Primary key and click Next.

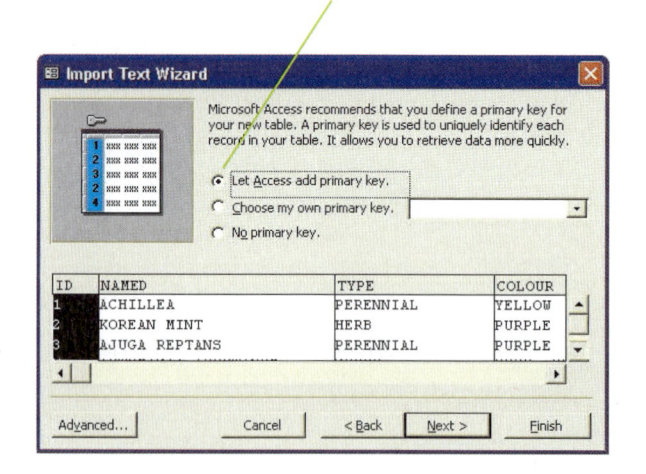

You must use the table name as specified in the exercise. This is a CLAIT Plus requirement.

8 Finally you will be required to supply or confirm the table name. Click Finish and the table will be created.

...cont'd

Hot Tip: When the table has been imported you should check to make sure it is correct. You can amend it in Design view if necessary, see page 76.

Don't Forget: Adding, removing and amending individual records in Table view is covered in New CLAIT.

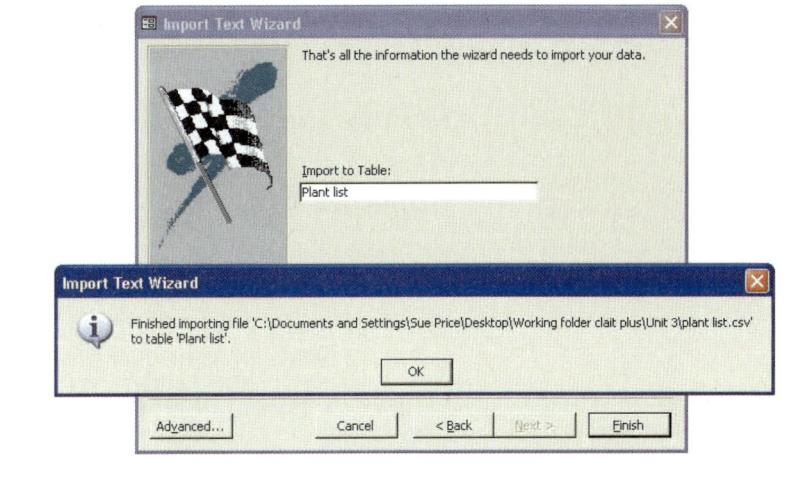

9 The message confirms that the table has been created from the original data file, and provides the full folder name and location.

Error messages

If the Wizard encounters any problems in importing the data it will display an error message.

Hot Tip: The errors may be a mismatch between the number of field headings and the number of fields, or between data type and field content.

Hot Tip: The .csv file should import without any errors. If you do get error messages, then you have probably missed a step in the Import process.

1 Access will create the table and also a table of errors. Open the error table, to view the field and row number of the errors.

2 If there are only a few errors, you could open the original .csv file in NotePad and check for the correct data. If there are many, then it would be easier to start the Import process again.

3. Databases | 81

Queries

Hot Tip: *Build your query one step at a time. Select your fields then run your query. Return to the design and add a criterion. Run the query again, and so on. If the query fails, then you know which step caused the problem.*

To create a query:

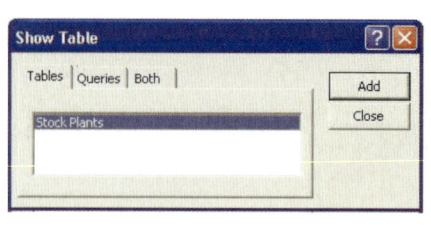

1. Select the Queries tab and click on Create Query in Design view. Select the table and click Add and Close.

2. Select the fields for your query from the window. You can double click on each field name, or click in the empty column and select from the drop down list.

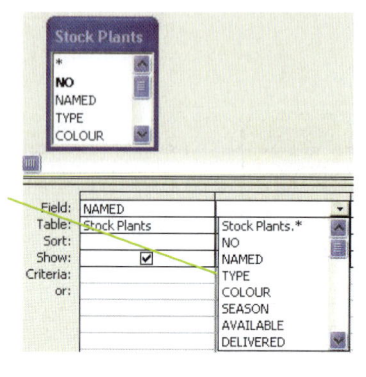

Beware: *If you select the same field twice it will show twice when you run the query, but with the field name Expr 100(n). Return to the design view and delete the duplicated column.*

And, Or, Not

Beware: *In normal English usage we would say "perennials and annuals". You should use OR, not And, in this query, as a plant cannot be both an Annual and a Perennial.*

These two queries shown above will return the same result. They are searching for "Perennials and Annuals". You would normally just use the single criteria row. Use the 'OR' criteria row for more complex searches, as shown below.

This query would limit the search to a Type (perennial) AND specific colours.

Using the 'OR' criteria row allows you to use multiple search criteria. For example, you could search for Perennials that are blue or Annuals that are white. You can have several levels of OR.

...cont'd

Use NOT as a quick way to exclude one value in the field and include the remaining. This query would exclude perennials.

Range operators
You will be expected to use the following criteria for selecting data:

= equal to
< less than
> greater than
<= less than or equal to
>= greater than or equal to

Access allows you to use the word 'between'. It is the same as typing the range operators >= AND <=.

In the example shown, the criteria used would select prices from £2 to £3 inclusive.

Wild cards
Access offers several symbols that can be used as 'wild cards' when creating queries and doing searches. You will need to understand and use the following:

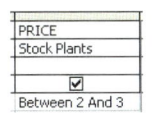

When you are entering criteria in a Currency field, you do not type the £ symbol.

*   this represents any or all character at the beginning or end of character strings
for example *ch finds each, such, teach, ch* finds church, chapel, challenge.
?   represents a single character
for example l?tter finds latter, letter and litter.
represents a single numeric character in a text field
for example 020# finds area codes 0207, 0208

*Using the database exercise downloaded from the Internet, try the effect of using the * either before or after the SH to see how the result differs.*

In the first example shown, the criteria is set to find Shrubs and Ev Sh (evergreen shrubs). In this instance both variations of the use of shrub are explicitly used.

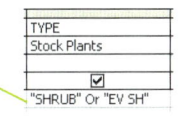

In the second example the wild card * is used to find any field that contains the value SH. Using the * both before and after the text would include all records that have SH. You only need to type *SH*, as Access will insert Like and the quote marks.

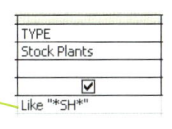

Calculated field

Number, Currency or Date data types can be used in calculations in queries.

To create a calculation in a query:

1. Select the fields for the queries as usual, then click in the next empty column and click the Build button.

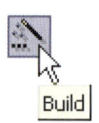

2. The Expression Builder provides a structured way to create the calculation. Initially the top pane will be empty but will display your calculation as you build it.

You could expand the list of Queries to use another query as the basis of your calculation.

3. Double click on the + next to Tables in the left pane to open the folder. Select from the list.

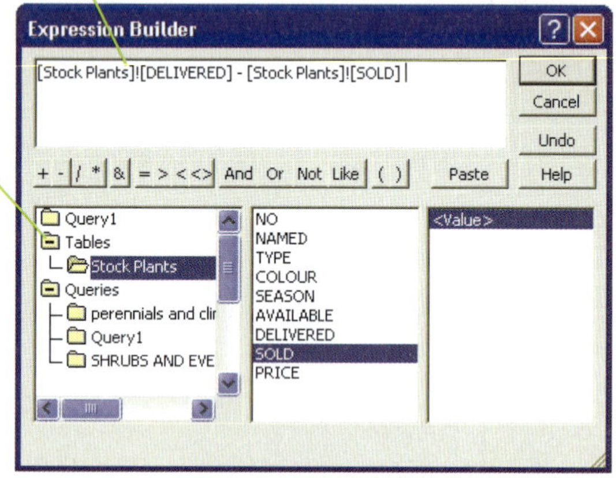

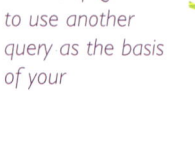

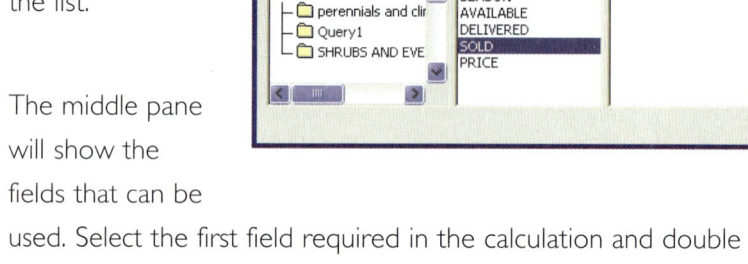

The Expression builder has a useful Undo facility!

4. The middle pane will show the fields that can be used. Select the first field required in the calculation and double click or click on Paste. It will be inserted at the top.

You can just type the expression if you wish. The format is Field heading : [field 1] Operator [field 2]. Where you have more than one table in the database, you should use the Expression Builder.

5. Click on the operator from the buttons in the middle. Select the second field and double click or Paste. Click OK when finished.

6. In Design view, widen the column to display the full expression. Delete the text Expr1 and type the required field name before the : (colon). This name becomes the heading for the calculated field.

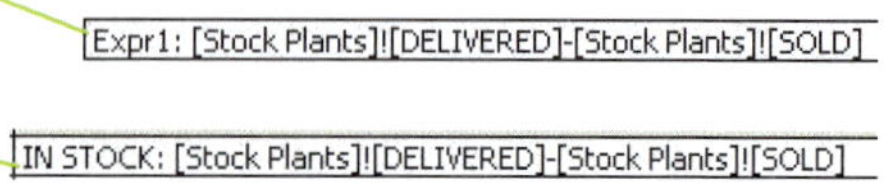

Expr1: [Stock Plants]![DELIVERED]-[Stock Plants]![SOLD]

IN STOCK: [Stock Plants]![DELIVERED]-[Stock Plants]![SOLD]

Forms

Creating and using forms is not required in Unit 3. It is needed if you decide to take Unit 11, Database Solutions.

Forms are used primarily for the entry and display of data in a database table. A form can be based on a full or partial list of field headings in a table or a query. To create a form in Access:

1. Select the Forms tab and click on Create form by using wizard.

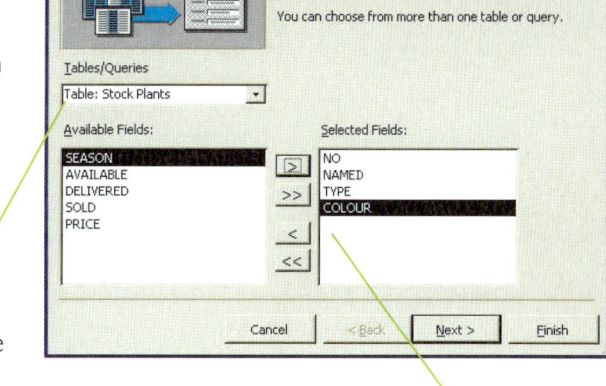

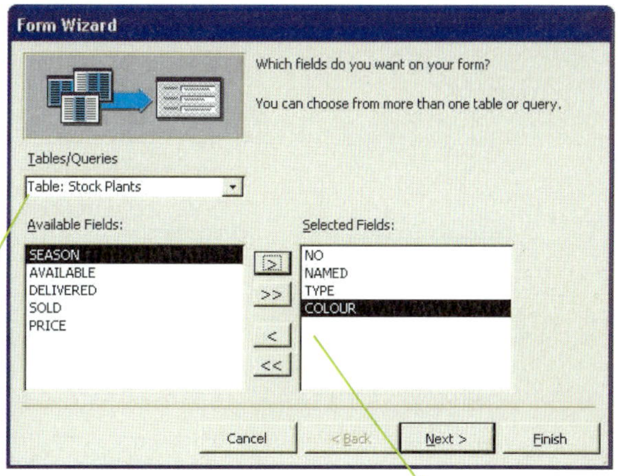

Using forms makes data entry easier and quicker by skipping unnecessary fields, and leaves fewer opportunities for errors.

2. Select the table or query to use as the basis for the form. Choose fields to include, or select all and click Next.

3. Select a format, a style, and a name from the following windows and click Finish.

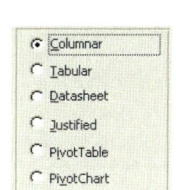

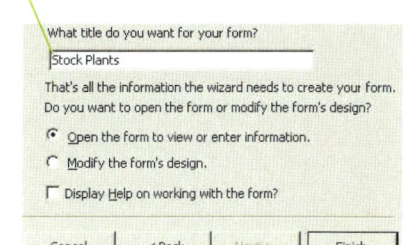

Autoform can only be used with tables. The Form wizard can be used with tables or queries.

Autoform

1. An Autoform can only be created when the Tables tab is selected. Click on the table to be used as the basis for the form. Then click on the New Object button and select Autoform.

Create labels

Access provides a labels wizard as one of its standard reports. To create labels:

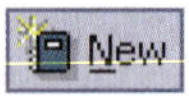

1. Select the Reports tab, and click on New in the toolbar.

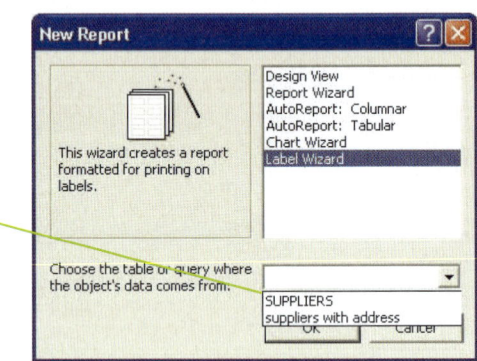

2. In the New Report window select Label Wizard. Choose the source table or query from the list and click OK.

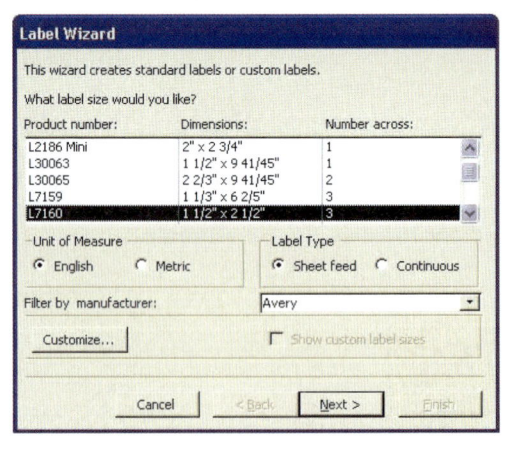

3. The wizard provides a large variety of labels. The list varies according to manufacturer, measurement or type of paper feed. The window displays product numbers, dimension and the number of labels across. Select a label style and click on Next.

The CLAIT Plus exercise may not indicate which size label to use. For Mailing labels, Avery L7160 is a good choice.

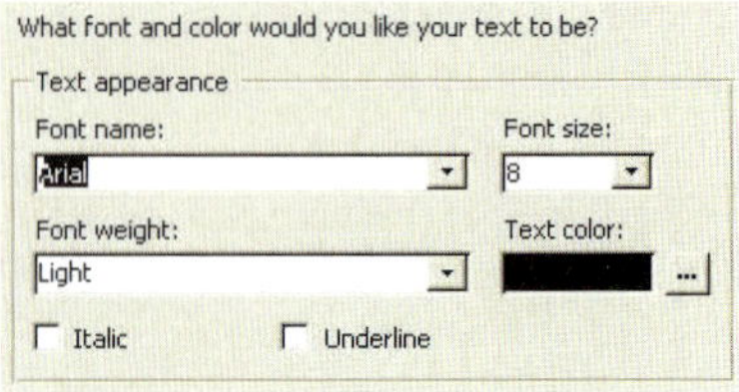

4. In this step you can select a font and format. It's probably best to stay with the default. Click Next to continue.

You can experiment with font sizes and formatting when the label is finished. Remember that you must be able to see all the data.

86 | CLAIT Plus in easy steps

...cont'd

> **HOT TIP**
> You can also type text onto the label, as in the example shown here. The words *Delivery charge have been typed. However, they should be on a separate line as otherwise the merge field {DELIVERY CHARGE} loses its formatting on the finished label.*

5 Select the first field for the label in the left pane and click the central arrow to transfer it. It will appear as a merge field with curly brackets. Press the space bar to separate two fields on the same line. Press Enter to move to the next line. Click next to continue.

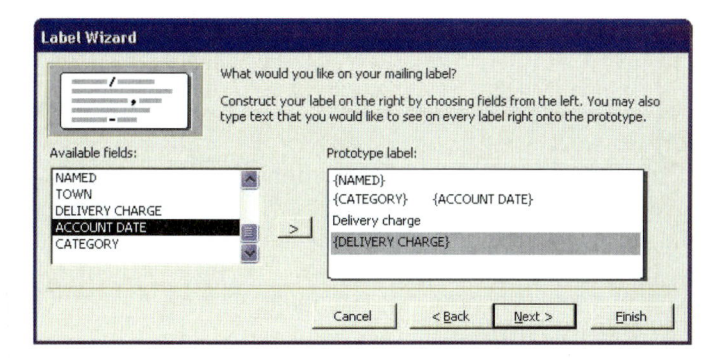

6 Select a sort order for the labels. You can select more than one field, for example by Account Date and then by Name.

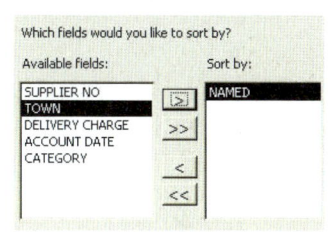

7 Provide a suitable name for the report and click on Finish.

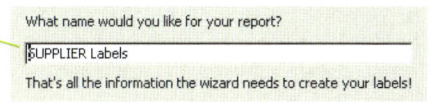

> **DON'T FORGET**
> *Check the exercise requirements to see if you need to include your name and details on the labels report. See page 93 for details on how to create a text box.*

8 The Report window switches between Design view and Print Preview. Check the layout in Print Preview to ensure that all the data displays. Switch to Design view to see how the label has been created.

3. Databases | 87

Report with summary

The Report wizard in Access provides most standard reporting requirements, such as grouping fields and calculating totals.

1 With the Reports tab selected, click on Create report by using Wizard.

2 Select the table or query for the report. With reference to the exercise requirements, select the fields to include and click Next.

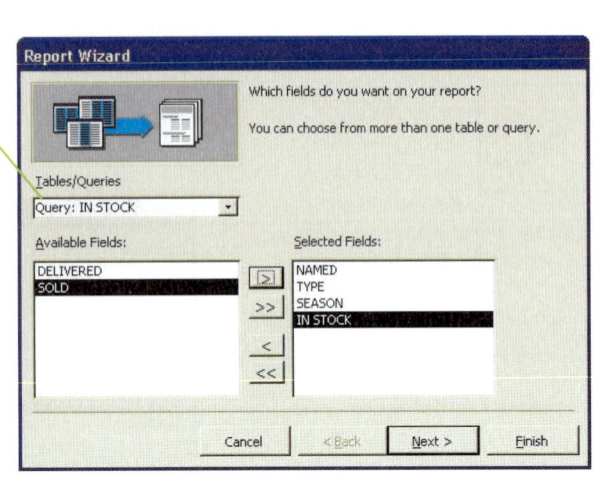

The order in which you select the fields is the order they will display in the report, so check the exercise.

For a simple report, skip Step 3.

3 Choose the main field to Group by. The right hand panel changes to reflect your choice, in this case Type.

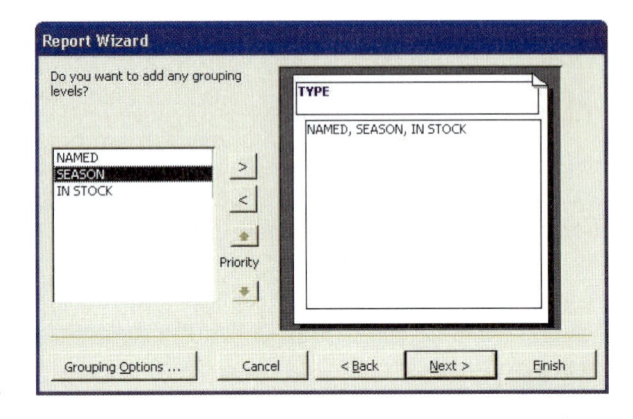

Whichever field you sort by in this window will appear first in the report. The CLAIT Plus exercise stipulates that you display the fields in a specific order, so skip the sort option here and create the sort order as a later step.

4 The Sort by window offers several levels of sort. You would click the down arrow to view the available fields. Skip the Sort option and click the Summary options button.

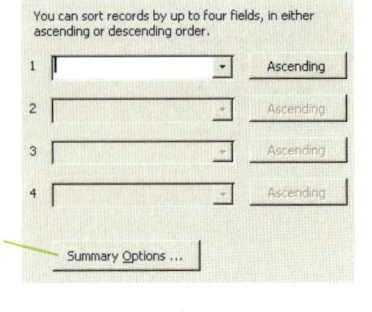

...cont'd

5 The wizard will show fields that can be used for calculations. Choose as required and click OK.

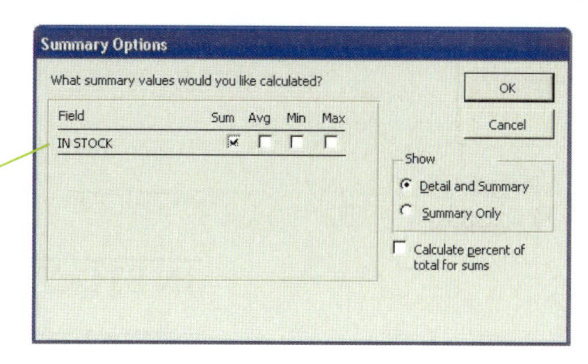

6 From the following step select a layout and orientation. Note that the box is ticked to adjust to the field width so all fields can fit on page. Even so, you may find that the report needs to be adjusted to show all the data.

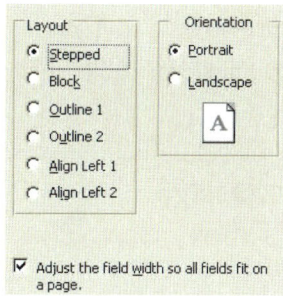

Try the different report layout styles to see the effect, especially if you are required to print the report on a specified number of pages.

7 From the next window select a style. It is worth experimenting with the different styles, as some use smaller fonts or less formatting and so get more data on the page.

8 The final window will request a report name. Access uses the name of the report as the title of the report, so it will appear as the heading. It can however, be amended later. Select to preview the report and click Finish.

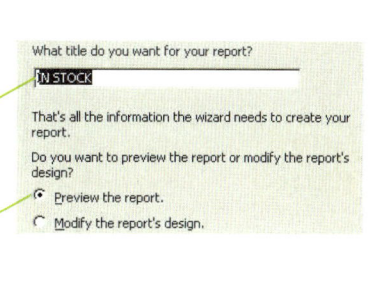

The title of the report is given in the exercise. If the title is long, then its best to supply a short name for the report, and amend the title later in Design view.

9 The report is displayed in Print Preview. Check the report carefully for truncated headings or data fields.

3. Databases | 89

Report design

The report produced by the wizard must be amended to comply with the exercise, and corrected where necessary.

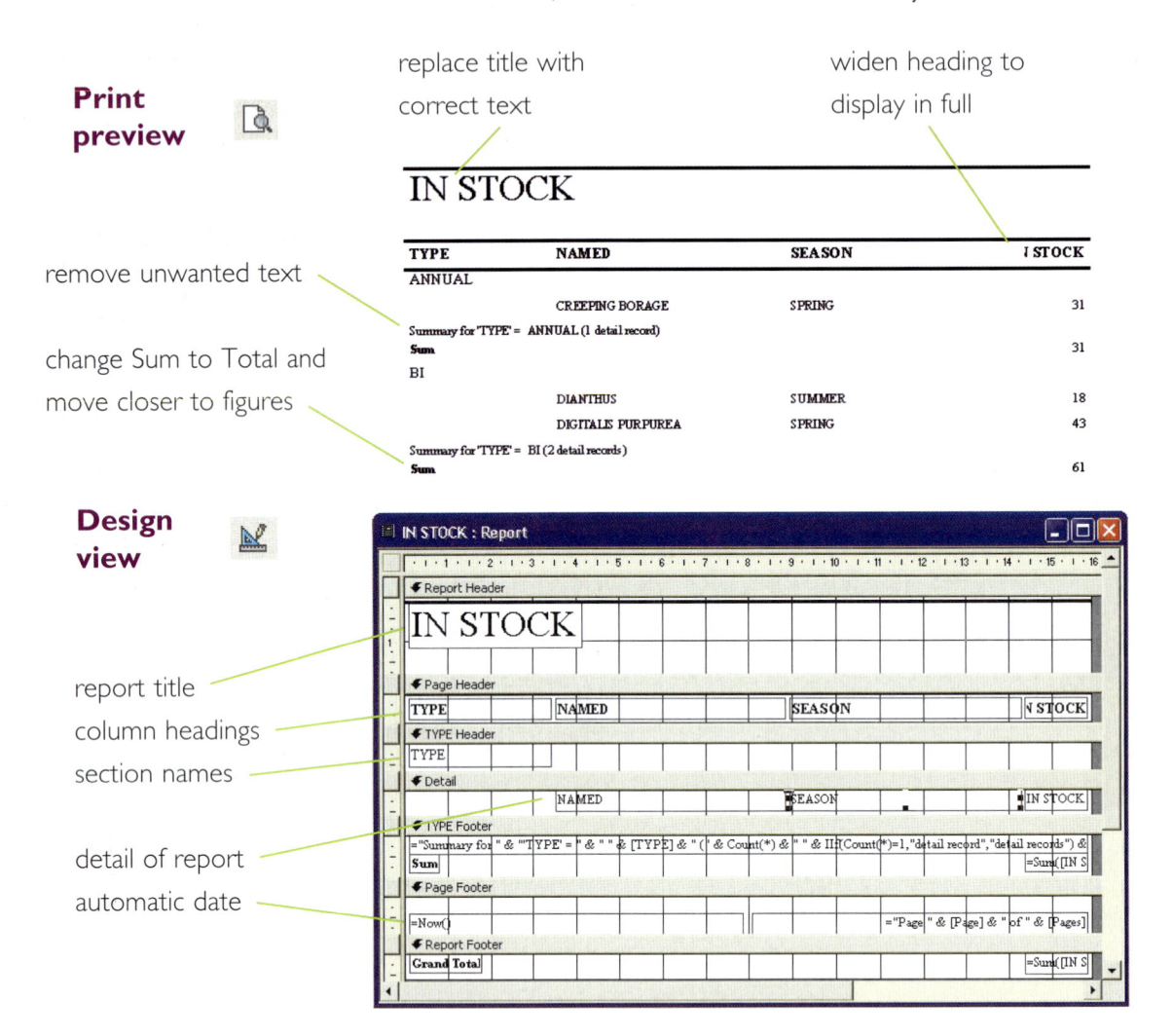

Print preview

replace title with correct text

widen heading to display in full

IN STOCK

TYPE	NAMED	SEASON	I STOCK
ANNUAL			
	CREEPING BORAGE	SPRING	31
Summary for 'TYPE' = ANNUAL (1 detail record)			
Sum			31
BI			
	DIANTHUS	SUMMER	18
	DIGITALIS PURPUREA	SPRING	43
Summary for 'TYPE' = BI (2 detail records)			
Sum			61

remove unwanted text

change Sum to Total and move closer to figures

Design view

report title
column headings
section names

detail of report
automatic date

Report Header — the report title, appears on the first page.
Page Header — the field headings, appear at the start of each page.
Type Header — this is the Grouping header in the report.
Detail — contains the data of the report.
Type Footer — has summary information for the grouping.
Page Footer — contains the date and page number.
Report Footer — may contain a Grand Total, only on the last page.

...cont'd

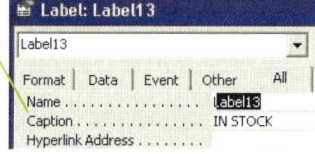

Each text box has its own Properties. With the text box selected, click on Properties and see the source and format.

Check for truncated data, and especially in longer data fields where complete words may be missing.

Sometimes changing the alignment of text can help with a spacing problem.

1. To amend the heading, click in the text box and type the new title. The box will expand as you type.

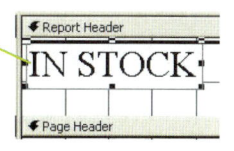

2. As an alternative, with the cursor in the heading text box, select Properties. You can change the Caption to the correct report title. You may then need to expand the text box in Design view.

3. For the body of the report, check in Print preview to ensure that you can see all the column headings and their associated data. You may need to narrow some columns and widen others. Remember to line up the column heading with the detail. Select a text box and move with the hand or resize with the arrows.

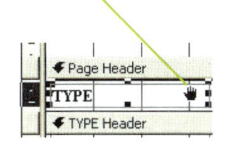

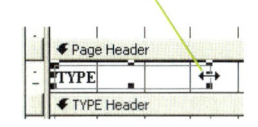

4. To delete the Summary text, click in the box or on the row heading to the left and press the delete key. Check the effect in Print preview.

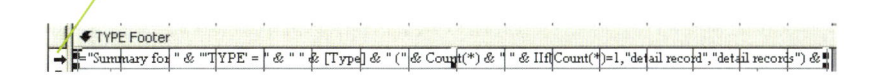

5. To format a Sum, Average etc. figure, select the box and click on its Properties. Click the down arrow in Format and select appropriately.

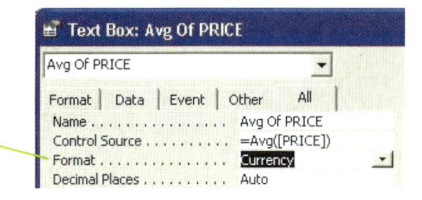

3. Databases | 91

Report controls

Headers and footers

Access reports automatically include the date and page number in the footer area. These can easily be removed by selecting each text box in Design View and deleting.

To insert a date and page number:

HOT TIP: The Page Header bar and the Report Title can be moved further down the page to make room for any text that needs to be left aligned.

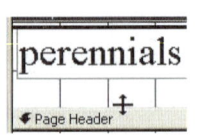

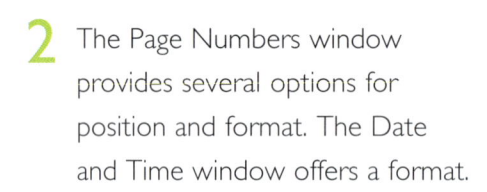

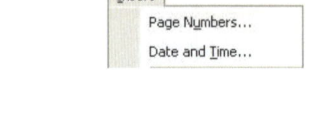

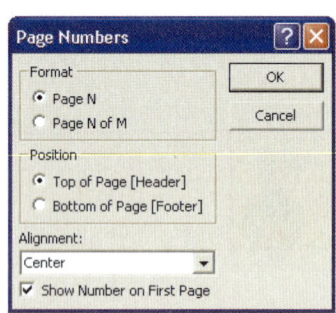

1. In Design view, select Insert, Page numbers, or Date and Time.

2. The Page Numbers window provides several options for position and format. The Date and Time window offers a format.

3. Unfortunately Access does not position them well, so you may need to move them to avoid conflict with other text. Check in Print preview.

Insert text

HOT TIP: Open the Toolbox by clicking on the Toolbox button.

1. Select the Label icon from the Toolbox, and draw a box in the required position. Type your name and centre number. You do not need to worry about the size as the box will expand as you type.

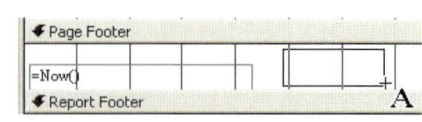

DON'T FORGET: Switch to Print preview to check the positioning.

2. If you have to create the text in the Header area, select File, Page setup and decrease the top margin size. This will provide a bigger area for the text. You can also move the Page Header bar as shown above.

...cont'd

HOT TIP: *The Text box tool creates two boxes, one for your automatic fields, and one with the Text number. It's best to delete the second box as it displays on the report.*

3 To insert automatic fields, select the Text box from the Toolbox, and draw a box. Type:

=Now()   for the date
=[Caption]   for the filename
="Page "&[Page]   for page numbers

Sorting and grouping

If it does not matter about the order in which fields are displayed, then it is easiest to select a Sort order as you create the report. To fully control the sort order and field order use the Sorting and Grouping facility in Design view.

DON'T FORGET: *Creating a 'grouped by' report was covered on page 88.*

1 Select the Sorting and Grouping button from the toolbar.

2 Click in the first Field Expression box and from the drop down box choose your field.

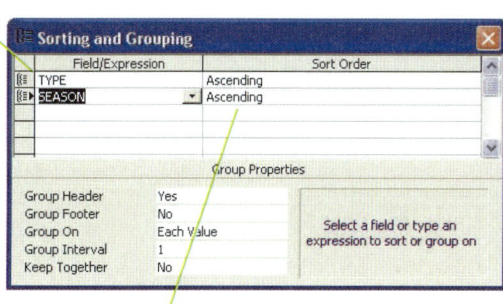

HOT TIP: *You can have several levels of grouping and sorting.*

3 In the Sort Order box, again click the down arrow and select ascending or descending.

4 Click in the Group Header box and select Yes for a grouped by header, or leave it as No to just sort the data. The field order will remain unchanged.

5 Click the Close button to return to the report. Select Print preview to see the finished report.

Checklist

You are allowed three hours to complete the OCR CLAIT Plus assessment.

When you have completed the exercise, run through a final check to ensure that you meet the specifications. Have you:

- used the correct file and table names
- created a new database table
- used the correct field names and field types
- applied the correct format to dates, currency and number fields
- selected data and used codes
- imported data successfully
- input new data accurately
- created queries using the correct criteria
- created reports with the required field headings in the specified order
- created reports using the correct sort order
- ensured that all the data displays on the reports
- included your name, Centre number and date on all prints
- produced the required number of prints
- proofread your prints

If you have followed the exercise that can be downloaded from the In Easy Steps web site, you can check your answers against the worked copies.

Marking

You are not allowed any critical errors. The following are considered critical errors:

- error in entering numeric data used in calculations
- missing title or field headings on any printout
- incorrect search results
- produces incorrect numeric values on reports/queries
- produces incorrect sort order
- a missing field in reports/queries/labels

Check with your tutor for a full list of critical and accuracy errors.

Desktop Publishing

This unit provides exploration of more advanced desktop publishing features. It includes complex document creation, linked text boxes, image control and commercial standards of printing.

Covers

Desktop Publishing | 96

Useful terms | 97

Set the paper layout | 98

The Master page | 100

Create styles | 102

Save, apply and modify styles | 105

Save template | 106

Text frame layout | 107

Create a multipage layout | 109

Link text boxes | 110

Text box options | 112

Text features | 114

Tables | 115

Image control | 116

Copyfit | 118

Printing | 119

Checklist | 122

Unit Four

Desktop Publishing

This unit follows a complete desktop publishing exercise. The image files, text files and the exercise can be downloaded from the In Easy Steps web site (see page 281).

Unit Four overview

This unit covers the following areas:

1. Using a design brief to create a multi page, custom sized document.

2. Creating a master page or template. This includes setting up Styles, standard header and footer text, using layout guides and setting document margins.

There are more Desktop Publishing topics in the Solutions unit, on pages 248-250.

3. Using standard editing marks and symbols to amend a supplied text file. This can be accomplished either before or after it is imported into the DTP application.

4. Importing and managing image files, including cropping, masking and resizing. You will also learn to manage text wrap around images, and how to layer text, shapes and images.

5. Managing DTP text facilities to apply styles, dropped capitals, create tables and bulleted text. It includes using text control facilities such as hyphenation, widows and orphans, leading and copyfitting.

In this unit we will be using Publisher 2002. Any substantial differences between software releases will be highlighted and alternative methods suggested.

6. Printing composite and colour separated prints. Understanding the use of crop and bleed marks, and the purpose and composition of commercially required prints.

Exercise files and documentation

You should have the following items:

- one or more text files
- the exercise
- a Design Layout brief
- one or more image files
- a House Style sheet

Useful terms

Desktop publishing uses a number of terms that stem from the printing processes used many years ago.

These are some of the desktop publishing terms you may encounter when undertaking this unit:

Banner - a main headline that goes across the top of the page, usually used for newspapers.

Bleed - printed colours which run all the way to the edge of the paper are known as bleeds. Bleed marks are indicated on the printed sheet.

Copyfit - resize the text to fit the text box. This may be to increase or decrease the text size, or the leading in between the lines of text.

Composite print - all the colours displayed on one print.

Crop marks - show where the page is to be cut when printed.

Cropping - cutting an image to remove unwanted background, or to fit a given area.

Although Publisher is a desktop publishing application, it is most useful for creating flyers, cards, banners etc., rather than books or large publications. It uses its own terms for some of the DTP functions, for example Spacing instead of gutter.

Drop cap - capital or upper case letter, set in a larger type size and extending into the lines of text below.

Gutter - the space between columns, also the two inside margins of facing pages.

Layering - superimposing text or images on each other. Layers can be selected and moved backwards or forwards.

Lead, or **Leading** - space added between lines of type to space text and provide separation of the lines. Originated from the strips of lead that used to be inserted between lines in hot metal type.

Kerning - character spacing, it can be used to close up or separate characters.

Process printing - printing colour images and text using four separate printing plates, with magenta, yellow, cyan and black ink.

***White Space** is used in DTP document design to give it some breathing room and make it more readable. OCR may include objectives related to this (see page 118).*

Reverse print - or reverse type, white characters set on a dark background. This can also be achieved by leaving the text inkfree, showing the colour of the background paper.

Widows and orphans - single lines of text at the end or beginning of pages, separated from the rest of the paragraph or heading.

4. Desktop Publishing | 97

Set the paper layout

To start the CLAIT Plus exercise, first study the various exercise pages thoroughly. The Page Layout document is very important as it contains much of the detail of page size, text frame position, text flow sequence and image placement. You will need to refer to it regularly, and should be completely familiar with its requirements.

Open Publisher and select New Blank Publication. The first step is to set the page size. Refer to the Page Layout sheet for the page dimensions. To create the correct size:

The standard desktop printer uses A4 paper, so the CLAIT Plus exercises are based on this. The page size stipulated in any exercise will always be smaller than A4. This allows for the printing of crop and bleed marks required by commercial printers, and the OCR course. See page 119 for more details on printing.

1 Select File, Page Setup.

2 Choose Custom from the Publication type pane. You will then be able to modify the page dimensions to those given in the exercise.

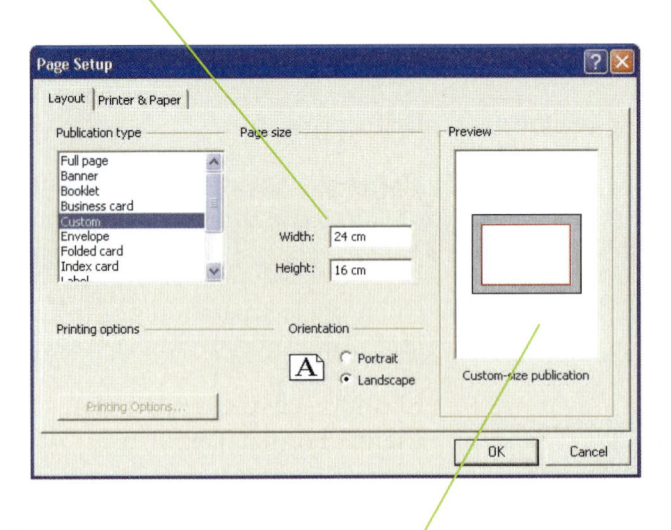

3 Select the orientation and view the result in the Preview pane. Click OK when finished.

4 The full page that you can now see shows the area available for use. Crop and bleed marks can be seen only in Print Preview.

...cont'd

Margins

Publisher inserts default margin guides on the new page. These will need to be changed to conform with the exercise. To reposition the guides:

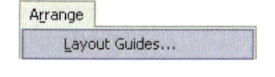

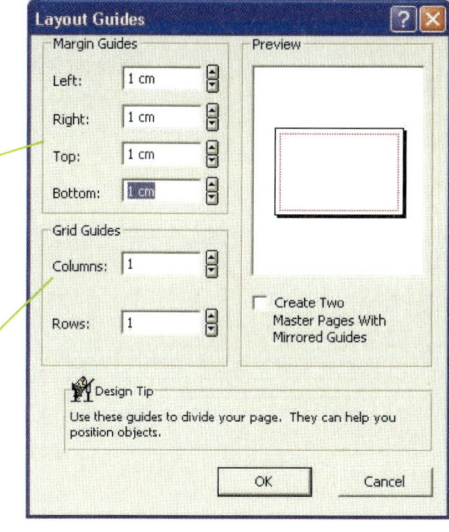

1. Select Arrange, Layout Guides. As you adjust the margins sizes, the result shows in the Preview pane.

2. Columns could be created using the Grid Guides to position the text frames required by the exercise. However, to achieve the level of accuracy required by CLAIT Plus, you should ignore this option.

You may find this a useful facility when designing your own layouts.

Using columns within a text frame was covered in New CLAIT.

In Publisher 2000, you must select Text Frame Properties.

Gutters

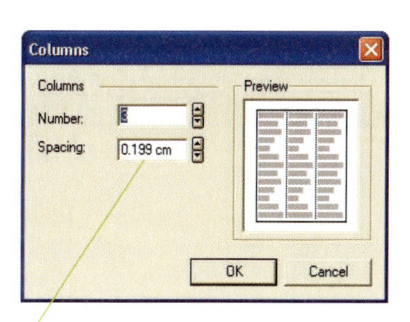

The gutter space between columns of text can be created in two ways. If you have designed your document so that text flows naturally from one column to the next in sequence, then you can use the Format Text Box option to create columns within the one text box. You can set the spacing (gutters) as required and it will be applied between adjacent columns.

If the text flow is done by linking separate text boxes, as will usually be the case with the CLAIT Plus exercise, then you will need to calculate the size and position of the text boxes to achieve a gutter space. This can be done using options within the Format Text Box facility, and is covered more fully on page 107.

4. Desktop Publishing | 99

The Master page

Headers and Footers in Publisher are similar to those in Word.

Publisher uses a Master page as a background page on which you can put text and images that you want to appear on every page, for example a company logo. Headers and Footers are part of the Master page, but in Publisher 2002 they are created via the View menu, rather than being entered directly onto the master page.

In previous versions of Publisher, you will need to select View, Background and create the Header and Footer text frames in the required position. You will then need to deselect the View Background option.

Headers and footers

To create Headers and Footers:

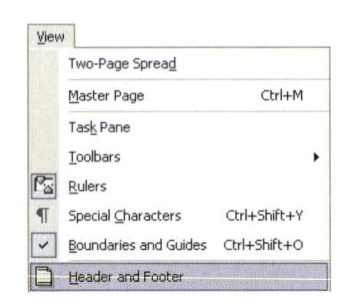

1 Select View, Headers and Footers. The Header text box should appear with the Header toolbar.

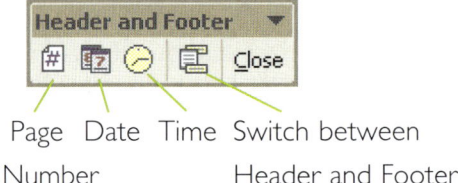

Page Number · Date · Time · Switch between Header and Footer

2 The toolbar provides only a limited number of automatic fields, and you cannot select a starting page number at this point. See page 101.

In Publisher 2002, having set your margin guides, the Header and Footer text frames are usually created correctly. They will honour the margin guides by being created outside the horizontal guide and level with the vertical guide.

Double click in the Header or Footer text box to edit the information.

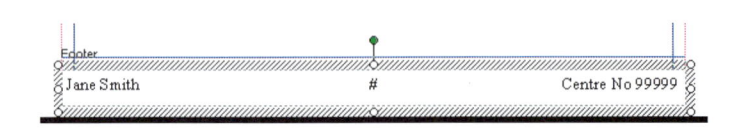

Jane Smith   #   Centre No 99999

3 The Header and Footer text boxes have preset centre and right align tabs. Type in the required text in the correct positions.

...cont'd

4 When you close the Header and Footer view you will return to the normal page view.

Page numbering

For standard page numbering you can use the Header and Footer process as described on the previous page. For more control over positioning and format, choose:

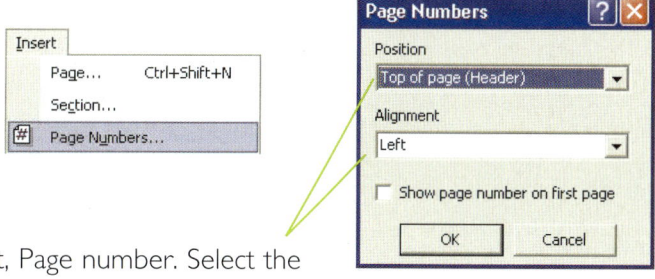

1 Insert, Page number. Select the page position and the alignment.

You can also select to show page number on first page.

> *To select a starting number in Publisher 2000, go to Tools, Options, and on the General tab you can type in a starting number.*

To select your own page number:

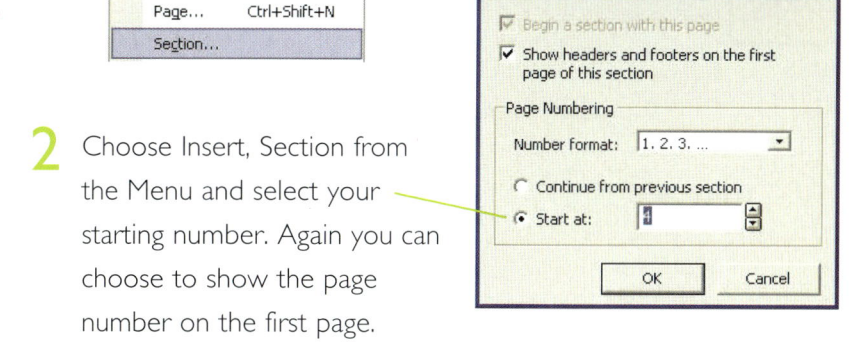

2 Choose Insert, Section from the Menu and select your starting number. Again you can choose to show the page number on the first page.

3 You will need to insert a page number with either the Header/Footer or Insert Page number method, before you will be able to see a page number specified using Insert Section.

4. Desktop Publishing | 101

Create styles

HOT TIP: *If the Task pane is already open, you can click the down arrow and select Styles and Formatting directly.*

HOT TIP: *In previous versions of Publisher, select Format, Styles and Formatting from the Menu.*

1 Select Format, Styles and Formatting. This will invoke the Styles and Formatting Task pane.

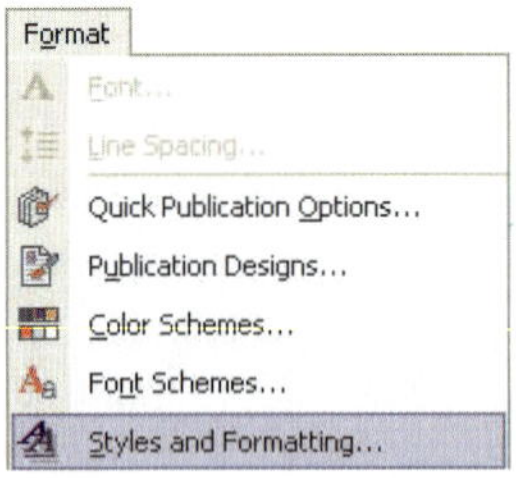

2 In a new document, Publisher has only two default options - to remove any formatting from existing text, or to apply the Normal style.

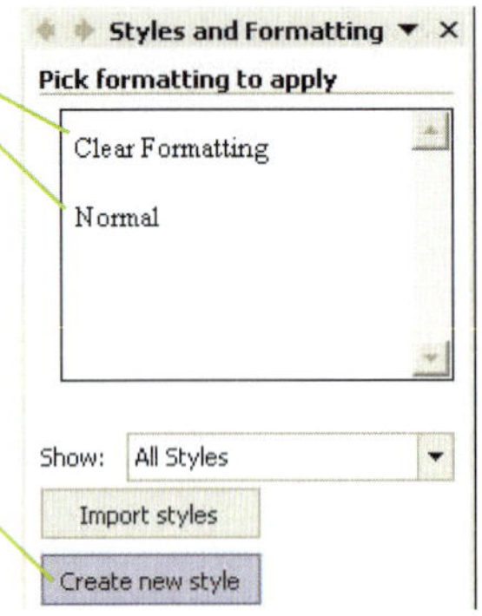

3 Select Create new style. Refer to the House Style sheet for the name and details of the various styles required.

4 Enter a name for the style. It will be based on Normal, as this is the only existing style.

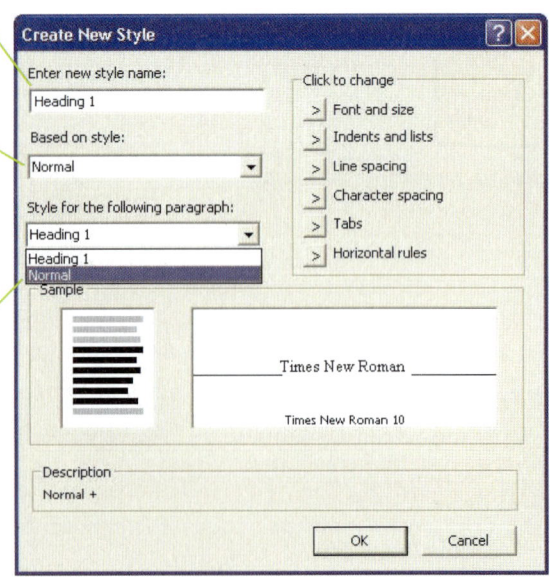

HOT TIP: *Once you have created a style, you can use its font or alignment to create another new style and bypass some of these steps.*

5 Select a style for the following paragraph. Again, you would select Normal.

6 From this window you will need to select most of the buttons in turn to set the font size, style, attributes such as underline, alignment and spacing.

...cont'd

Font size and alignment

Standard serif fonts are Times New Roman and Century Schoolbook. Sans serif fonts are Arial and Microsoft Sans Serif.

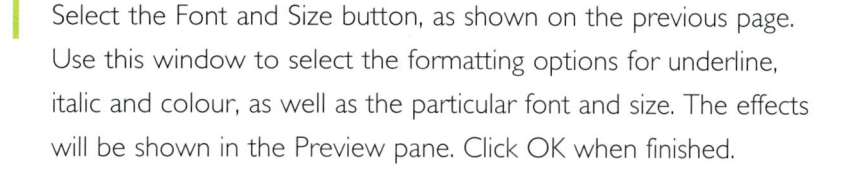

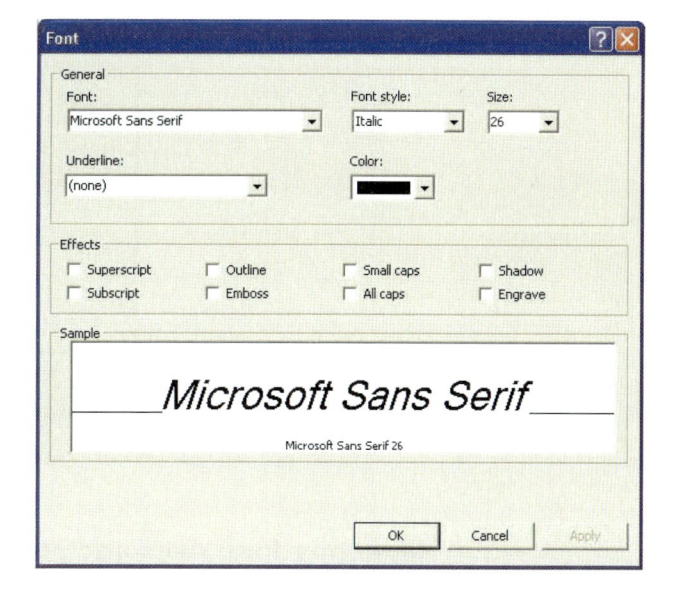

1. Select the Font and Size button, as shown on the previous page. Use this window to select the formatting options for underline, italic and colour, as well as the particular font and size. The effects will be shown in the Preview pane. Click OK when finished.

The Indents and Lists button, surprisingly, is where you set the text alignment.

If you need to set the Line Spacing, you can use the shortcut here and save a couple of steps.

2. Select the Indents and Lists button. Select any indentation required or click in Bulleted or Numbered list. You will then have the option to select from a variety of bullet styles, sizes or a new bullet altogether. The Sample pane allows a preview.

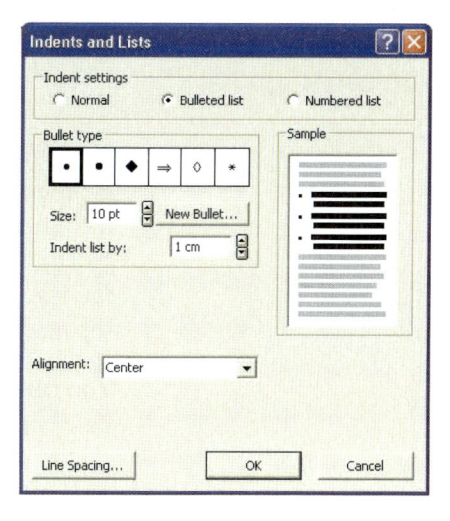

4. Desktop Publishing

...cont'd

> **Hot Tip:** *Spacing between lines is also known as Leading, see Useful Terms on page 97.*

Line spacing

1 Spacing Between lines does not need to be altered when creating a heading or subheading style, but you may need to amend it as a final step when copyfitting the text. See page 118.

> **Hot Tip:** *In word processing you would usually set 1.5 or double line spacing for selected paragraphs. In DTP you can adjust line spacing (Between lines) by very small amounts. Note that the measurement is in sp, whereas the before and after paragraphs is in point size.*

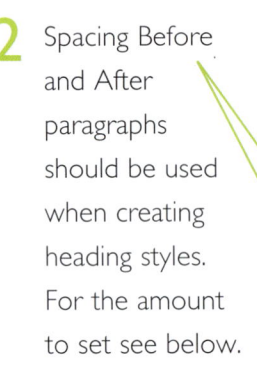

2 Spacing Before and After paragraphs should be used when creating heading styles. For the amount to set see below.

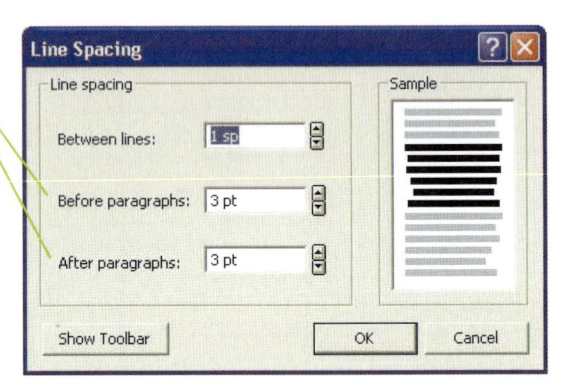

3 Spacing before and after paragraphs in the main text of the document should be set to the same values as for heading styles.

Selecting font sizes and spacing

You will be required to use a font size from a range of sizes for each heading and text style. It is a good idea to select the smaller of each of these ranges to start with, as it is easier to work with too much space, rather than too much text.

To achieve consistency in spacing, a CLAIT Plus requirement, a simple approach is to set the Before paragraph spacing to zero, and the After paragraph spacing to 6pt. (6pt is approximately a half line space). This means that the Heading 1 text will start at the top of the text box, leaving no white space. Subheadings will always be separated from the following text.

You can apply this rule to the body text style, so that the spacing between paragraphs is consistent, everywhere on the page.

104 | CLAIT Plus in easy steps

Save, apply and modify styles

Save the style

1. When you have selected the font, alignment and spacing click OK to save the style. You will need to repeat each step for each of the styles stipulated on the Style sheet for the exercise.

2. The styles created will be displayed in the Task pane, in the font style, size and alignment chosen. Hover the mouse over them to view and check the full description.

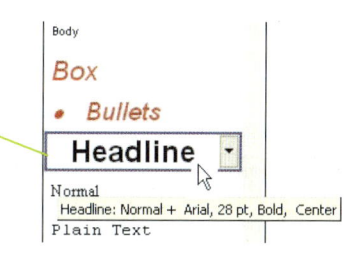

You will apply styles later in the exercise after you have saved the template.

Apply the style

1. To apply a style, simply click in the text to be formatted, and click on the style in the Task pane.

When applying styles, try starting with the body text style. Use Ctrl+A to select all the text and apply the body text style. Then select the headings individually. If you do the headings first you will have to apply the body text a paragraph at a time. When you do the body text first you also have a better idea of how much space you will have left for headings.

Modify the style

1. Select the style to be modified from the Task pane.

When you have modified a style, it should automatically be applied to each occurrence of the style.

2. Click on the down arrow on the right of the style and select Modify. The Change Style window offers the same option as the Create Style window.

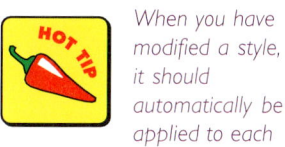

4. Desktop Publishing | 105

Save template

If you were creating a template in a business environment, you could include logos or watermarks as part of the template.

Now you have created the page layout, headers and footers, and styles, you need to save it as a template.

1 Select File, Save As. Publisher opens the My Documents folder.

2 Click on the down arrow in the Save as type box and select Publisher Template. The destination folder changes automatically to the Templates folder, where other templates are listed.

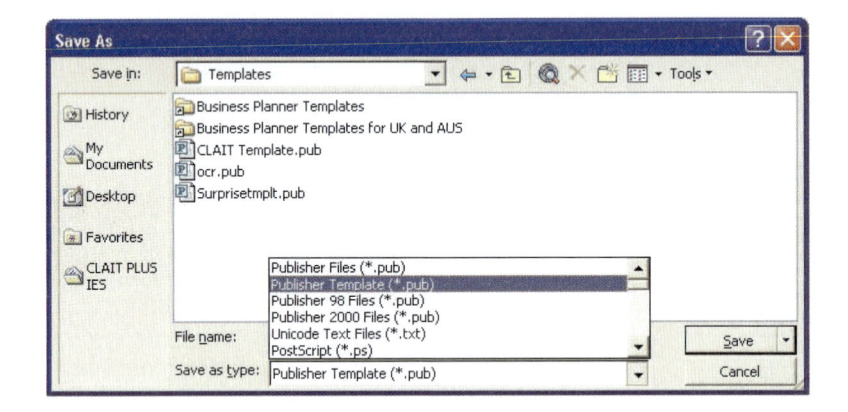

To use templates in older versions of Publisher, use the Templates button at the bottom of the Wizard panel.

3 Name the template file and click Save. The file will be saved with the .pub file extension.

Use the template

1 You must first close the template. Otherwise any further actions, such as importing text, could be saved as part of the template.

Create New creates a new document, not a new template.

2 Select File, New, From Template. Select the template and click Create new. You can now save the file as a standard file.

106 | CLAIT Plus in easy steps

Text frame layout

Don't Forget: On this page we look at how to create a layout that uses a number of text boxes of identical size, to fill the page, margin to margin.

For example, to calculate the text box dimensions, given:

Page width	24cm
Page Height	16cm
L/R margins	0.5cm
T/B margins	1.0cm
Gutters	1.0cm
No of boxes	3

Text width = 24 - (2x0.5) - (2x1)
= 21cm
Text box width = 21 ÷ 3
= 7cm
Text box height = 16 - (2x1)
= 14cm.

Don't Forget: Text boxes were referred to as text frames in earlier versions of Publisher.

Don't Forget: Creating a text box was covered in New CLAIT.

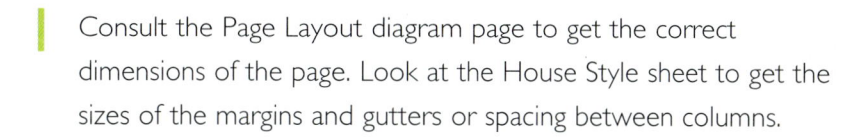

Hot Tip: Having created one box the correct size, you can copy and paste the rest of the text boxes. Make sure to avoid resizing when moving them into position, see page 108.

1. Consult the Page Layout diagram page to get the correct dimensions of the page. Look at the House Style sheet to get the sizes of the margins and gutters or spacing between columns.

2. Calculate the text box widths taking into account margins and gutters by using the following formulae:

   Text width = Page width - Left/right Margins - Gutters.
   Text box width = Text width ÷ No of text boxes.

3. To calculate the text box height required to fill the page, use this formula:

   Text box height = Page height - Top/bottom Margins.

4. Draw a text box of any size. Right click the text box and select Format Text Box. Select the Size tab. Set the height and width dimensions as calculated.

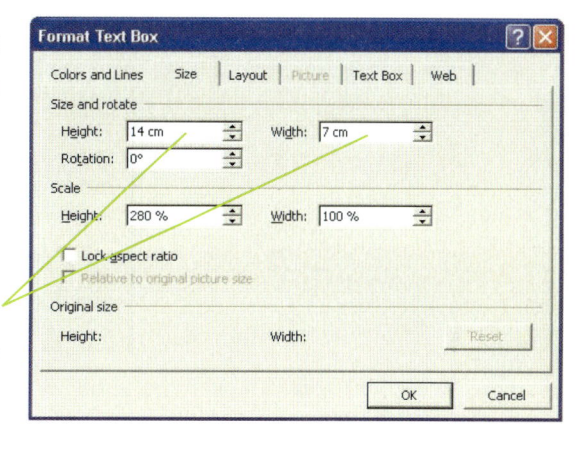

5. Switch to the Text Box tab and change the margins to zero. This ensures that your text fits right to the edges of the text box so that your margins and spacing are correct.

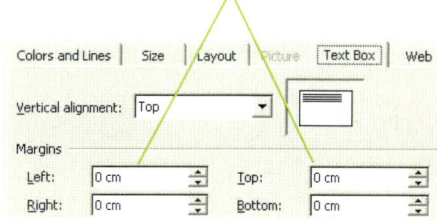

4. Desktop Publishing | 107

...cont'd

Position text boxes

> **Hot Tip:** *If you have positioned the first text frame correctly, the Position on page figures should be the same as the margin size.*

1. Position the first text box on the left-hand layout guide, and make sure it fits to the top and bottom guides.

2. To position the second text box accurately, right click inside it and select Format Text Box. Choose the Layout tab.

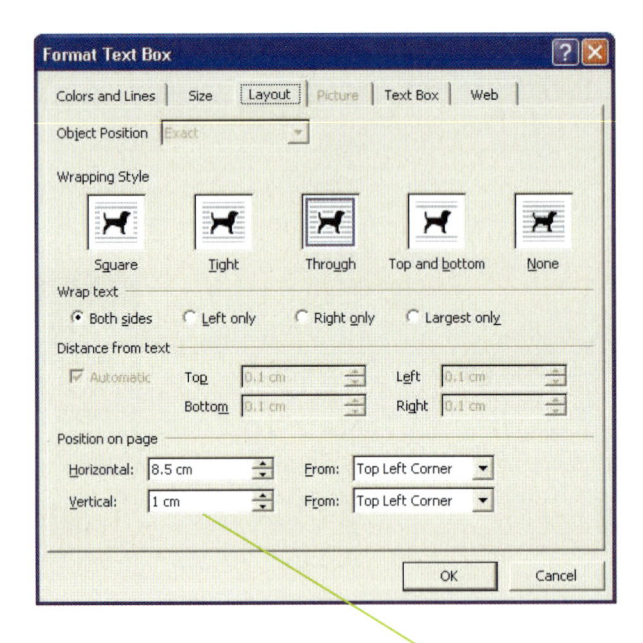

> **Don't Forget:** *The figures used to calculate the text box size are now used to calculate the vertical position.*
> *Text box (7cm) plus margin (1cm) plus gutter (0.5cm) = 8.5cm.*

3. You will need to adjust the Position on page settings. Note that the default position is measured from the Top Left Corner. In the exercise the margin is set to 1cm, so the Horizontal position on the page is 1cm. To calculate the Vertical position, add together the text box width plus one margin plus one gutter spacing.

4. When you have positioned all the text boxes, they should fill the page. You should check visually to confirm that you have measured and calculated correctly.

108 | CLAIT Plus in easy steps

Create a multipage layout

When you have created your first page layout, you can add more pages to the document and copy the layout automatically.

To move from page to page in a multipage document, use the page navigation icons at the bottom of the screen.

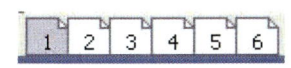

1. Select Insert, Page.

2. Select the Number of new pages. You would normally insert the pages After current page.

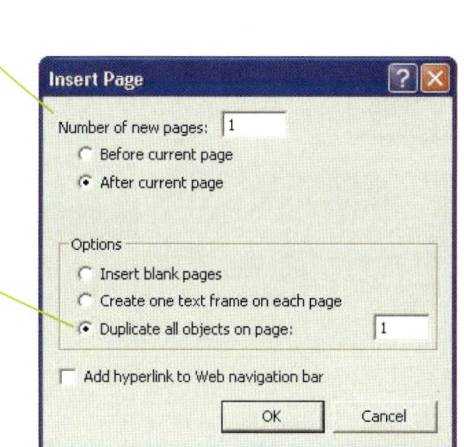

To duplicate a page layout where you have more than one layout in the document, first select the page you wish to duplicate.

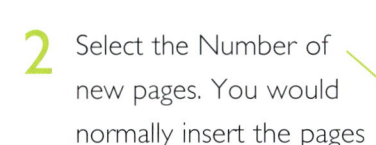

3. Select to Duplicate all objects on page. The pages will duplicate Page 1, as that is the only page in the document at the present time.

The supplied text file

You will be given a text file as your source data. The exercise will indicate which text is to be used as headings and subheadings. The exercise will also indicate any amendments which need to be made to the text.

It's a good idea to make the amendments to the text before you import it into Publisher. Although you can edit text in Publisher, you will need to zoom in to read it, and the text flow from one text box to another makes editing more difficult.

The notation used for text amendments is covered in detail in Unit One, Create, Manage and Integrate Files, see page 28.

Open the text file in Word, and make the changes. You can save it as a text file, or as a Word file. When you insert a text file in Publisher, it will look for all forms of text files. Word documents will be converted for use in Publisher as they are imported.

It is worth printing the text file before you import it. You can then make sure that all the text is displayed in the finished publication.

4. Desktop Publishing | 109

Link text boxes

Refer to the Page Layout diagram in the exercise for the text flow sequence.

With all the text boxes created, you are now ready to insert the text.

1. Click in the first text box and select Insert, Text File. Navigate the folders to the file, select the file and click OK.

The procedure illustrated here shows the sequence when the links are created as you insert the text. However, you can link the text boxes before you insert the text file if you prefer. Publisher handles the process well, either way.

2. With the text frames unlinked, Publisher will fill the first frame with text. It then offers to flow the text for you. Select No so that you can control the sequence yourself.

   Microsoft Publisher
   The inserted text doesn't fit in this box. Do you want to use autoflow?
   To have Publisher automatically flow text throughout your publication, asking for confirmation before it flows into existing boxes, click Yes. To connect boxes yourself, click No. For information on connecting text boxes, press F1.
   [Yes] [No]

If you change your mind during the process of linking boxes, just press Esc to stop. The jug will disappear and revert to an arrow.

3. You will now see the symbol for 'text in overflow' at the bottom of the first text box.

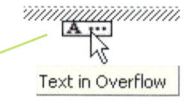

   Text in Overflow

4. Click on the Create Text Box Link button on the toolbar, and the mouse pointer will become a jug. When you position the jug inside a text box, it tips. Simply click in the next sequential box to create the link.

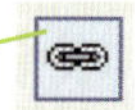

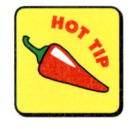

You can still navigate from page to page when the mouse pointer is a jug. When you move the mouse onto the page navigation icons it changes back to an arrow. It will become a jug again in the text area.

5. Click again on the Create Text Box Link button and select the next box. Repeat until you have placed all the text.

6. Check the last text box to ensure that you have no text in overflow. It's a good idea to make a note of the last few words of the text file to make sure that they are always displayed. This is essential when you need to copyfit the text. See page 118.

...cont'd

The Break Text Box link button is inoperative when the final text box is selected.

Disconnect text boxes

You may find that the exercise requires you to change the text flow, or perhaps you need to make a correction.

1 Select the last text box that is correct.

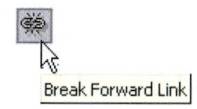

2 Click on the Break Forward Link to unlink boxes. The text will disappear from the next text box in the sequence, and the current text box will once again show the Text in Overflow symbol.

3 Click on the Create Text Box Link button again and continue as before.

Navigate the links

Linked text boxes are referred to as a story. The text in the text boxes is treated as a single object. This means that you can format all the text at once, and use utilities such as Find and Replace.

Not all the text boxes will be linked. Tables, for example, will usually be in a separate text box.

1 You can use the Frame Navigation icons, which appear at the top and bottom of text boxes, to move backwards and forwards through the text boxes in sequence.

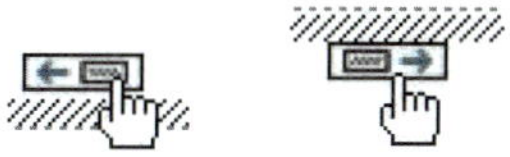

2 Publisher provides navigation buttons on the toolbar.

3 You can still use the cursor to move through the text, if for example you need to edit the text. It will automatically jump to the next text box in sequence.

4. Desktop Publishing | 111

Text box options

1. Click in the text box and then right click. Select Format Text Box. Use the Colour and Lines tab to select a Fill colour.

2. Click the down arrow to select More Colours or Fill effects.

Standard text boxes are automatically transparent. Select a Fill colour and you can then set a degree of transparency.

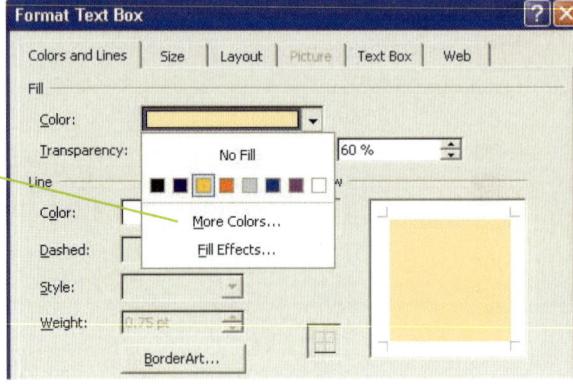

3. Select a Line Colour, and then options of Dashed, Style or Weight, or even Border Art. The Preview pane indicates the current choice.

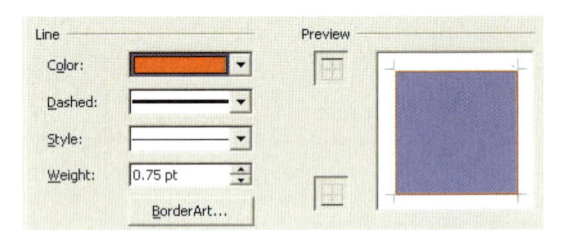

Use Ctrl+T to make a text box transparent.

Rotating text

4. Select the Size tab to Rotate text. Clicking the up arrow on the Rotation option rotates the text clockwise.

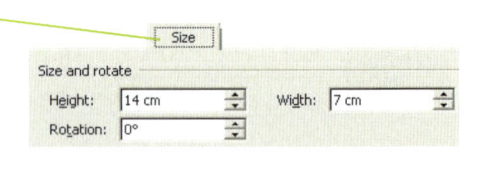

5. You can rotate the text box freehand. Position the mouse over the green Rotation handle and drag to the required angle.

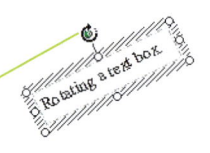

112 | CLAIT Plus in easy steps

...cont'd

Text wrapping refers to the way text wraps around the outside of another text box or an image frame. Within the text box you can select any standard alignment such as centred or justified.

Text wrapping

The text box has two position definitions, In Line and Exact.

1. The In Line option is only available when the text box is positioned within another text box. With In Line text, the only Wrapping style available is Square.

To become familiar with the effects of text wrapping styles, it's a good idea to experiment with just a sample image and sample piece of text.

2. With In Line, you can choose the Horizontal alignment of Left, Right or Move object with text. This means that the text box will maintain its position within the text, even if you add or delete text.

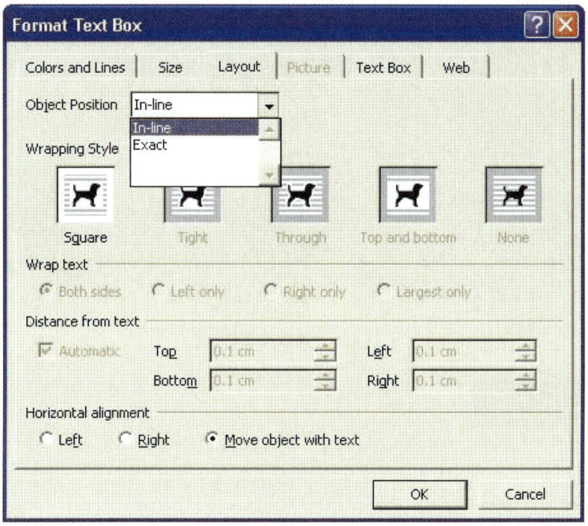

You will need to specify Exact as the Object Position if you wish to rotate the text box.

You can also use Position on page to set the position exactly.

Text wrap is also covered in the Solutions unit on page 248-250.

3. The Exact object position means that you can position the text box anywhere on the page. With Exact you can choose any of the Wrapping Style and Wrap Text options.

4. In some instances, for example text on text, you may find that the default Distance from text of 0.1cm is too little. Deselect Automatic and adjust the measurement. This option is only available if you select the Square Wrapping Style.

Text features

Dropped capitals

> **Hot Tip:** Dropped capitals are initial letters of a paragraph that descend into the text.

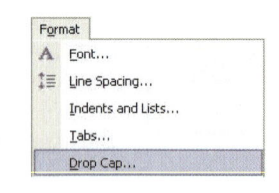

1. Select the first paragraph then click Format, Drop Caps. You can select several paragraphs at once, but do not include any headings.

> **Hot Tip:** Use F9 to zoom in and out.

2. Select from the options where the letter descends one, two, three or four lines. Use Custom to create your own. Select Remove to set the capital back to normal.

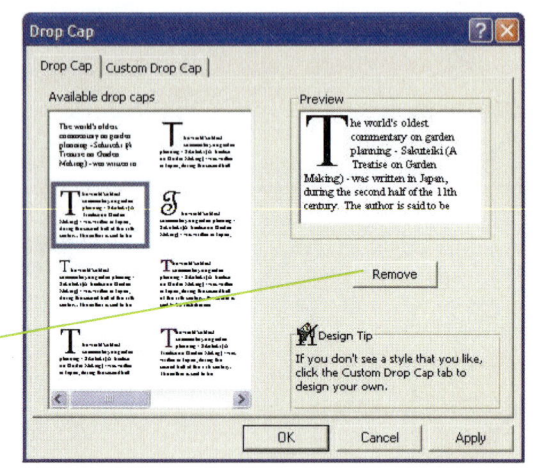

Reverse text

> **Hot Tip:** Reverse text is created by showing white text on a dark background.
>
> This is reverse text

3. Select the text box and fill with colour. You can use the Fill tool or Format Text Box. Select the text and change the colour to white.

Hyphenation

> **Hot Tip:** To control hyphenation for all new text boxes you must change the default. Select Tools, Options, and the Edit tab. Deselect the option to Automatically hyphenate in new text boxes.

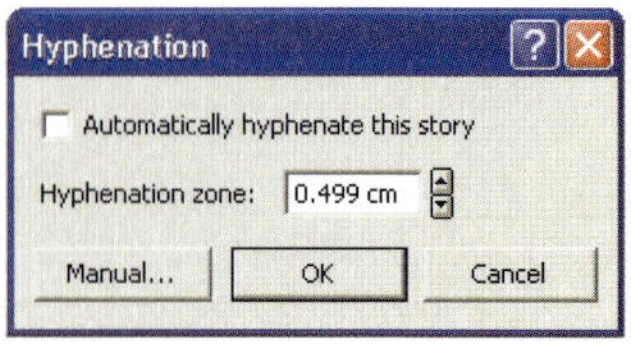

4. Select Tools, Language, Hyphenation and deselect Automatically hyphenate this story. Linked text boxes are referred to as a story. When you change the hyphenation option, all the linked boxes are affected. Remember to check the hyphenation setting for any unlinked boxes.

Tables

If you are familiar with tables in Word, you will find Publisher tables easy to use.

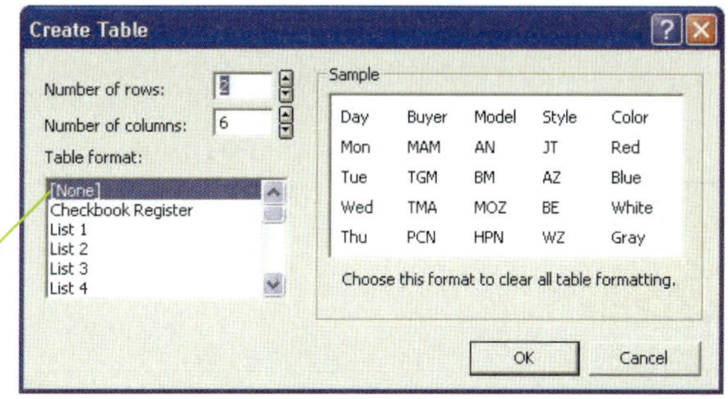

For the CLAIT Plus exercise you are unlikely to use any of the Autoformat options.

Apply the formatting required by the exercise. You may need to adjust column widths and alignment.

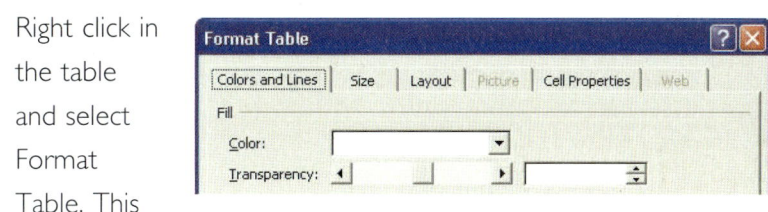

If you must specify a particular size for your table, make sure that the option Table, Grow to Fit Text, is not selected.

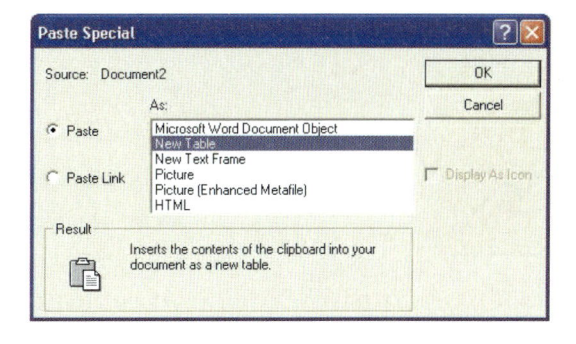

Publisher has no option to convert text to table, as offered in Word.

1 From the Menu select Table, Insert Table.

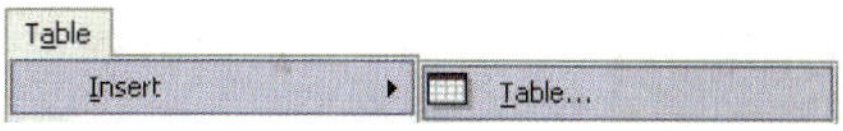

2 Select the number of columns and rows. The default format of None creates a simple table and is the best choice.

3 Right click in the table and select Format Table. This window offers functions similar to those of Format Text Box. You can, for example, select a Fill colour, specify a size, select a text wrap and set a position on the page.

4 If the text is already in the supplied file, you can cut and paste it into Word and use the Word facilities to convert it. To paste the table back into Publisher select Edit, Paste Special.

4. Desktop Publishing | 115

Image control

Don't forget: Basic procedures for inserting image files was covered in New CLAIT.

1. To set the size, position and text wrap options, right click the image and select Format Picture. You will see options similar to those used for Text boxes.

2. Right click the picture and select Show Picture toolbar. The toolbar provides quick access to some of the most used functions.

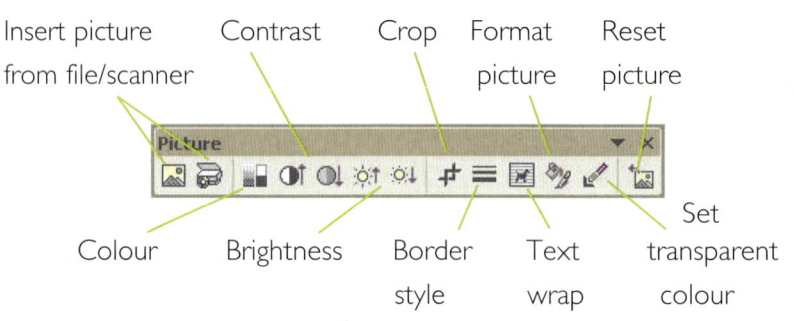

Don't forget: You can place the image in an Exact position, or In Line, where it moves with the text.

Insert picture from file/scanner — Contrast — Crop — Format picture — Reset picture

Colour — Brightness — Border style — Text wrap — Set transparent colour

Hot tip: Use Alt+ arrow keys to nudge an object (text box, autoshape or image) into a precise position.

3. To resize the image you can drag the corner, or use the Size / Scale option in Format Picture. Tick Lock Aspect ratio to keep the proportions.

Hot tip: To maintain the picture's position press Ctrl as you drag.

4. Click on the Crop tool to select it. Click again to turn it off. Position the crop tool on a crop point and drag.

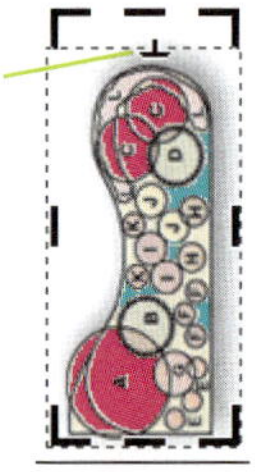

5. To crop accurately, select Format Picture and the Picture tab and specify the amount to be cropped. With either method the original file remains intact.

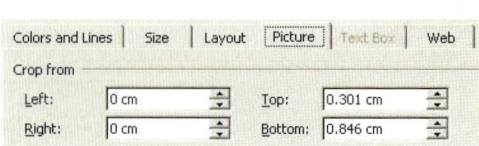

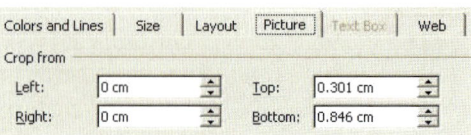

Hot tip: If you crop a picture by a negative amount, it will increase the white space around the picture. This can be useful when trying to copyfit the text.

116 | CLAIT Plus in easy steps

...cont'd

> **HOT TIP**
> *The Transparency tool lets you to select a colour to make transparent, allowing the background colour to show through.*

6 The Picture toolbar provides the facility to Edit Wrap Points on the picture, allowing you to take advantage of irregularly shaped objects.

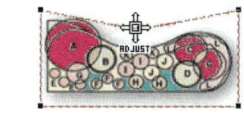

> **HOT TIP**
> *As part of the exercise you may be required to place images, text or Autoshapes on top of one another. This is known as Layering.*

Layering objects

7 Select the object and click on Arrange, Order.

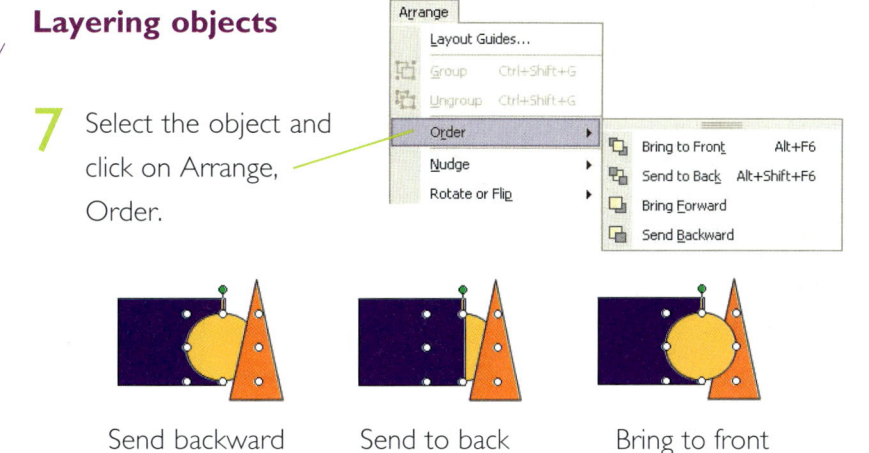

> **HOT TIP**
> *If an object disappears completely from view, select the front object and use Send to back.*

Send backward   Send to back   Bring to front

Grouping objects

To ensure that layered objects maintain their relative positions when moving, you can group them, which locks them together.

> **HOT TIP**
> *To work with the objects individually, Ungroup them, click away to deselect all, and then click on the one you want.*

8 Select one object and hold down the Ctrl key. The cursor will display a + sign. Click on the second object. From the menu select Arrange, Group. You will see the Grouped symbol and the frame will encompass all grouped objects.

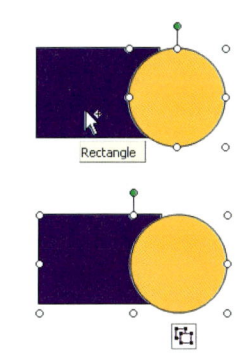

> **HOT TIP**
> *To quickly Group and Ungroup, click the Grouped symbol.*

9 To Ungroup, select the object and click Arrange, Ungroup.

4. Desktop Publishing | 117

Copyfit

The Style sheet will indicate page size, margins, space between columns, font sizes, styles and alignment. You must adhere strictly to all these specifications.

Copyfitting the document means making the document fit the specified pages and layout, without leaving excess areas of white space, or overlapping text and images unless specified. The final instructions will indicate other criteria which must be met.

1. Widows and Orphans are not allowed. A Widow is a single line of a title or paragraph on its own at the bottom of a column. An orphan is a single line at the top. Whilst Word offers Widow and Orphan control, Publisher does not. It is therefore a case of fine tuning the document to prevent it happening.

Hyphenation is covered on page 114.

2. Paragraph spacing must be consistent. This can be achieved through the Styles and Formatting facility, see page 104.

Adjust the line spacing between lines by very small amounts. You may find the default increment of 0.25 is too much. Remember to check that the final text box is not indicating Text in Overflow.

3. Leading (the white space between lines) must be consistent. Adjusting the Leading on the Body text style is one of the major tools used to copyfit the material. Select the Body text style and select Modify. Select Line Spacing and adjust the Between lines measurement.

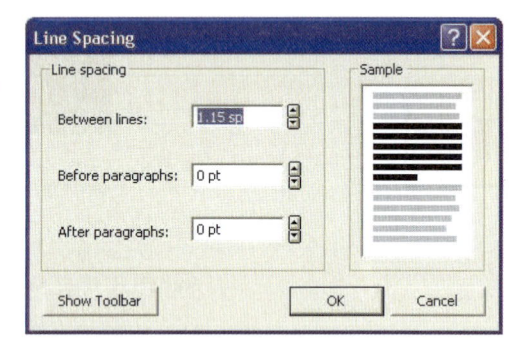

When you have modified the Body text spacing, press Ctrl+A to select all the text, and then click on the style name.

4. Unless otherwise specified, you are normally limited to 10 mm of white space in the document. This is equivalent to two blank lines, and could be a useful tolerance.

If you need to adjust heading and subheading styles remember to stay within the sizes specified.

5. You can adjust image sizes to help in the copyfitting process, but remember to keep the proportions.

Printing

Bleeds allow you to indicate chapters or sections by showing different colours at the edge of the paper.

Crop marks and Bleed marks

Crop marks show where the paper should be cut. To print crop marks the paper needs to be 2.54cms larger in both height and width than the page size.

Bleed marks show the furthest point for printing images and text. To print to this point you must also select Allow bleeds. Bleeds allow you to print a background or colour right to the edge of the paper.

1. Select File, Print. From the Print window select Advanced Print Settings.

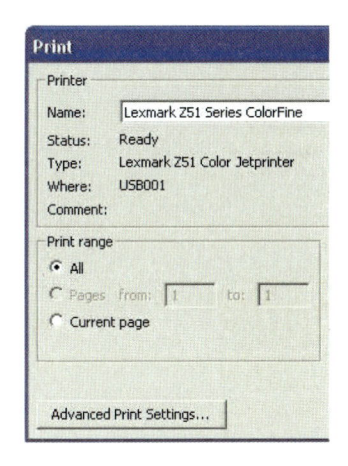

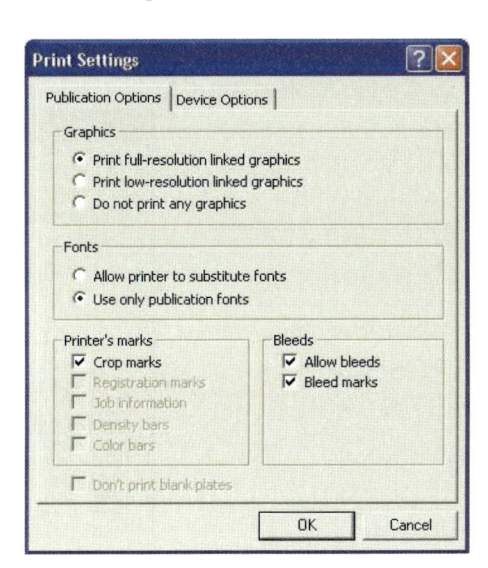

If you are printing on a laser or older printer, you may find that it has inbuilt fonts. Select Use only publication fonts to ensure that you get the fonts you specify.

2. Make sure that the boxes for Crop marks, Allow bleeds and Bleed marks are ticked. Click on OK.

Crop marks are the inner lines that are separated. Bleed marks are the joined corners.

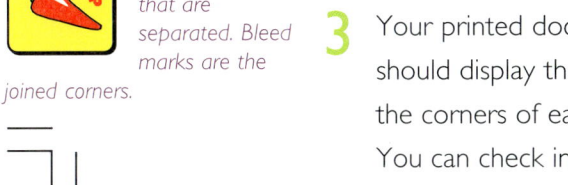

3. Your printed document should display the marks in the corners of each page. You can check in Print preview before you actually print.

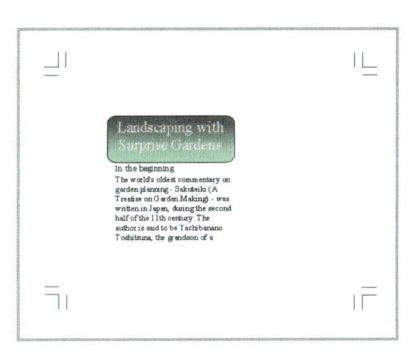

4. Desktop Publishing | 119

...cont'd

When using a commercial printing company in a business situation, you should check with them to find out in what format they want the file, and discuss with them the colour selection.

Composite print

The composite print is the print you would normally get from Publisher, with all the colours showing on all the pages. Just select File, Print and follow the normal procedure.

Colour separated prints

Colour separated prints are used by commercial printers to see how the colours are laid out in the publication. They divide into two types, CMYK and spot colours. To print colour separations:

1. Select Tools, Commercial Printing Tools, and Colour Printing.

2. Composite RGB is the default print setting.

The four Process colours are Cyan, Magenta, Yellow, and Black.

3. Select Process colours (CMYK) to see the colours to be used in the publication. Then click on OK.

When using CMYK colours, Publisher converts all the colours in the document to those values, regardless of the original colour. In a working environment you should check the effects of the colour change.

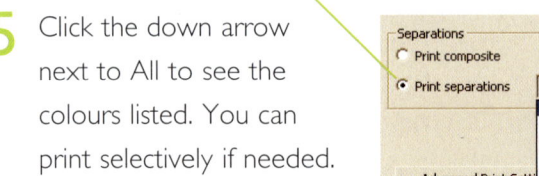

4. Go to File, Print. At the bottom of the Print window click to select Print separations.

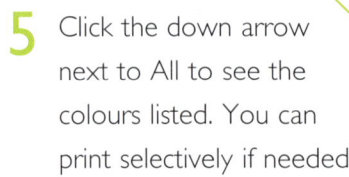

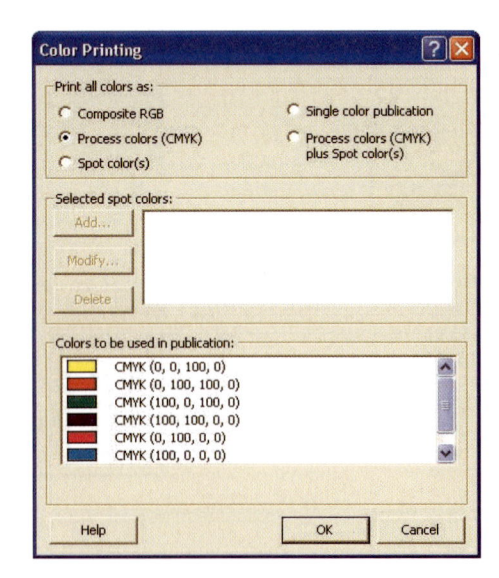

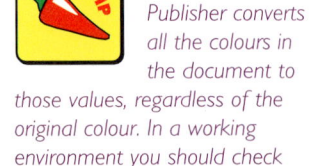

5. Click the down arrow next to All to see the colours listed. You can print selectively if needed.

120 | CLAIT Plus in easy steps

...cont'd

composite

6 The four colour separated prints will be printed using the greyscale. Each print will identify its colour in the footer area.

cyan    magenta    yellow    black

You could start with a plain monochrome document and add spot colours to it to enhance or brighten it.

Spot colours

Using spot colours is a way of introducing colour to a publication at a reduced cost. If you select one colour, (black is automatically included) Publisher will convert all colours except for black to shades of the spot colour. If you choose two spot colours, it applies spot colour two to identical matches and the rest to shades of spot colour one.

When you remove colours from this window, you will delete them from the publication. Save the file before you remove any, so that you can restore them if necessary.

1 When you select Spot colours Publisher allows you to add, modify or delete colours from the document. The bottom pane reflects the effect on the publication.

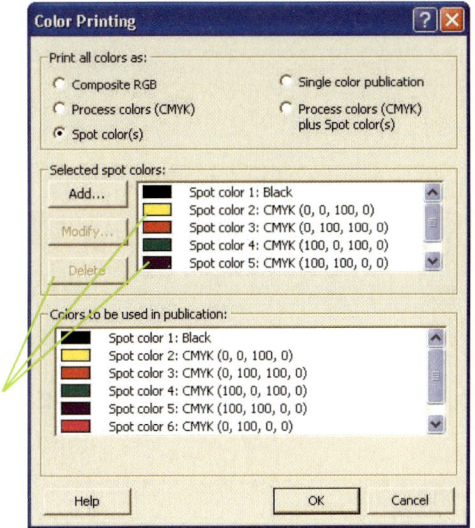

Follow the printing process as for the CMYK prints above.

2 Click on the colours not required and then Delete.

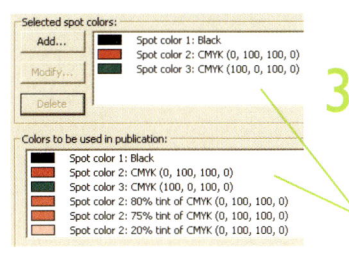

3 The application recognises the depth of the original colour that has been deleted and applies a related equivalent shade of the spot colour. The example shows the effect of removing all colours except red and green.

4. Desktop Publishing | 121

Checklist

You are allowed three hours to complete the OCR CLAIT Plus assessment.

When you have completed the exercise, do a final check to ensure that you meet the exercise requirements. Check you have:

- followed the page layout diagram
- created the required page size
- kept all objects on or inside the margins
- amended the text as required
- linked the text boxes in the correct sequence
- created and applied styles
- modified the styles and applied the modification
- cropped and positioned the images as required
- copy fit the document ensuring:

    text and graphics are not superimposed
    there are no widows and orphans
    hyphenation is controlled
    paragraph spacing is consistent
    leading is consistent
    there is no more than the permitted amount of white space

- included your name, Centre number and date on all prints
- produced composite and colour separated prints
- proofread your prints

If you followed the exercise that can be downloaded, you can check your answers against a worked copy. Remember though, that there may be some differences depending on image size, font size and styles used.

Marking

You are not allowed any critical errors. The following are considered critical errors:

- any specified text files are missing or incomplete
- any specified images are missing
- failure to print colour separated prints

Check with your tutor for a full list of critical and accuracy errors.

Presentation Graphics

This unit covers creating a slide presentation using PowerPoint. Topics include creating a house style, inserting diagrams and charts, and using transitions, animations and timings in the presentation.

Covers

Presentation Graphics | 124

Getting started | 125

The Slide Master | 126

Create the slides | 129

Organise the slides | 130

Create a hyperlink | 132

Tables | 133

Charts | 134

Organisation chart | 136

Transitions | 137

Animation effects | 138

Timings | 140

The slide show | 141

Speaker notes | 142

Print screen | 143

Print | 145

Checklist | 146

Unit Five

Presentation Graphics

Unit Five overview

This unit covers the following areas:

This unit follows a complete Presentation Graphics exercise. The exercise, image and text files used can be downloaded from the In Easy Steps web site (see page 281).

1. Using a design brief to create a multi-slide presentation. The design brief covers details of the Master slide, text styles and slide presentation effects.

2. Creating a master slide. This includes defining styles, inserting an image and creating standard footer text.

3. Using supplied text files in the presentation. You will also have to enter and edit text.

More Presentation Graphics features are covered in the Solution unit on pages 251-252 and the MOS unit on page 274.

4. Inserting and controlling objects such as tables, organisation charts and graphs.

5. Applying transition and animation effects to the slides.

6. Managing the slide show with timings, hidden slides and hyperlinks. You will also have to insert, delete and sort slides.

In this unit we will be using PowerPoint 2002. Any substantial differences between software releases will be highlighted and alternative methods suggested.

7. Printing the slides, handouts and speaker's notes. You will also have to print a screenshot of the slides showing that transitions, animations and timings have be created.

Exercise files and documentation

You should have the following items:

- two text files
- the exercise
- one image file
- a Design brief

Getting started

PowerPoint has some features and settings that should be understood and possibly adjusted before you start to create the presentation.

HOT TIP *From the Menu, select View, Task pane, if it does not appear automatically.*

1 The Task pane, available in PowerPoint 2002, is especially useful. Initially it offers a list of New presentations or to Open an existing one. Click the down arrow next to New Presentations to see those that are available.

HOT TIP *You can also use this pane to sort the slides.*

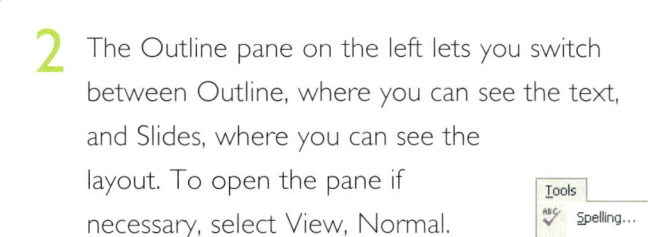

2 The Outline pane on the left lets you switch between Outline, where you can see the text, and Slides, where you can see the layout. To open the pane if necessary, select View, Normal.

BEWARE *This is a very important step if you are to maintain the text size as stipulated.*

3 PowerPoint will automatically resize your text to fit the place holders. To turn off this feature select Tools, AutoCorrect and deselect the two AutoFit options.

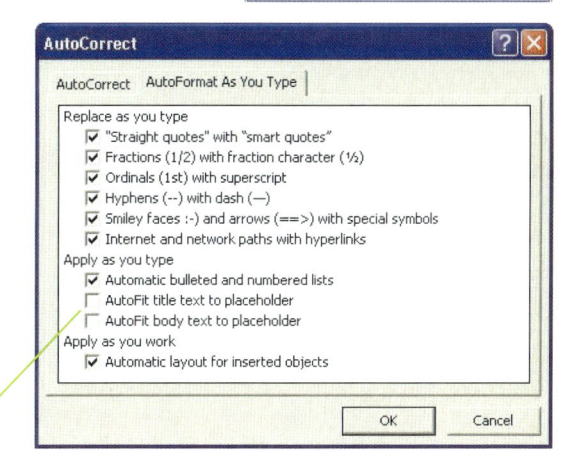

HOT TIP *You can use drawing guides to ensure that your presentation is centred on the slide. Select View, Grid and Guides. Make sure that Snap objects to grid is selected. Click Display drawing guides on screen and click OK. You will see two fine guide lines.*

4 Select Tools, Options and the Spelling tab. Note how PowerPoint will ignore words in uppercase unless otherwise instructed.

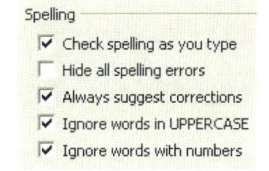

5. Presentation Graphics | 125

The Slide Master

You can have several slide masters. This allows you to have a variety of standard but different designs, used throughout the presentation.

The slide master is used for several purposes. It allows you to create styles that can be applied consistently throughout the presentation, thus giving the show a professional appearance. It is used for text that you would like to appear on every slide, such as date or designer name. You can also use it for company logos or images that you wish to be a standard part of the presentation.

Slide master styles

In this step you are creating the heading or title style. When you close the Slide Master and start entering text, the font size and style that you have selected here will be applied to all headings.

1. From the Menu select View, Master, Slide Master. The text boxes that are displayed are placeholders. Click in the title text box. All the text should be highlighted. You can now set the font size, style, colour and alignment as required by the exercise. You should not type any text.

2. The main or body text box displays five levels of bullet point. Select each bullet point in turn and again choose a font size and style according to the exercise. If the exercise only specifies two levels of bullets, you do not need to change the others.

Note how the ruler indicates the bullet point positions. Drag the bottom square to increase the degree of indentation. For promoting and demoting bullet points, see page 129.

3. To select your own bullet style, click on Format, Bullets and Numbering. You can also adjust the size of the bullet point, or apply a colour. Select Customise to choose from an even greater choice of symbols. Click on OK when finished.

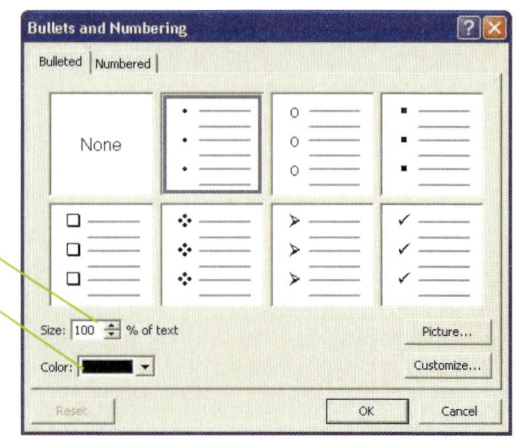

...cont'd

Slide master text

<date/time>   <footer>   <#>
Date Area   Footer Area   Number Area

HOT TIP — To position any of the footer fields elsewhere, see Step 5 below.

1 The footer place holders indicate the default position of date, footer text and slide number. Initially they are inactive. To insert any of the required fields select View, Header and Footer.

HOT TIP — If you select a Fixed date, then you must supply a date.

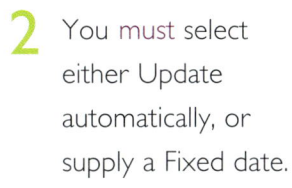

2 You must select either Update automatically, or supply a Fixed date.

BEWARE — Your date must use the English format of day/month/year.

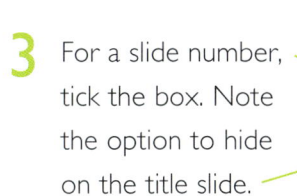

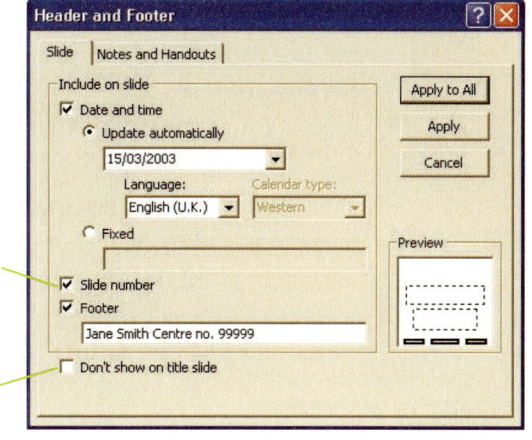

3 For a slide number, tick the box. Note the option to hide on the title slide.

DON'T FORGET — You do not normally need to add text to the Master slide, other than through the Header/Footer facility.

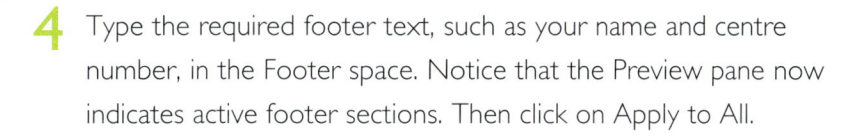

4 Type the required footer text, such as your name and centre number, in the Footer space. Notice that the Preview pane now indicates active footer sections. Then click on Apply to All.

HOT TIP — You can also select Insert, Slide number, or Insert Date. In either case you will be presented with the Header and Footer window.

5 You can reposition any of the footer text boxes in the usual way. To help with fine positioning, select the text box and press Ctrl and the arrow keys to nudge it into place.

6 To relocate the date, position the cursor in the text box, perhaps after your name, and select Insert Date and Time. This displays a specific Date and Time window.

...cont'd

Inserting images was covered in New CLAIT.

Slide master image

1. Select Insert, Picture, From File. You will need to navigate through the folders to locate the file. Select the file and click on Insert.

2. The image will be inserted into the centre of the slide. Using the four-headed cross, drag to the position specified in the Design Brief.

If you find that you need to make the image smaller, once you start inserting the text, you must return to the Slide Master to make the changes.

3. You may need to resize the image. Always use the corner handles so that you maintain the correct proportions.

Background colour

The background colour, dates and slide numbers can be added to all the slides without using the Slide master. However, as it is all part of the setup it's a good idea to apply them at the beginning.

Try to keep the background light if you are going to print the slides, but always follow the exercise Design Brief.

1. To apply a background colour to all the slides, select Format, Background, pick a colour and Apply to All.

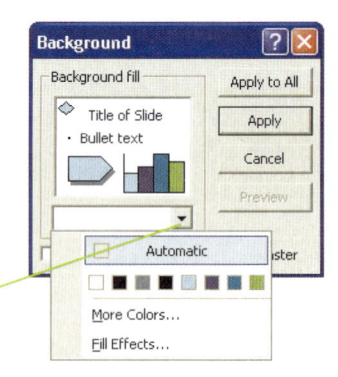

2. For a greater choice of colours or effects click the down arrow and select from the options.

Close the Slide master

To begin entering the text into the slides you must close the Slide master.

1. Select View, Normal. Alternatively click on Close Master View on the Slide Master View toolbar.

128 | CLAIT Plus in easy steps

Create the slides

Remember to use the Taskbar at the bottom of the screen to switch applications. You could also tile the screen and have both applications visible at the same time by using right click on the Taskbar and selecting Tile Horizontally or Vertically.

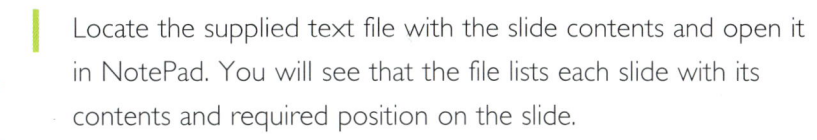

1 Locate the supplied text file with the slide contents and open it in NotePad. You will see that the file lists each slide with its contents and required position on the slide.

2 You can select the text in NotePad, copy and paste it into PowerPoint. This eliminates the need for typing and reduces the opportunity for data entry errors. However, you can only select the contents for one text box at a time.

In previous versions of PowerPoint, use Common Tasks to get a new slide.

3 Select the appropriate layout for the first slide from the Task pane. Copy and paste the text from NotePad. When you have created the first slide, click on New Slide on the toolbar, or press Ctrl+M. Continue until you have created all the slides.

You can use the keyboard shortcuts of Ctrl+C to copy and Ctrl+V to paste. Avoid copying blank lines and text information such as Heading or Bullets.

Promote and demote bullets

Select the text to be adjusted. This could be a single line or several lines. Then click the Increase or Decrease Indent button on the toolbar (or press the Tab key).

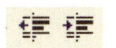

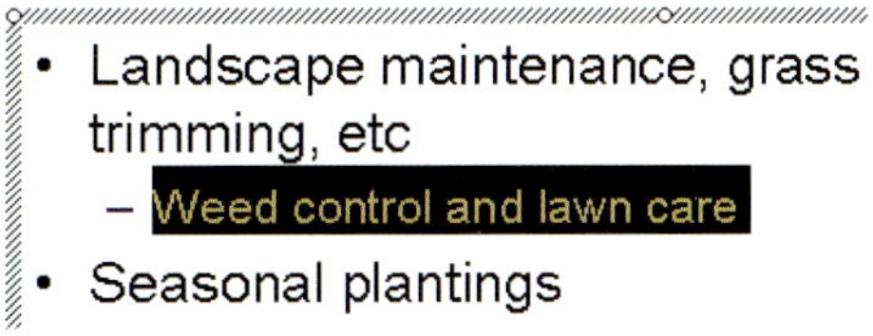

- Landscape maintenance, grass trimming, etc
  - Weed control and lawn care
- Seasonal plantings

The Find and Replace utility has been used in several units and also in New CLAIT.

Find and Replace

Make sure that you get the correct spacing before and after replaced text. Using large fonts in PowerPoint means that mistakes show up very clearly. Use Edit, Replace to start the process.

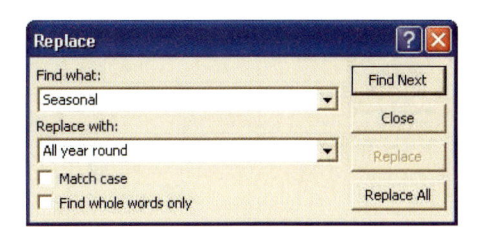

Organise the slides

1. As you create the presentation, you will normally select New Slide from the toolbar, and then choose the layout from the Slide Layout Task pane.

2. When you insert a slide into the presentation between existing slides, the new slide is inserted after the current selection. For example, to insert a slide between slides 2 and 3, select slide 2.

3. Slides can be moved using the Outline view on the left side of the screen. Select the slide to be moved, hold down the left mouse button and drag. You will see a small box attached to the mouse, and a line will appear between slides. Release the mouse button when the line is in the correct position.

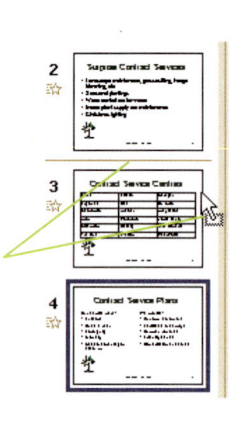

From the Status bar at the bottom of the screen select Slide Sorter view.

Normal view | Slide sorter | Slide show

4. You can also use the Slide Sorter view to move and rearrange your slides. Select View, Slide Sorter. To move the slide just drag and drop as before.

Save your file before you rearrange or delete slides from your presentation. After you have deleted files, save the file with a different name.

5. To delete a slide, just select the slide and press the delete key on the keyboard. A vertical flashing bar will indicate the former position of the deleted slide.

...cont'd

Hide a slide

Whichever method is used, the slide remains visible, but its slide number underneath is displayed as crossed through.

1 To hide a slide in Normal view, select the slide and from the Menu choose Slide Show, Hide Slide. Repeat the process to show the slide.

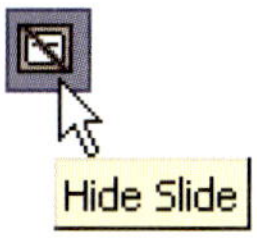

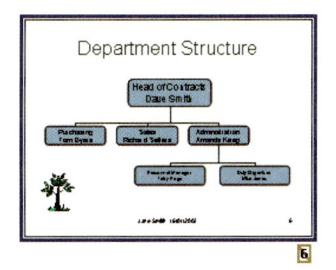

2 The Slide Sorter view has a dedicated Hide Slide toggle button. Select the slide and click the button.

Link to another slide

PowerPoint provides Action buttons which are pre-defined hyperlinks and bear familiar icons. They are the buttons used in most programs to move forwards or backwards, last page, Home etc. They can be used as hyperlinks in the CLAIT Plus exercises.

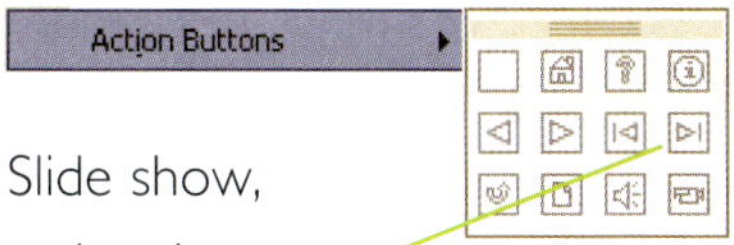

1 To insert an Action button select Slide show, Action Buttons. Click on the appropriate button, for example End. The panel will disappear and the mouse will become a cross symbol.

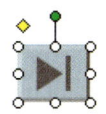

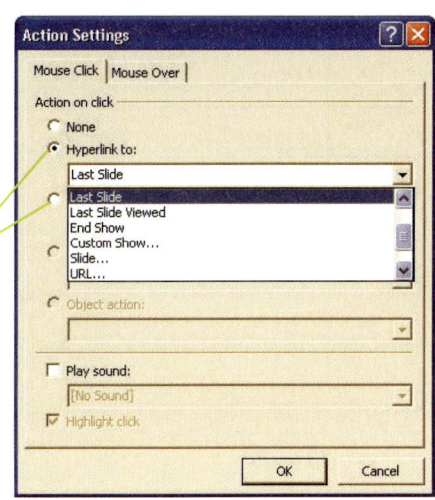

The mouse pointer will become a hand when it's over the hyperlink, during the Slide Show.

2 Draw a small square and release the button. The Action Settings window will appear. Check that the Hyperlink is to the correct destination. Click OK. The hyperlink will become operational in the Slide Show.

5. Presentation Graphics | 131

Create a hyperlink

For CLAIT Plus you can use the Action button, as described on the previous page, for your hyperlink.

1. To create a true Hyperlink in PowerPoint, select Insert, Text box. Draw a small text box in the required position.

2. With the text box still selected, click on the Insert Hyperlink button.

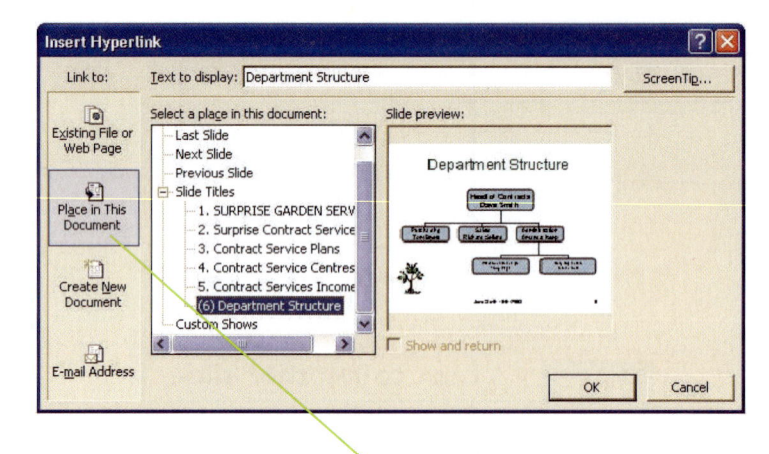

3. From the side panel select Place in this document. The middle panel will then provide a list of pages. Select the page to be linked.

Alternatively, in Step 1, you could have selected some existing text to be used as your hyperlink.

4. The title of the page will be shown in the Text to display space and the contents in the Slide preview pane. You can amend the Text to display to something brief or cryptic.

5. Click on OK to create the hyperlink. The text on the slide will now be underlined, but the hyperlink will only be active in the Slide Show.

6. You can select an image or create an AutoShape and use that as your hyperlink button.

Tables

To change an existing slide into a table layout, it's a good idea to insert a new slide with the table defined and cut and paste the text.

1 From the Slide Layout Task pane scroll to find Other Layouts and select the Title and Table slide.

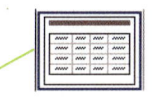

2 Follow the instructions to add the table. Choose the number of columns and rows and click OK. The inserted table will fill the free space on the slide.

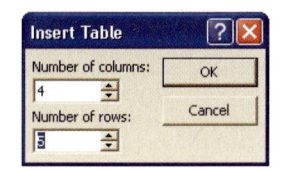

3 Add the table text as required, applying the styles dictated in the Design Brief.

Correct

Incorrect

4 You must ensure that no text overlaps the image, so you may need to shrink the table frame. Position the mouse on the central resize handle at the bottom and drag upwards. Make sure you have the correct mouse symbol. All the rows will resize proportionally.

5 To set a tab within the table, position the cursor within the cell. To the left of the Ruler is the Tab selector. Click on it repeatedly until you see the style of tab required. Move the mouse to the Ruler above the cell and click on the lower part of the Ruler. The tab marker will appear.

Tables in PowerPoint work in the same way as in Word, see page 29-30. You can press Tab to move from cell to cell and press Tab in the bottom right cell to add a new row.

Word and PowerPoint use the same process for setting and using tabs. See page 32 for more information.

6 You will need to set a tab for each of the cells in the column as PowerPoint will not let you select the column and then set the tab.

7 To use the tabs in the table, click in the cell and press Ctrl+tab. The cursor will move to the tab location. Then type the text.

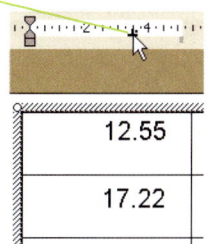

5. Presentation Graphics | 133

Charts

PowerPoint uses the Office Chart program to create and mange graphs and charts.

1. To create a chart, scroll through the Slide Layout Task pane to find and select a suitable layout.

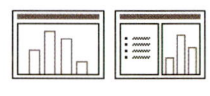

2. Double click to add the chart. A sample datasheet with dummy data and a template chart will open.

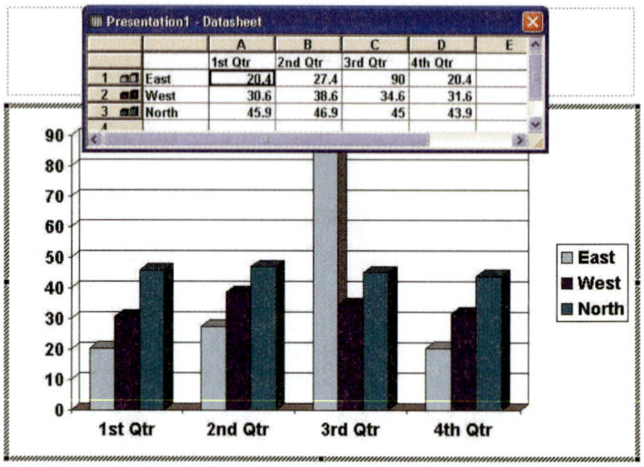

It's useful to have completed the New CLAIT or CLAIT Plus Graphs and Charts unit before starting this item.

3. Change the headings and the data in the datasheet to that given in the exercise. The chart will be amended as you enter the data.

4. To change the chart type select Chart, Chart type from the Menu. Note that the Chart entry on the Menu is only available when the chart is selected.

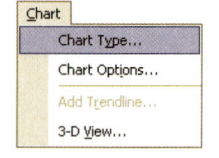

5. Select from the list of chart types. The Preview pane offers a choice of styles within the chart types. You can use the Press and Hold button to see your data illustrated.

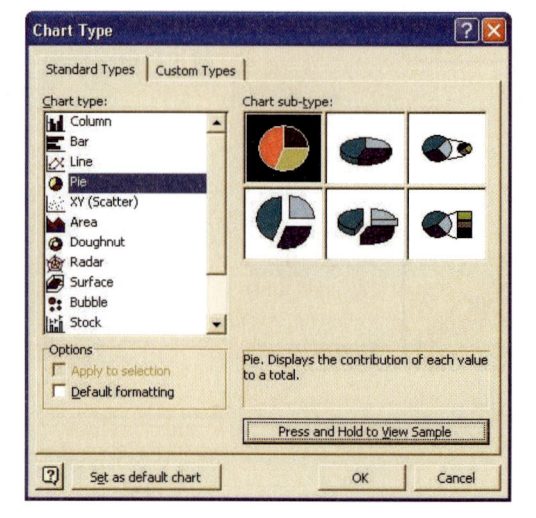

Don't be unduly alarmed if initially your chart does not look as you would expect. You might need to make some amendments to how the data is interpreted. See page 135.

134 | CLAIT Plus in easy steps

...cont'd

The Data entry on the Menu is only available when the chart is selected.

6 The chart program may need to re-interpret the new data, especially if you are changing from the default column chart to a pie chart. Select Data, Series in Rows, or Series in Columns, whichever is appropriate.

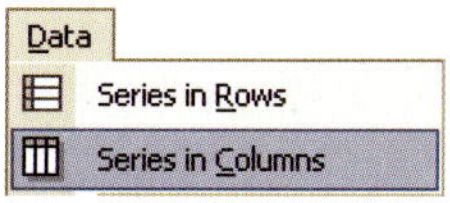

Before changing the data series

After changing the data series

To finish editing the chart, click outside the chart area or press Esc. To edit the chart, double click inside the chart area.

7 To make changes to the chart display, such as remove the legend or apply values, select Chart, Chart Options. Select the Titles tab if you wish to add a chart title. Click on the Legend tab to add or remove the chart legend. The Data Labels tab lets you display Category names, Values and Percentages.

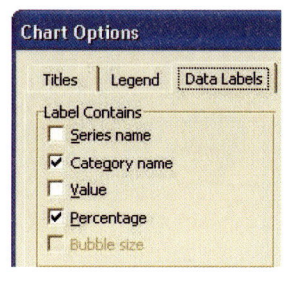

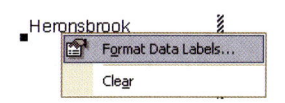

8 To select a font size and style for the data labels, click inside the chart area and single click one of the labels to select it. Right click the label and choose Format Data Labels. It's a good idea to deselect Auto scale.

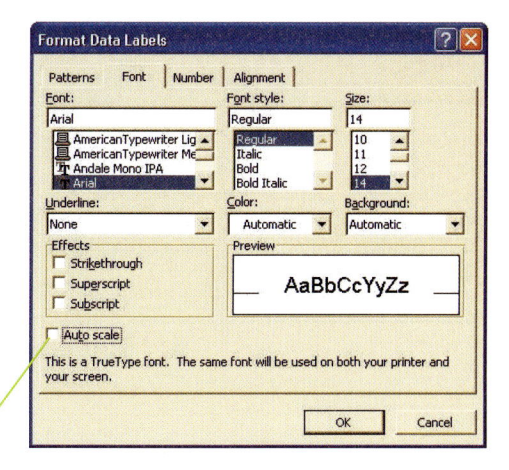

When the label is selected it has a black dot either side. Click again once it is selected and it will be framed. This allows you to move it away from the chart if it appears too close.

5. Presentation Graphics | 135

Organisation chart

1. The Slide Layout pane includes a slide for an Organisation chart. Once selected, click in the centre of the slide to open the Diagram Gallery.

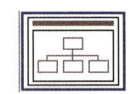

2. Select the Organisation Chart and click OK. When you click in the chart area the Organisation Chart toolbar appears.

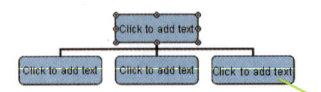

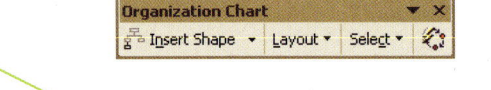

3. Click inside any of the text boxes to enter the details. The text boxes will expand as you type.

BEWARE: *The Organisation Chart will only honour the font size you have specified as long as there is space available. If you need to enter a significant amount of text, the font will resize.*

4. You can work with the text boxes individually, or you can select a Level or Branch using the Organisation toolbar. This allows you to apply font sizes and styles to several text boxes at once.

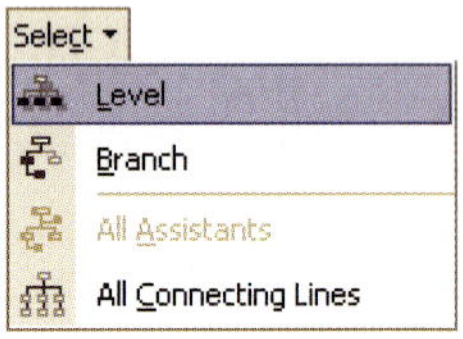

HOT TIP: *Check the text in the text boxes carefully to ensure that it does not overlap the outlines. If it does, then the frames can be resized. Sometimes just clicking inside the frame solves this problem.*

5. To add a new entry, select the relevant text box and choose Insert Shape from the toolbar.

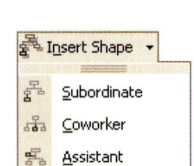

6. To drag and place individual frames if you need to adjust the layout, select Layout, AutoLayout.

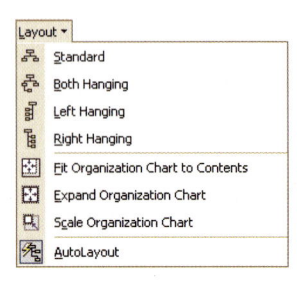

7. Click outside the drawing area when you have finished.

136 | CLAIT Plus in easy steps

Transitions

A transition defines how the slide appears on the screen when you run the slide show.

For the CLAIT Plus course, it's easiest to select a transition and click the button Apply to All Slides.

1. In Normal view or in Slide Sorter view, select the first slide. From the Task pane select Slide Transition.

In previous versions of PowerPoint, select Slide Show, Transitions. This also lets you set the timing and other options.

2. To apply the transition, just click on your choice from the list in the Task pane. If the AutoPreview box at the bottom of the Task pane is ticked, you should see the effect immediately.

For a professional looking presentation, you should limit the number of different transitions you use.

3. You can adjust the speed of the transition effect, and add sounds.

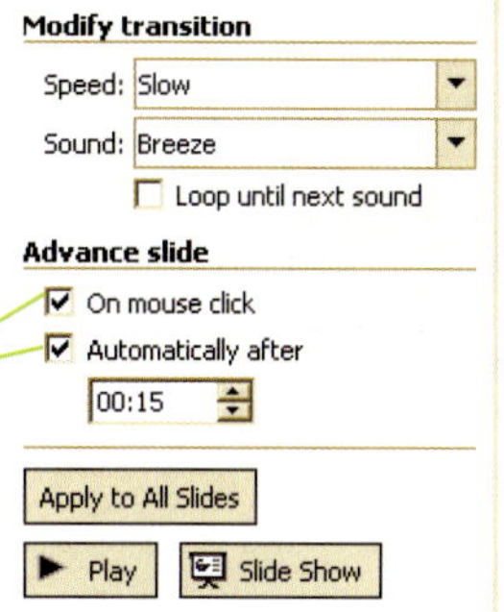

It's a good idea to select Advance slide on Mouse click. It can be quite frustrating and time consuming to have to wait a set amount of time when you are setting up the show.

4. To advance to the next slide you can choose both Mouse click and Automatically after a period of time. This way you have the advantages of both methods and can go to the next slide when you want.

5. For a quick set up, you can apply the same transition to all slides. To apply the same transition to several separate slides, press Ctrl and click each of the required slides. Then select the transition. To remove a transition select No transition from the Task pane.

6. When you view the slides in Slide Sorter view you will see that each slide has a symbol at the bottom left corner indicating that a transition has been applied.

Animation effects

The CLAIT Plus exercise may refer to Animation effects as Builds.

Animation effects are applied to the individual text boxes and objects that make up the slides.

1. From the Task pane select Animation Schemes. They are added to the slides in the same way as Transitions are added. You can apply the animations to individual slides or to all. Press the Play button to see the effect.

If the CLAIT Plus exercise requires you to add just one animation to each slide, use Slide Design - Animation Schemes. Custom Animation is when you need to apply several effects.

2. To apply different animation effects within the same slide, choose Custom Animation from the Task pane

For earlier versions of PowerPoint, animations can be added in the Slide Sorter view. Click the down arrow on the toolbar next to Preset Animations, or select Slide Show, Animations to see the full list. The effects can be applied to individual lines of text.

3. Next select a text box within a slide and click on Add Effect. From the drop down menu select one of the four options, and within that option choose an effect.

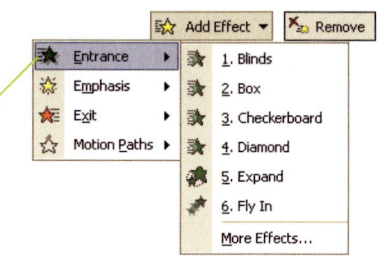

4. You can choose when the text appears by clicking on Start and selecting from the options.

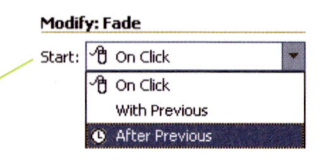

5. You can also choose the speed at which the text appears. This does affect the overall timings for the presentation, although in Slide Sorter view the timings shown below each slide remain the same. See page 140 for setting timings.

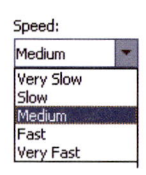

...cont'd

6 Each of the slide objects that has an animation effect applied will be listed in the Task pane. When you hover the mouse over the entry, the applied effects will be listed.

7 When viewed in Normal view, the slide will display numbered elements when Animation effects have been applied.

> **HOT TIP**
> *When working with bulleted text, you can make each bullet point appear separately. Click on each bullet point in turn and select Start After Previous.*

8 The effects can be customised even further for each object. Select the item in the Task pane and choose from the items listed.

9 Press Play at the bottom of the Task pane to see individual slides, or Slide Show to see the whole presentation.

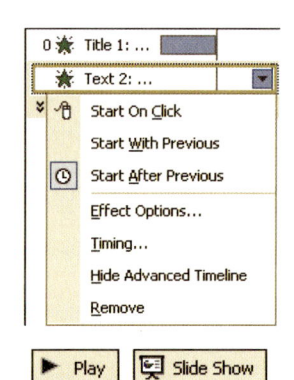

5. Presentation Graphics | 139

Timings

You can be in Normal view or Slide Sorter view when you apply timings to your slides.

While you are still working on setting up the slide show, it's a good idea to keep the On mouse click box ticked as well, so that you can move to the next slide when you want.

1. Select the Slide Transition Task pane. In the section to Advance slide, make sure that the box is ticked to Automatically after.

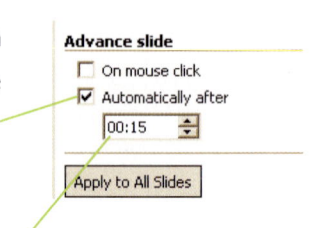

2. Set the time specified on the Design Brief.

3. Click on the button to Apply to All Slides. In the Slide Sorter view, you will see the time set underneath each slide.

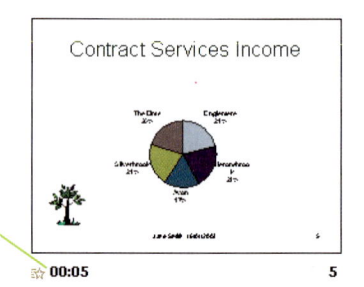

4. You can modify the transition speed, but this does not generally affect the slide timings.

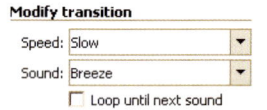

5. If you apply animation effects to the slide, the timings may be affected, although the timings shown underneath each slide will not be altered.

This is not required by the CLAIT Plus exercise.

For sophisticated presentations, you can adjust the timings as you view the show. This gives you much greater control over individual slides and individual animations. When you have finished the show you will be prompted to save the timings. Timings set in this way will override any others.

This topic is covered in greater detail in the Presentation Graphics Solutions unit, see pages 251-252.

The Slide Show

1 The Slide Show can be started from several points, including the Task pane and the navigation buttons on the bottom left of the screen. You can also press the F5 function key.

2 To stop the show at any point, press the Esc(ape) key on the top left of the keyboard.

3 By default the slide show will end with a black slide. To change this setting select Tools, Options. Select the View tab and deselect End with black slide.

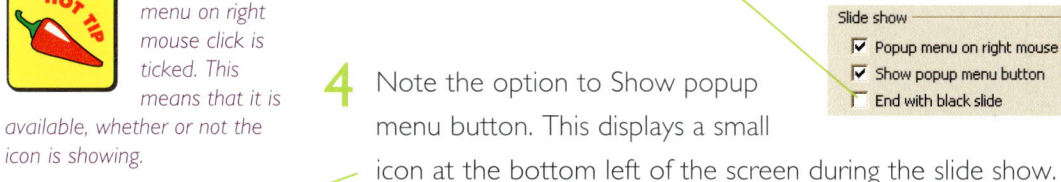

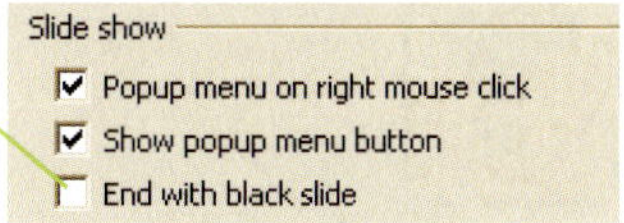

Note that Popup menu on right mouse click is ticked. This means that it is available, whether or not the icon is showing.

Slide show
- ☑ Popup menu on right mouse click
- ☑ Show popup menu button
- ☐ End with black slide

4 Note the option to Show popup menu button. This displays a small icon at the bottom left of the screen during the slide show.

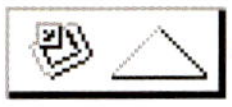

5 Click on the Popup menu button to display a list of options. The Go button takes you to the Slide Navigator window, where you can select which slide to view next. Speaker Notes displays any notes you have entered for that particular slide. You can select Pointer Options, including a pen colour. Screen offers Pause or Black screen.

Next
Previous
Go ▶
Meeting Minder...
Speaker Notes
Pointer Options ▶
Screen ▶
Help
End Show

For the CLAIT Plus exercise you should save the file in the standard PowerPoint .ppt file format.

6 PowerPoint offers several save options. As well as a regular PowerPoint file, you can save the file as a PowerPoint show, with the .pps file extension. The presentation will always then open as a slide show. You can also select Pack and Go from the file menu. This opens a wizard which prepares the show to be used on another computer. See the MOS unit, page 274 for more details.

Speaker notes

1. Speaker notes can be viewed in the Normal PowerPoint window. They are displayed in a separate pane at the bottom of the screen. The pane can be expanded by dragging the divider upwards with the mouse.

2. PowerPoint also offers a separate Notes window. Select View, Notes Page.

The speaker notes have been provided for the exercise in a separate .txt file.

3. To insert the provided notes into PowerPoint, open the text file in NotePad. The file will be presented in the same format as the slide contents file.

4. Copy and paste the notes a slide at a time into the presentation. See page 129 for copying and pasting between the two applications.

5. To format the notes text to a specified font and size you must be in the Notes Pages view. The normal style options then apply.

Print the Notes

1. Select File, Print. In the print menu select Notes pages.

To print a particular Notes Page, the slide must be the one currently selected in Normal view.

2. In the Print range, All, Current slide and Selection can be used to selectively print Notes Pages as well.

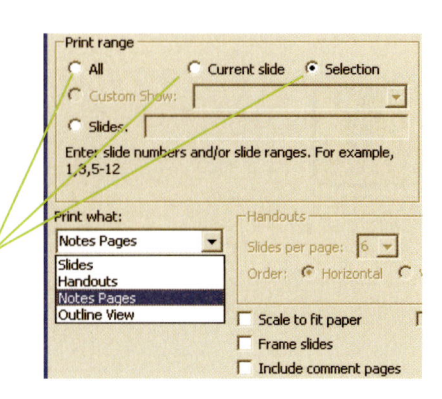

142 | CLAIT Plus in easy steps

Print screen

To demonstrate that you have applied transitions, animations and timings to all the slides you must provide a screen snapshot.

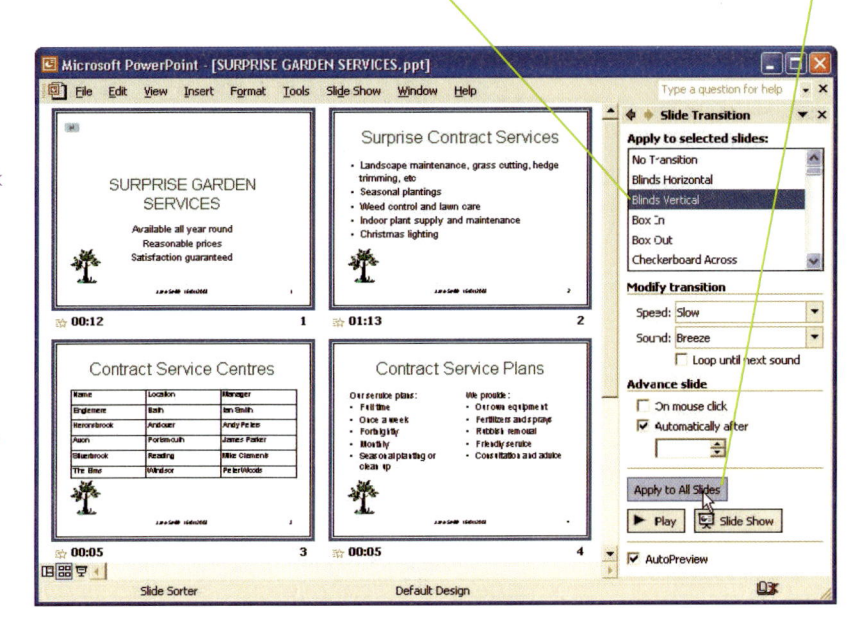

In PowerPoint 2000 and previous versions, the application of transitions and animations was indicated by two separate symbols, as shown below. Unfortunately in Office XP, PowerPoint 2002, Microsoft have combined the two icons, so you can no longer identify that both actions have been applied.

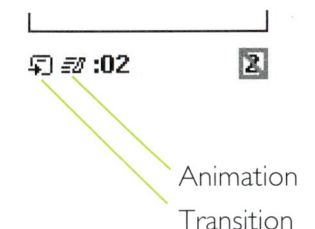

1 Go to Slide Sorter view. This shows the transitions/animations icon underneath each of the slides.

2 You must select all the slides. Click on the first slide and press Shift and click on the last. They should now all have a blue frame.

3 Select the Transitions Task pane and make sure that a transition is selected.

Animation
Transition

4 Position the mouse over the button to Apply to All Slides. The button will turn blue. Whilst it is still blue, press the Print Screen keyboard key. In this way you demonstrate that all slides have been selected, a Transition chosen and Apply to All Slides clicked.

The Transition and Animation should already have been applied. If it hasn't, then make sure you click the Apply to All Slides button.

Creating a screen print was also covered in Unit 1, see page 23.

5. Presentation Graphics | 143

...cont'd

5 Open Word and select the Paste from Clipboard button. The image will be pasted into the document.

6 Click away from the image to deselect it, and press Enter a couple of times to give yourself a little space.

7 Return to the PowerPoint window and this time select Slide Design - Animation Schemes. Select an animation and once again position the mouse over the Apply to All Slides so it turns blue.

To help with checking your final prints, it would be useful to expand the images and identify in the Word document which screen print shows Transitions and which Animations.

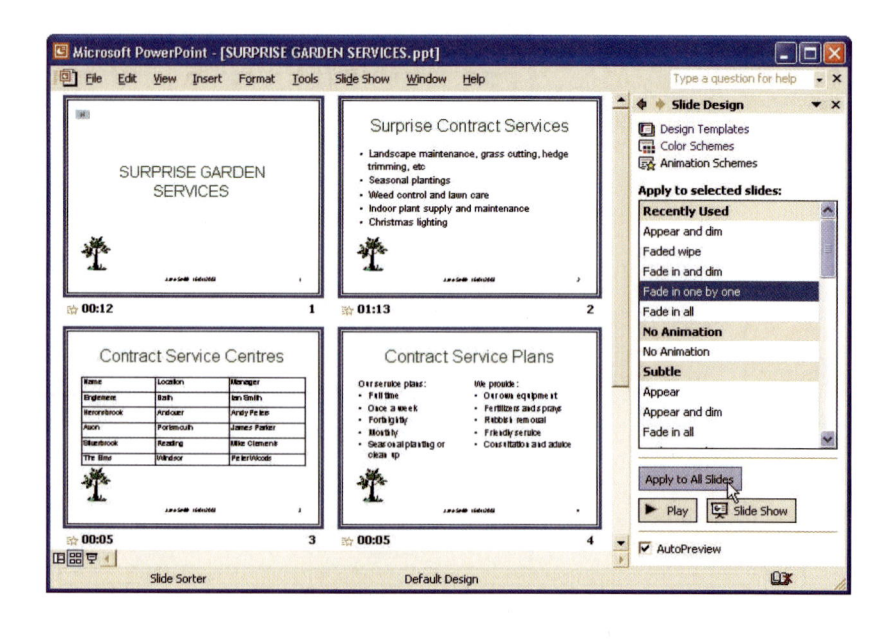

8 Capture the screen with the Print Screen key and paste the image into Word. Add your name and details to the Word document, and save and print the file.

9 These prints also indicate that timings have been applied to each slide.

Print

> **HOT TIP:** For printing Notes, see page 142.

1. Print Preview provides some print options, and can be used as a shortcut in certain circumstances. You can, for example select slides, handouts or Outline view, and you can access items such as Header and Footer.

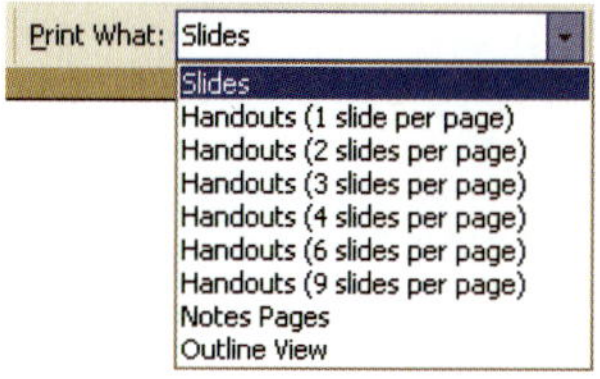

2. Use the main Print menu, File, Print, for the full range of options. To print specific slides, click in Slides and enter the slide numbers, separated by commas or hyphens.

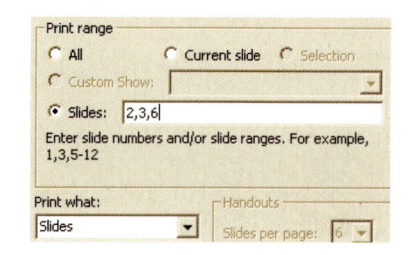

> **HOT TIP:** The Print Range selection of All, Current slide, Selection and Slides is applied whether you are printing Slides, Handouts, Notes or Outline View.

3. Click the down arrow in Print What and select Handouts. You can then select the number to be printed on each page, and see the layout in the small preview window.

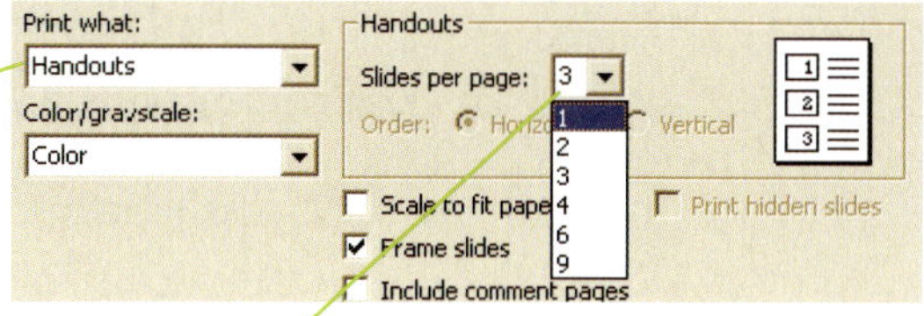

4. Outline View will print the document with just headings and bullet points. It can be selected from the Print What box.

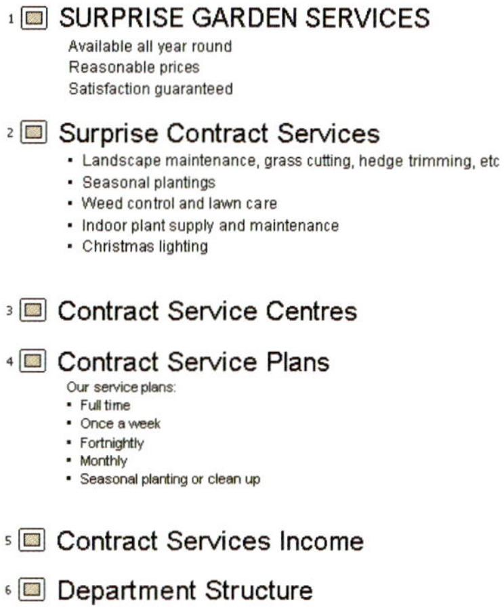

> **DON'T FORGET:** It's worth checking Print Preview before you print, to make sure that you have the right style of print.

5. Presentation Graphics | 145

Checklist

You are allowed three hours to complete the OCR CLAIT Plus assessment.

When you have completed the exercise, do a final check to ensure that you meet the exercise requirements. Make sure that you have:

- set up the Master slide according to the Design Brief
- applied a background colour to all slides
- included header/footer text on each slide, including date and slide number
- inserted the correct text on each slide
- inserted the required images and objects
- amended the text as required
- rearranged, deleted, hidden and linked slides
- applied transitions, animations and timings to each slide
- inserted the speakers notes from the supplied text file
- included your name, Centre number and date on all prints
- produced the required number and style of prints
- amended the text as required
- proofread your prints

You can check your answer against those in the Worked Copy folder, if you downloaded the exercises from the Internet. You may find some subtle differences depending on image sizes and fonts used.

Marking

You are not allowed any critical errors. The following are considered critical errors:

- title slide in wrong order or a missing slide
- data incorrectly imported or inserted
- failure to insert specified graphic/logo
- failure to embed a chart or organisation chart
- numeric data for the chart not absolutely correct
- failure to hide slides or to create a hyperlink to a hidden slide
- speakers notes attached to wrong slide

Check with your tutor for a complete list of critical errors and accuracy errors.

146 | CLAIT Plus in easy steps

Computer Art

This unit shows how to create a piece of art work using Paint Shop Pro. You will see how to use editing tools to size, layer, make transparent and recolour images. It also introduces the concept of animating images, using Animation Shop.

Covers

Computer Art | 148

The software | 149

Building the art work | 151

Create the canvas | 152

Insert images | 153

Layer images | 154

Working with layers | 155

Edit and retouch tools | 156

Tool and colour options | 157

Coloured area selection | 158

Text | 159

Shapes | 160

Deformation | 161

Text effects | 162

Print | 163

Animation | 165

Checklist | 170

Unit Six

Computer Art

This unit follows a complete exercise for Computer Art. The image, text files and the exercise can be downloaded from the In Easy Steps web site (see page 281).

Unit Six overview

This unit covers the following areas:

1. Creating a canvas to a specific size and overlaying a variety of images.

2. Using image editing tools to improve pictures by removing marks and unwanted objects.

See pages 253-255 for Digital Imaging Solutions. The unit covers the use of scanners and digital cameras, as well as photographic editing.

3. Working with colouring tools to change or swop colours, and to set colour transparency.

4. Using vector graphics to create objects such as lines and shapes, using facilities to fill the shapes with colour, textures or gradients.

5. Adding text to the art work. You will cover how to add the text using Paint Shop tools, or using Microsoft's Word Art.

6. The relationship between image resolution and print resolution, and print size and print quality.

In this unit we will be using Paint Shop Pro v7, and Animation Shop 3.

7. Creating and displaying an animated image.

Exercise files and documentation

You should have the following items:

- the exercise files
- the exercise
- the Design Brief for the art work and the animation

The software

The assignment exercises for this unit require a combination of computer applications. There are numerous sets of products that you could use on your own system. OCR does not make any recommendations or suggestions, but the education centre where you take your CLAIT Plus courses may require that you use their specific choices.

> **HOT TIP**: *You may have photo editing software supplied with your scanner or digital camera. You could use this to practise the exercises, but make sure that it can handle all the functions specified in the CLAIT Plus syllabus, since these applications are often Lite (lower function) versions.*

Jasc Software options

These are the products that have been used to illustrate the steps in the exercises. Other graphics and animation editors would have similar tools and functions.

- Paint Shop Pro 7
- Animation Shop 3

These products are shareware and you can download trial 30 day versions from the Jasc Software web site http://www.jasc.com. Animation Shop 3 is included as an extra component with the retail copy of Paint Shop 7.

> **HOT TIP**: *It's always possible to make use of other applications for functions that you need to develop your computer artwork, for example, the WordArt options in Word or Publisher.*

...cont'd

Microsoft options

These are applications you could consider, if you have Office 2000 and if they are included in your particular edition.

- PhotoDraw 2000
- GIF Animator

The PhotoDraw 2000 product has now been discontinued, and there is no obvious Microsoft application for Office XP users.

GIF Animator was supplied with FrontPage 2000 and Image Composer. It was also available as a free download on the Internet, but can no longer be obtained in this way.

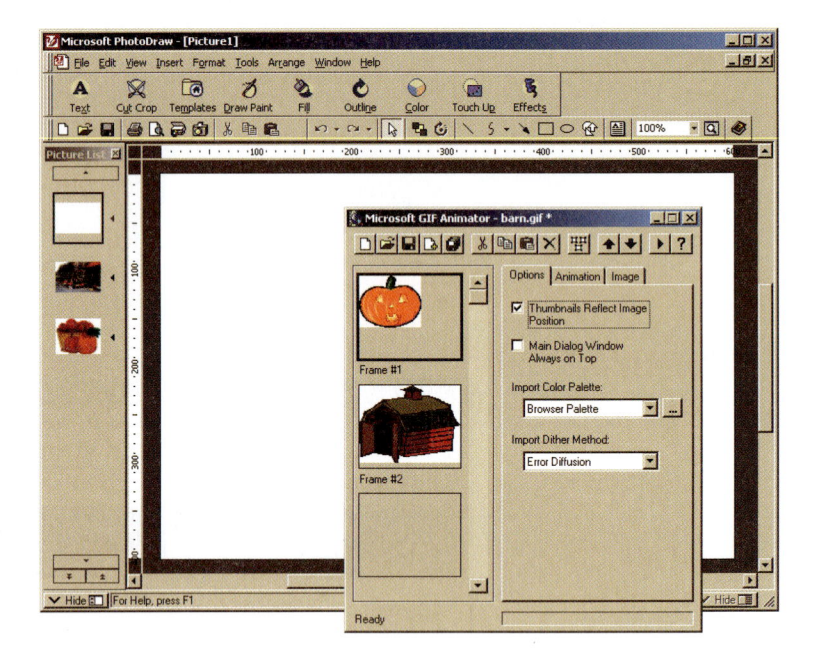

Image Ready is supplied as an extra component with Photoshop 7.

Adobe options

This is arguably the highest function solution which would satisfy professional requirements.

- Photoshop 7
- Image Ready

However, this is a relatively expensive product. A lower cost alternative would be:

- Adobe Photoshop Elements 2

You can convert layers to animation frames in Adobe Photoshop Elements 2, so you don't need a separate animation application.

Building the art work

See page 154-155 for working with layers.

Later in the unit we will introduce and work with other tools such as colour, text and shapes.

Zoom level

To cancel a selection, click with the right mouse button.

Some of the tools, such as Deformation, can only be used when you are working with a particular layer or selection. If the tool is not enabled, then you are not on the correct layer.

The art work you are going to create starts with a canvas which sets the size of the finished work. The process requires you to work in layers, with the canvas being layer one. Each image that you use will be opened in a window, copied and pasted onto the canvas as a separate layer. The individual file window can then be closed.

Working with layers in this way means that you can select a specific layer with which to work. You can also insert layers to create effects or change factors such as the brightness or hue.

As you work with each layer, you will need to select components on that layer to resize, move, colour etc. Here we introduce the selection tools, but there will be more information on how to use them as you work through the exercise.

The Selection tools

Arrow if the image is too large for the screen, select the arrow, move to the image, press and hold the left mouse button. The arrow becomes a hand that lets you move the image, so that hidden areas appear.

Zoom use the left mouse button to zoom in, the right to zoom out. The zoom level is shown on the Title bar.

Deformation use this to resize, skew and distort layers, floating selections and images. Resize using the middle or corner handles. Drag the corner with the right mouse button to resize maintaining proportions.

Crop using the mouse draw a box. The area inside the box will be kept. Double click inside the box to action the crop, or click on the Crop Image button.

Mover this can move either a selection or a layer, just click with the left mouse button and drag.

Selection and Freehand selection draw a box or freehand shape around the area you want. When you release the button the area becomes a marquee which can be moved or copied.

Magic Wand selects content using colour and opacity as its selection criteria.

6. Computer Art | 151

Create the canvas

Paint Shop Pro remembers anything that you specify. Next time you open this window it will have the details and dimensions that you set this time.

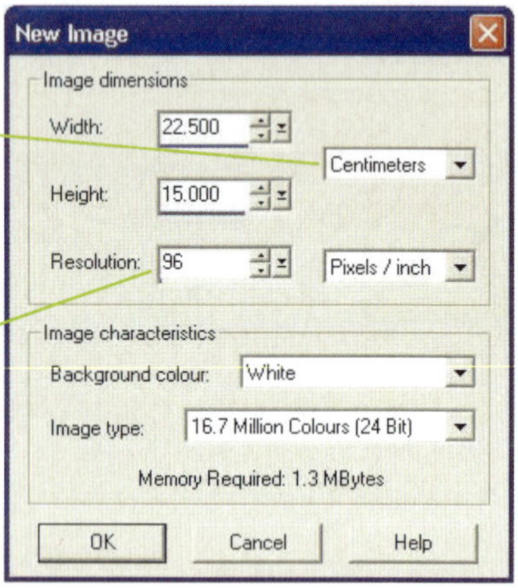

An image resolution of 96 dpi (dots per inch) is suitable for images intended for web pages. Image resolutions of 150 or 300 are typically selected for images to be printed.

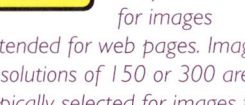

Once you have created the canvas, the size and the resolution are directly linked. If you change the image resolution, the physical dimensions will change as well.

Print resolution is a separate issue, see pages 163-164.

The canvas is your starting point. It lets you set both the size and resolution that will be used by the whole art work.

1. Paint Shop Pro opens with an empty grey screen. Select File, New or the New icon.

2. Choose the measurement units first, (inches, centimetres or pixels) and then the size.

3. Select the resolution.

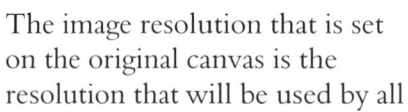

The image resolution that is set on the original canvas is the resolution that will be used by all the images. The resolution, once set, controls the size of the finished product and should not be changed.

Take, for example, an image with a size of 10 cms by 8 cms and a resolution of 150 pixels per centimetre. When you place it on a canvas with a resolution of 300 pixels, it will shrink to 5 cms by 4 cms. If you place it on a canvas at 96 pixels, it will grow to approximately 15.6 cms by 12.5 cms. The same number of pixels are distributed at the canvas resolution.

The resolution also affects the memory required to work with the art work. At 96 pixels/inch the memory required is 1.8 MBytes, at 300 it is 17.9 MBytes.

4. Finally, select the background colour. Choose white or another colour rather than transparent to help ensure that you cover right to the edge with the layered images. The canvas is the white area inside the cross-hatching.

152 | CLAIT Plus in easy steps

Insert images

1 Open your first image as you would open any file. It will open in a new window.

> **HOT TIP**
> When you bring in an image take note of the details at the edges, so that you are sure you have the complete picture as you work.

2 The whole picture is treated as if you have already selected it. Click on Edit, Copy, or use the Copy button.

3 Select Window from the menu and choose Image 1, ie the canvas.

> **HOT TIP**
> Select Layers on the menu to see the layers listed. You should have Layer 1: "background", Layer 2: "layer 1".

4 Select Edit, Paste as new layer. The image will be placed, in the middle of the canvas.

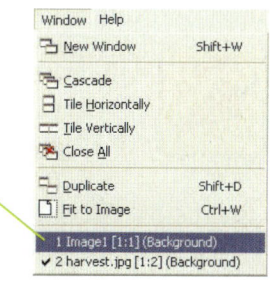

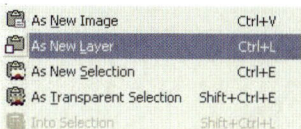

5 If the image is smaller than the canvas, you will see all of it and any background canvas not covered. Select the Deformation tool and drag the corners with right mouse button to fill the canvas.

> **HOT TIP**
> When the proportions of the image and the art work are different, you will have to fit to one dimension and allow the image to overlap on the other.

6 If the image is bigger than the canvas, you will see just the centre. Zoom out and select the Deformation tool. The perimeter of the image will be indicated. Shrink to size using the right mouse button to drag the corners whilst keeping the proportions.

6. Computer Art | 153

Layer images

As you build the art work, you will probably need to super-impose one image over another. The images may be from different sources and may have different proportions or perspectives. To enable a new image to blend, you may have to size it proportionally and remove the background. Layers make this easier to manage.

Save your file as Artwork1.psp before you start working with the next image.

1. Open your next image, it will open in a new window.

See page 157 for more information on selecting colours.

2. Copy the whole image to the Clipboard. Switch to the Canvas window, Artwork1.psp

3. Select Layers, New Raster layer and name it appropriately. Click OK to accept the remaining defaults.

Vector layers allow you to create and resize vector objects, (text and autoshapes). Raster layers allow you to resize and deform all objects.

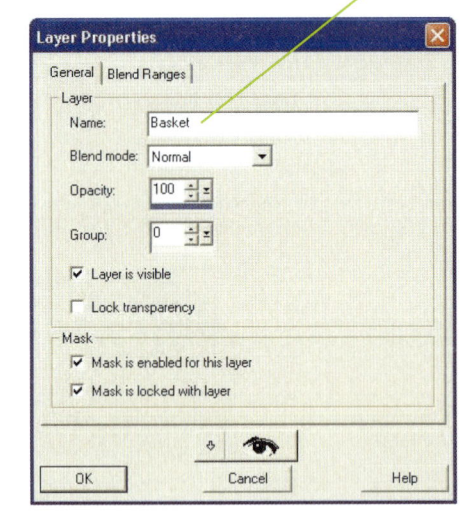

Check that the background colour specified for the art work matches the background of the image. The background will then be eliminated when you Paste As Transparent Selection.

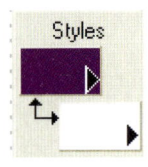

4. Use Edit, Paste, As Transparent Selection. Drag the image to its required position and select the Deformation tool. Resize the image as necessary.

154 | CLAIT Plus in easy steps

Working with layers

When you save your file in the .psp format, the layers remain. When you reopen it you can still access individual layers. When you save the file as a .gif or .tif the layers will be merged.

Layers function as in the same way as sheets of transparent acetate, such as you would use on an overhead projector. You can write (paste) on them, work with each independently, lay one over another, or group and shuffle them.

Working with layers gives you the flexibility to amend particular elements of your art work at a later stage, when for example you realise that something needs to be moved slightly.

At this stage in your art work, you should have created several layers. Selecting Layers from the toolbar will display a list of options and list the layers you have created. You can work with the layers using this list or you can use the Layer Palette toolbar.

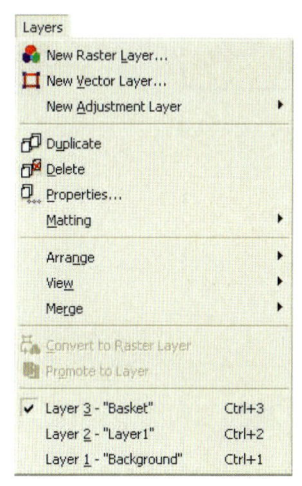

To display the Layer Palette toolbar, select View, Toolbars, and tick the appropriate box.

Right click the toolbar for a list of options. For example, you can rename Layer1 to a more meaningful name, such as Craftshop.

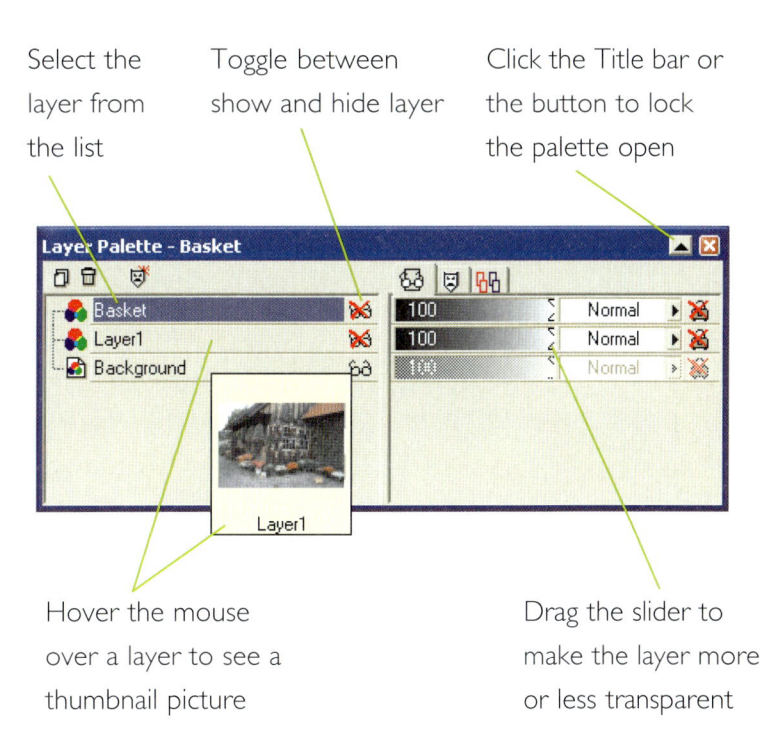

Select the layer from the list

Toggle between show and hide layer

Click the Title bar or the button to lock the palette open

Hover the mouse over a layer to see a thumbnail picture

Drag the slider to make the layer more or less transparent

6. Computer Art | 155

Edit and retouch tools

Paint Shop Pro provides several tools that allow you to remove scratches, marks and unwanted items from your pictures.

When using the colouring tools, use the left mouse button for the foreground colour and the right mouse button for the background.

The Colouring tools

Dropper use it to select foreground and background colours. See page 157 for more details.

Paintbrush this and other painting tools, including Colour Replacer and Eraser, can only be used on raster layers.

Clone brush copies one part of an image to another. See below for how to use it.

Colour replacer this replaces one colour in the image with another. You can replace fore or background with brush strokes, or double click to replace throughout.

Retouch use it to paint with the effect, to lighten, highlight and make other such changes.

Scratch remover removes scratches and cracks. You must merge layers or a transparent image to make it available.

Eraser will replace colours with the background colour or transparency.

Each of the painting tools has options to let you select size, density etc. See page 157 for more details.

To repair and remove unwanted items from the image:

1. Using the layer palette, select the layer that needs editing and use the Zoom feature to close in on the working area.

2. Select the Clone brush. Right mouse click to select an area to copy. Move the mouse to the object, press and hold the left mouse button to activate.

Paint Shop Pro has an extensive Undo facility.

3. Experiment with the other tools, select Undo between each attempt to get the best effect.

156 | CLAIT Plus in easy steps

Tool and colour options

All of the colouring, selection and effect tools have associated options which allow you to select characteristics such as shape, density, width etc. Select the Tool Options button to open the window, which will float over the image. As you switch from one tool to another, the Tool Options window will change to the new tool.

Use the Lock button to lock the window open, or unlock and allow it to collapse and expand as you move over it.

Clone brush options

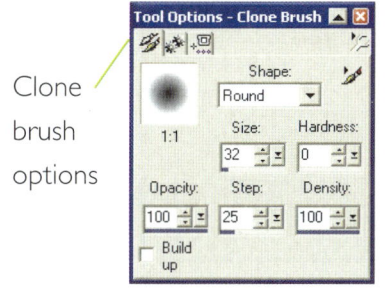

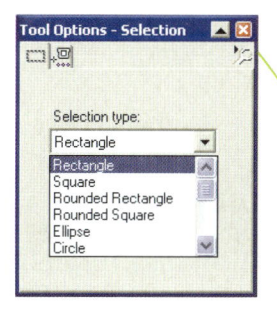

Selection tool options

Colour options

If the image is a .gif file, it will have a maximum of 256 colours and will show a limited palette. The colour palette shown below is 16 million.

When you want to select a colour to use with any of the painting tools:

1 If the colour is on the image, select the Dropper and click on the colour, left mouse button for foreground, right mouse for background.

2 To select a colour from the colour palette, take the mouse to the fore or background box. It will change to the dropper, automatically, simply click.

Click the arrow to choose between Solid, Gradient, Texture or Null colour options.

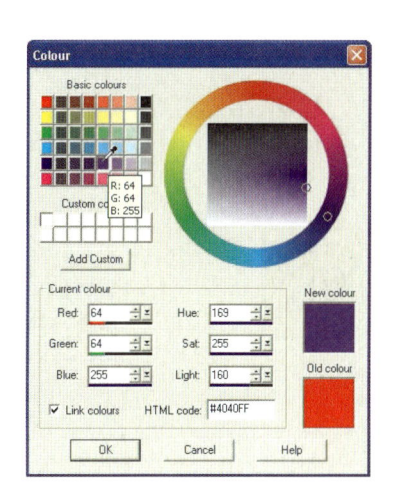

3 Select the colour from the full range, or specify numerical values.

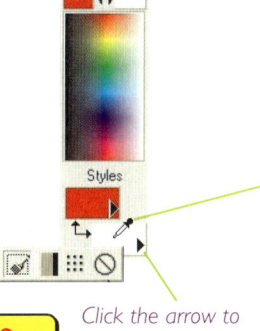

6. Computer Art | 157

Coloured area selection

Magic Wand

1 Select the Magic Wand, position the cross on the target area and click with the left mouse button to create the outline.

> **HOT TIP** *In the example illustrated, the Magic Wand cross was placed at the centre of the circle. A tolerance of 2 selected just the inner circle, 11 selected the rectangle and 16 selected the whole object.*

> **HOT TIP** *Change the Hue and Saturation values in the Colourize window, to see the effect immediately. Hue is the shade and Saturation is the depth of colour. With Saturation set at a constant 128, try:*
> *Hue = 0 for red shades*
> *Hue = 85 for green shades*
> *Hue = 170 for blue shades*

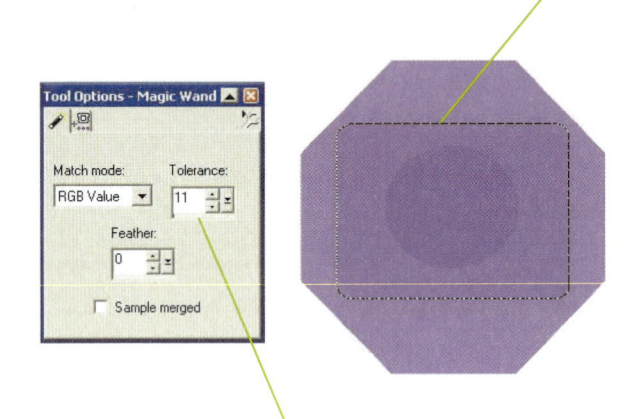

2 If necessary use the Tool Options window for the Magic Wand to select a Tolerance level.

3 From the Menu choose Colours, Colourise. Change the Hue and Saturation values to change the colours.

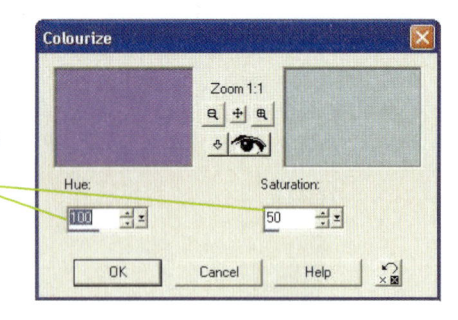

Red Eye and other effects

Select Effects, Enhance Photo, to view the complete list of available effects. Red Eye Removal shows the current state in the left pane and in the right, any adjustment. You can zoom in and out to help select the area, or use a hand to move the right pane image. Just click on the red eye in the left pane to perform the correction.

> **HOT TIP** *The Red Eye Removal window is similar in design to the Colourise window with two panes, and adjustment options below. It offers Human eye and Animal eye, and a Hue of Grey, Blue, Brown, Green and Violet.*

Text

Text

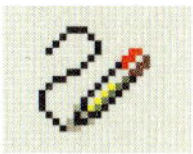

Draw

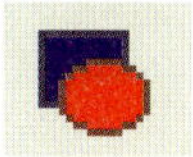

Shapes

Object Selector

Text and shapes are both vector graphics and are managed using similar procedures and controls.

1 Select the Text tool, and click on the canvas. Type your text into the Text Entry window and select the font, size and position. See page 167 for an illustration of the Text Entry window.

The foreground and background colours of your artwork become the Stroke (outline) and Fill colours for the text. To change the colours and styles:

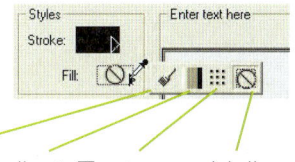

2 Click on the arrow right of the Stroke or Fill colour box in the Text Entry window. Select between Solid, Gradient, Texture or Null.

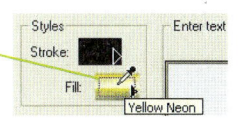

3 When you have chosen an effect, click on the new colour area to open and select from the full colour palette.

Vector text enables you to move, resize and rotate the text.

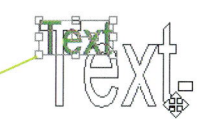

4 Finally, select Create as Vector and click OK. Use the corner or middle handles to drag and resize.

If you right click away from the text you will lose the selection handles. To work with the text again, select the Object Selector tool and click within the text area.

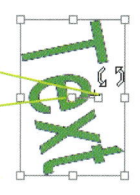

5 Use the Rotation handle to rotate the text. Position the mouse over the centre point/handle, to move the text.

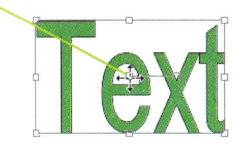

Although you are able to resize and move the text, it is not possible to create any special effects as it is created as a vector drawing. See page 161 for applying deformations.

6. Computer Art | 159

Shapes

1. Click on the Shapes icon and select the shape from the Tool Options window which provides a drop down display of those available.

2. Draw the shape and adjust the size using the selection handles, as for text.

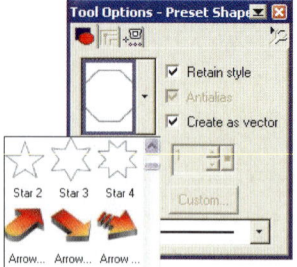

3. To make any other adjustments to the shape, select the Object Selector and click on the shape. The Tool Options window changes to display Properties for the object.

If the Tool Options window is not visible, right click the shape and select Properties.

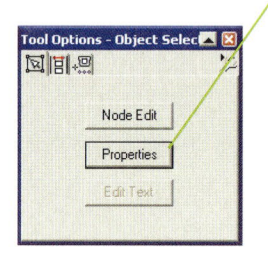

4. Click the arrow on the Fill box and choose Solid, Texture, or Gradient (as shown here). You can select from a list of preset styles. To amend a style or set a degree of transparency, click on Edit.

You can rotate the gradient angle by spinning the handle in the colour box.

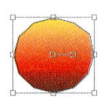

5. The style chosen is immediately applied to the object.

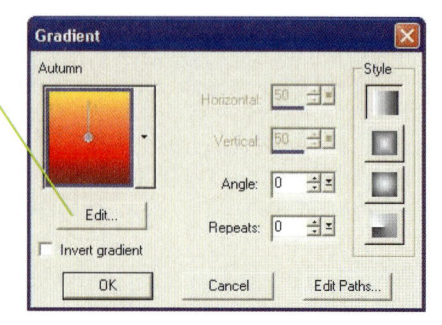

160 | CLAIT Plus in easy steps

Deformation

If you create two objects, such as text and a shape, and convert them to a raster layer, you will no longer be able to select them individually.

Both text and shapes can be reshaped or deformed, but first you must convert them to a raster format. This means that instead of being composed of a series of points and calculated lines, they become a collection of pixels.

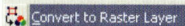

1 Having created your text, select Layers, Convert to a Raster Layer. The mouse pointer becomes a No Entry sign when on the canvas.

2 Select the Deformation tool. The text or shape should automatically be framed. It can be resized as before.

3 To deform it press and hold Shift as you drag. You will notice that the oblong with the cursor becomes oblique.

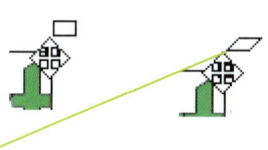

4 Drag the text in any direction to create the desired effect.

You must deselect the Deformation tool to be able to continue with other tasks such as copy and paste.

Curved text

Paint Shop Pro combines shapes and text to create curved text, referring to it as Text on a Path.

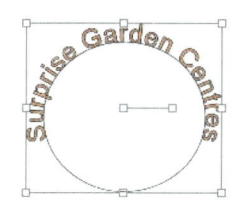

1 Create a shape and deselect it to remove the framing handles.

2 Select the text tool and move the mouse to the edge of the shape. You will see a curved shape to indicate curving text.

3 Create your text, make sure to select Create as Vector text and click OK. The text will wrap around the shape.

Text effects

1. Insert a new vector layer, and then create your text, selecting a reasonable size and using Create as Vector text.

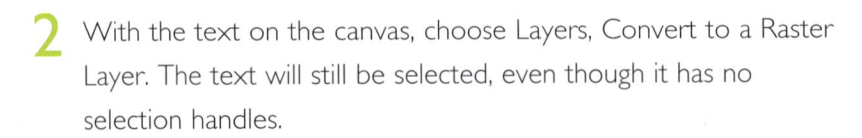

Try the various effects in combination.

2. With the text on the canvas, choose Layers, Convert to a Raster Layer. The text will still be selected, even though it has no selection handles.

3. Select Effects, 3D Effects and choose an effect.

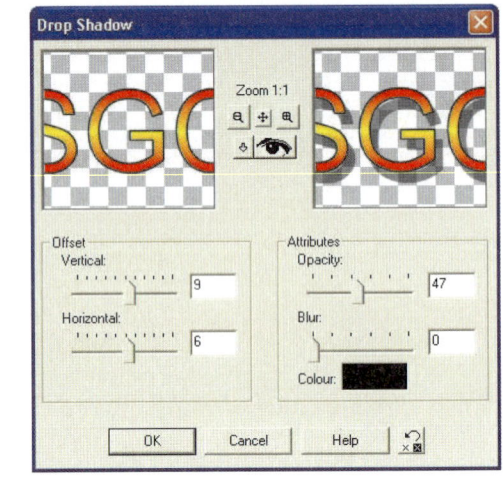

The Drop Shadow window is the typical approach used by Paint Shop Pro to enable you to add effects. The left pane shows the current view and the right pane the effects of changing the settings. You can zoom in and out, move the area displayed and Preview the canvas using the Eye.

This text was created using gradient fill, drop shadow, inner bevel and then reshaped with the deform tool.

WordArt

Microsoft includes WordArt in its Office suite of programs. This can be used in conjunction with Paint Shop Pro.

Paint Shop Pro offers such an overwhelming range of text effects and enhancements that, in practice, you may find it easier to create your text with a specific tool such as Microsoft's WordArt which has predefined effects. The text can be copied from Word and pasted into Paintshop using the Clipboard.

1. Open Word and select Insert, Picture, WordArt. Select a style from the Gallery and enter the text.

2. Use the WordArt toolbar, to reselect a shape or change the colour or other attributes.

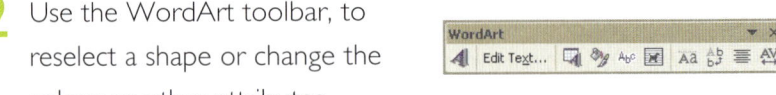

162 | CLAIT Plus in easy steps

Print

1 Add your name and Centre number to the print by selecting Image, Image Information. This window shows the art work resolution and size.

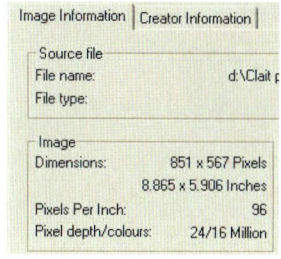

2 Select the Creator Information tab and add your name and centre number in the Title. This is the only user information that will print with the image.

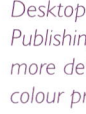

See Unit 4 Desktop Publishing for more details on colour printing.

3 Use File, Page Setup to choose the orientation and to select between Colour, Greyscale and CMYK prints.

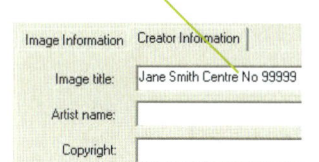

Note that Page Setup has an option to Fit to page. Make sure it is deselected or it will change the size of your print.

Controlling the print resolution (dpi) or quality of your image is a CLAIT Plus requirement. To set the print resolution:

1 Select File, Print and choose the Properties button. Choose the Paper/Quality tab. The quality settings control the printer resolution and will usually be set to Normal.

The resolution settings available depend on your particular printer, so you may find that you are unable to match exactly those required by the exercise.

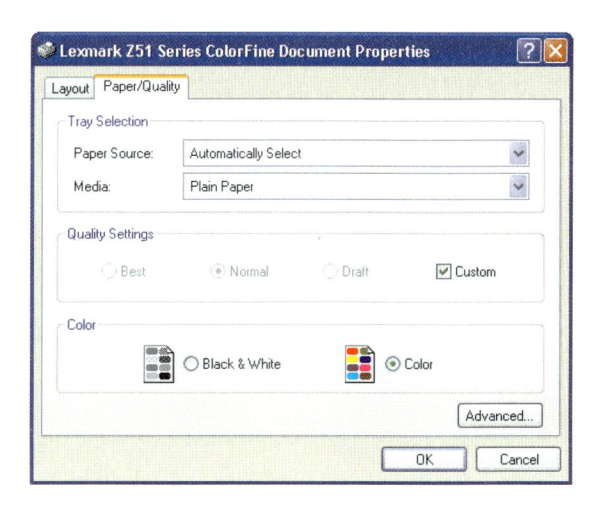

6. Computer Art | 163

...cont'd

This sets the print resolution, not the artwork resolution. Changing the art work resolution would change the artwork size.

2 Tick the Custom box and click on the Advanced option. Select the resolution closest to that required by the exercise.

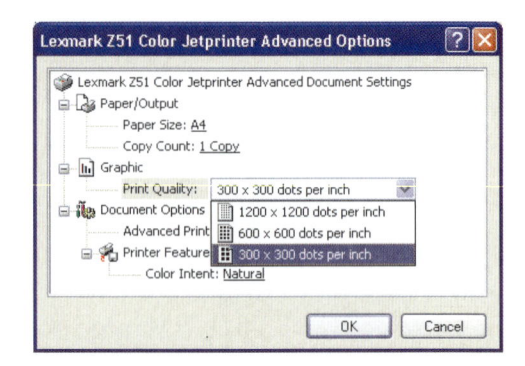

3 To provide the required screen print, press Alt+Print Screen. Open Word and paste the image from the Clipboard. You can then add your name and details and save it as a Word file.

The higher the print resolution, the longer it takes to print.

4 Click OK to return to the Print window. Tick the boxes to Print corner and centre crop marks.

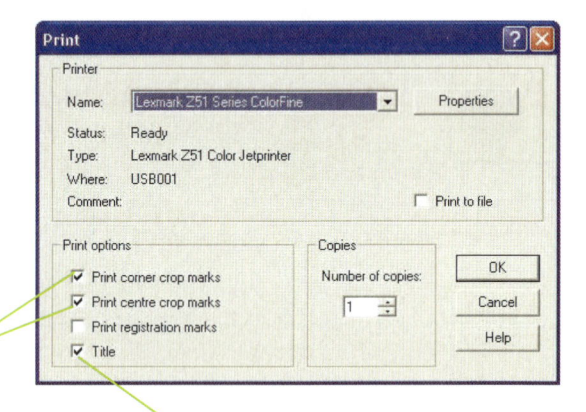

5 Also tick the box to include the Title, which is your name and centre details. Click OK to print the file.

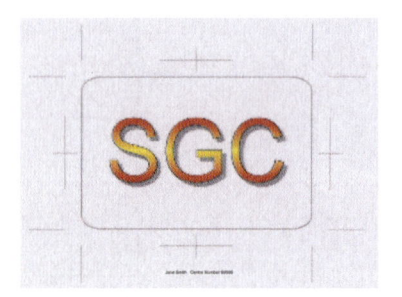

Animation

You can create a whole range of effects by changing colour, position, size, shape and rotation.

You are going to create an animation .gif file to be used as a banner on a web site. To do this you will create a series of images that will create the impression of change. Each image will be created in the graphics editor, Paint Shop Pro. The images will be saved as separate .gif files and then assembled in Animation Shop to create the 'movie'.

The Paintshop Pro background is set to white so that you can paste images with a white background and let the banner show through.

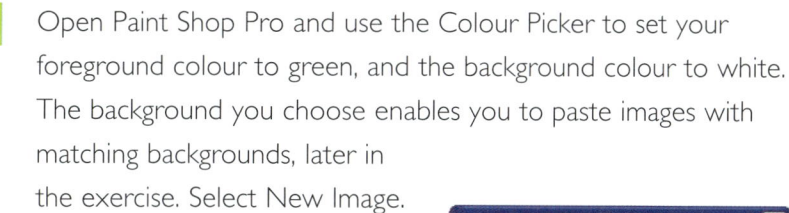

1. Open Paint Shop Pro and use the Colour Picker to set your foreground colour to green, and the background colour to white. The background you choose enables you to paste images with matching backgrounds, later in the exercise. Select New Image.

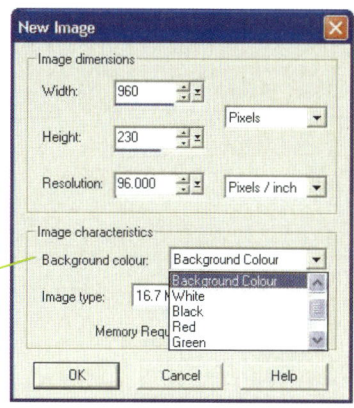

2. Create the canvas as specified, this time using pixels as the measurement unit. Select a Resolution of 96 and set the canvas to Background Colour.

To simplify: fill the foreground with colour, which will then be used as the 'background' or back cloth of the banner.

3. To colour the canvas, select the Fill tool and use the left mouse button to Fill the banner.

4. Select View, Grid and Guide Properties, and set the spacing to an appropriate measure.

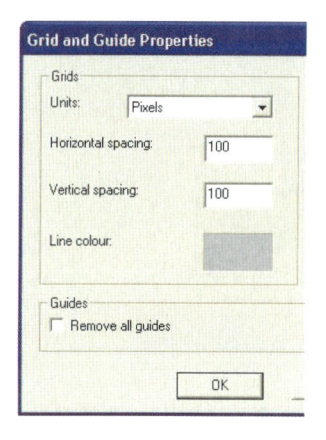

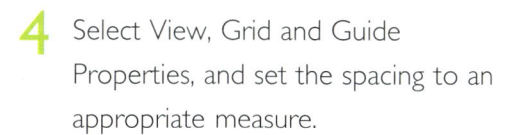

We are going to be using the image of a pumpkin which is about 200 pixels wide, so we have used 100 as the grid spacing. The grid enables us to move and rotate the pumpkin a standard amount each time.

5. Select View, Grid to display the Grid.

6. Computer Art | 165

...cont'd

As the canvas colour is white and the background to the barn image is white, the barn background will be transparent.

When the frame is saved, the selection will be merged into the rest of the picture and saved as a single layer.

6 Open the Barn.gif image, copy it and select Edit, Paste, Paste as a Transparent Selection. Position according to the Design Brief and save the file as frame1.gif

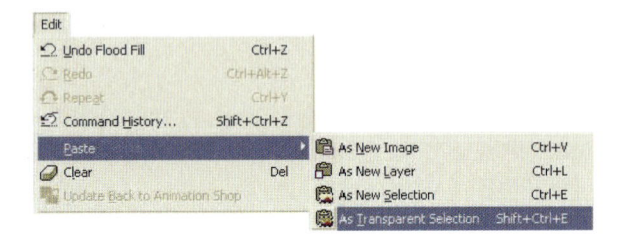

7 Open pumpkin.gif, copy and paste it as a transparent selection into frame1.gif. Leave the pumpkin selected (with the outline flashing) and save the file as frame2.gif.

Remember to use File, Save As, otherwise you will overwrite the previous step.

8 With the pumpkin still selected, move it proportionally (about 100 pixels) to the right. Then choose Image, Rotate and rotate 90 degrees to the right, simulating a rolling pumpkin. Leave the pumpkin selected and save the file as frame3.gif.

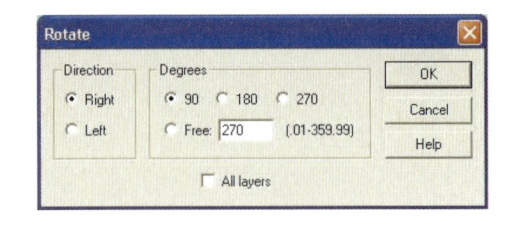

The more intermediate images you create, the more realistic the motion will appear.

9 Repeat these steps until you have the required number of images, making sure that the pumpkin reaches the barn.

166 | CLAIT Plus in easy steps

Final frames

As a refinement, you could show just the edge of the pumpkin in the doorway.

1. Delete the pumpkin leaving only the barn and save the file again. If you are following the exercise this should be frame 8.

2. Select the Text tool, position it at the top centre of the green and click. Type your text, pressing Enter to create a new line.

See the Web Animation solutions section on pages 257-259 for using a different approach to the animation process.

3. Choose the text colour, size and alignment. Make sure to choose Create as Vector, which will allow you to resize and click OK.

4. Drag the corner handles to resize the text to fit the available area. Use Save As to save the file as frame9.gif.

6. Computer Art | 167

Animation Shop

Animation Shop 3

This application is used to assemble images created in Paint Shop Pro or elsewhere. It provides a wizard which steps you through the animation process.

HOT TIP — As Paint Shop Pro and Animation Shop are from the same software company, many of the tools are identical. They also have a link between programs through the File menu.

1 With Animation Shop open, select the Animation wizard.

2 In the first step you will choose Same size as the first image frame, as we have made all the frames the same size. Click Next.

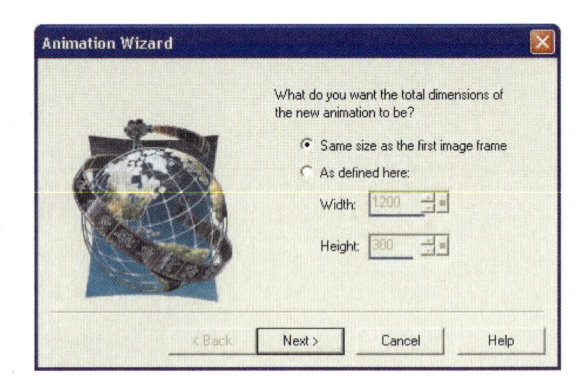

HOT TIP — If your frames were irregularly shaped, or had rounded corners, you could use transparent to let the underlaying web page show through.

3 In the next step you can choose either Transparent or Opaque. As the picture will fill the canvas, it doesn't matter which you choose. Continue through the wizard, accepting the defaults.

HOT TIP — You can set a display time for individual frames later, so check the exercise and in the wizard choose the predominant timing.

4 Add the images you created in Paint Shop Pro, and use the Move Up and Move Down buttons to sort the images into the correct sequence. On the next step click Finish to create the animation.

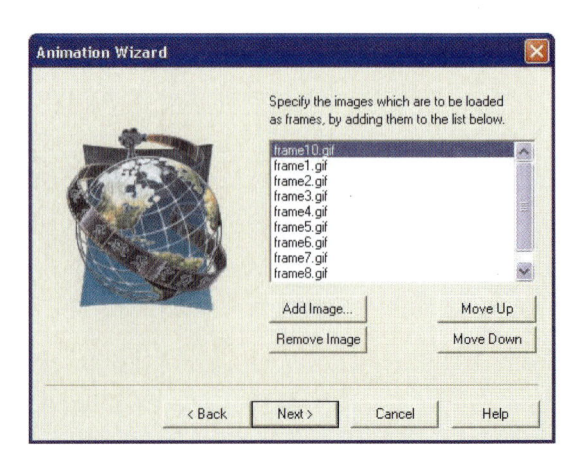

HOT TIP — Check the order of Added files as frame10 actually appeared first in the list. If you use Move Up for frame10, it will be put at the bottom of the list.

Run the animation

The .gif file format is suitable for use on a web site as the files are small, but still retain 256 colours, and of course the format supports multiple images for animation.

1. Initially only the first frame is visible. Change the Zoom level so that you can see most of the frames. They will be displayed in their sequence, with the timings shown underneath.

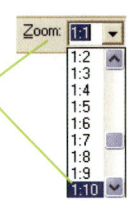

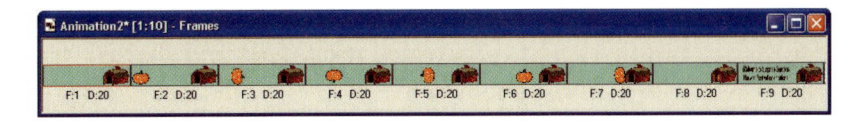

The red outline indicates a selected frame. Frames can be copied, moved and deleted using toolbar icons or through the Menu.

2. Run the animation by selecting View, Animation, or using the toolbar button. The animation runs in a separate window which you need to close to return to edit the frames.

3. To set an individual time, right click the frame and select Frame Properties. The display time is set in 1/100th seconds. Repeat for each frame where necessary.

Choose View, Preview in Web Browser to see the full effect. The same optimisation procedure will take place unless you have already saved the animation.

4. Save the animation as welcome.gif. During the save process the file will be optimised for web use. Select between higher quality or lower file size.

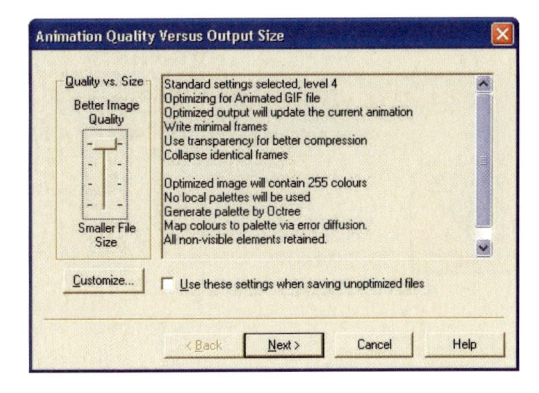

5. To provide a screen print, resize the window to show all the frames. The print should show the file name and type in the title bar, and the timings for each frame. Follow the instructions for a screen print described on page 164.

6. Computer Art | 169

Checklist

You are allowed three hours to complete the OCR CLAIT Plus assessment.

When you have completed the exercise, do a final check to ensure that you meet the exercise requirements. Check that you have:

- the correct artwork size
- inserted all the required images
- positioned the images in the correct location
- created text effects and shapes
- used transparency and gradient fill
- printed the art work and checked the dimensions
- provided a screen print of the printer resolution
- created the required number of images for the animation
- run the animation
- provided a screen print of the images with timings and file name
- checked that your name and centre number is on all prints
- proof read your printouts

If you followed the downloadable exercise you can check your final copy against a sample in the Unit 6 Worked copy folder.

Marking

You are not allowed any critical errors. The following are considered critical errors:

- a missing or incorrect image
- a missing text item (in its entirety)
- a missing frame in an animation
- a missing frame duration
- failure to print in colour

Check with your tutor for a full list of critical and accuracy errors.

Web Pages

In this unit you will learn how to present information for use on the Internet. You will use FrontPage to create a web site structure with several web pages, hyperlinks and a variety of data formats. You will also become familiar with HTML concepts and code.

Covers

Web Pages | 172

HTML & HTML code | 173

Meta-variable tags | 175

FrontPage | 176

Download files | 177

Create the web folder | 178

Import the files | 179

Create a template | 180

Create Meta tags | 182

Navigation table | 183

Font formats and styles | 185

Save the template | 186

Insert text and image | 188

Tables | 191

Forms | 192

Feedback and hyperlinks | 195

Checklist | 196

Unit Seven

Web Pages

This unit follows a complete exercise to create a web site structure and web pages. The exercise, images and text files used, can be downloaded from the In Easy Steps web site (see page 281).

Unit Seven overview

This unit covers the following areas:

1. Downloading files from the Internet. The files will include text files, image files and one or more completed web pages.

2. Using a web site map to create a web structure. The web site will consist of a home or index page, and some related pages.

3. Creating a web page with standard text, styles, background and images to be used as a template for all the pages in the site.

See the Solutions units, Web Animations (pages 256-259) and Web Pages (pages 260-262) for other topics and features.

4. Importing images and pages into the web folder. You will then insert text and image files to create the pages.

5. Manipulating text to apply formats and to create a feedback form.

6. Creating, testing and troubleshooting links, both internal and external.

In this unit we will be using FrontPage 2002. Any substantial differences between software releases will be highlighted and alternative methods suggested.

You will also develop an understanding of HTML code and web page structure. The unit covers some of the basic concepts and code used by the HTML language, and you will be able to apply this knowledge to create code for yourself.

Exercise files and documentation

You should have the following items:

- access to the web site, to be able to download the exercise files
- the web site map and standard page content details
- the house style sheet and exercise

HTML

The CLAIT Plus syllabus says 'A familiarity with raw HTML code would be advantageous, but is not required'.

When you have some items on your web page, select View, Reveal Tags to show the start and end of various formats.

See page 175 and 182 for more information on Meta tags.

FrontPage indicates HTML code in blue, user data and settings are shown in black.

Web pages are created using HTML (HyperText Markup Language). This is a plain text language that can be interpreted by all Internet browsers. The code can be created in any text editor, including NotePad, Word, a desktop publisher or a dedicated HTML code generator, such as FrontPage.

Some knowledge of HTML is advantageous if you wish to create and manage your own web site, even if you use FrontPage.

This is an example web page plus the HTML code that is used to define it.

The page has two sections, the head and the body, all of which is enclosed between an opening and a closing HTML tag.

The head section contains META tag information such as Author and Title. It also is enclosed between specific head tags.

The body section starts with a <body tag and indicates background colour (bgcolor). It uses the hexadecimal code for the colour, (FFFFFF is white).

It contains tags for heading levels, (h1, h3), and alignment.

```
<html>
<head>
<meta name="author" content="Jane Smith">
<meta http-equiv="Content-Type" content="text/html; charset=windows-1252">
<title>Surprise Gardens</title>
</head>

<body bgcolor="#FFFFFF">

<h1 align="center">Surprise Gardens</h1>

<h3 align="center">Surprise Garden Centres</h3>

<p align="right">Surprise Gardens Home Page</p>

<p align="left">
<img border="0" src="image/Surprise%20Logo.wmf" width="115" height="129"></p>

</body>
</html>
```

The <p> and </p> tags are start and end paragraph markers. Paragraphs contain text or objects such as images. The image details shown here are alignment, border size, source or folder location including image name, and the size.

The final HTML tags close the body section, </body> and the page.

7. Web Pages | 173

HTML code

Although you are not required to write HTML code for yourself, it can be useful to understand its construction and know some standard syntax.

Meta tags use only > at the end of each line.

- HTML statements usually open with <tagname ...> and close with </tagname>
- All code should be in lower case. This allows it to be understood by any operating system and server.
- Meta tag text, file names and attributes such as size, are enclosed between quotation marks. Plain text is typed without quote marks.
- Each page is defined as one <html> ... </html> statement.

If you type your own HTML, you must ensure that you have matching start and end tags. Statements without the correct syntax are ignored.

For sample exercises creating and using HTML code visit http://www.w3schools.com/html/html_examples.asp

Code	Purpose
<html>	start web page
</html>	end web page
<head>	start head section
</head>	end head section
<body followed by attributes such as link colour, background colour >	start body section, insert particular code and finish with >
</body>	end body section
<p>	start paragraph
</p>	end paragraph
<h1 followed by attributes such as alignment >	start heading level 1, 2, 3, etc finish with >
</h1>	end heading level
<img>	start image
src=""	folder/file name of image
</img>	end image
<ul>	start a bulleted (unordered) list
<li>	start the list item
</li>	end the list item
</ul>	end of bulleted list
<ol>	start a numbered (ordered) list
</ol>	end of numbered list
href="filename.htm"	hyperlink
href="http:// ..."	
bgcolor="#hexnumber"	background colour
	blank line

Professional web site creators prefer to write HTML code as succinctly as possible as it makes the files smaller and pages faster to load. HTML editors and text processors add some HTML code of their own to the page. This is a particular concern with Word when you save files in .htm format.

174 | CLAIT Plus in easy steps

Meta-variable tags

Meta tags, or Meta-variable tags as they are often known, hold data that can be used by Internet browsers and search engines to identify and index your web site. They are contained in the head data in the HTML code, and consist of two types.

System variable tags

These control the action of browsers and are used to refine information provided by the headers. You do not normally need system variables to index your site and they are not included in the exercise requirements.

For the CLAIT Plus course you will usually work with three sets of user Meta tags, but there are many more that you would need to investigate if you were to develop and publish a web site. See FrontPage 2002 in easy steps, for further details.

User variable tags

User tags specify information about a document using sets of data with name and content/value. In the exercises you will work with the following User variables:

- author – used for company, web creator, or in this course for your name, centre number and other required details. It could, on a live site, be the subject of a search

- keywords – terms and words that identify the contents of your pages and that browsers might enter into a search. The words should be separated by commas. You would on a live site include common misspellings and different word forms to increase the opportunities for your page to be found

- description – a short definition of the page contents.

Other tags that you should be familiar with are:

- resource-type – you would put Document for an HTML page, it would be the only tag needed for indexing purposes

- distribution – normally you would use Global

- robots – these can be used to avoid search engines indexing the page or following links to private or member only pages

Meta tags can be used to exclude web pages from being indexed by a search engine.

When you use FrontPage to create your web page, it inserts some of its own identifying Meta tags which can be left untouched.

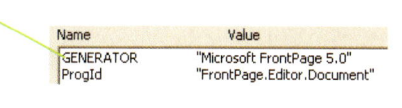

Name	Value
GENERATOR	"Microsoft FrontPage 5.0"
ProgId	"FrontPage.Editor.Document"

7. Web Pages | 175

FrontPage

FrontPage provides you with various ways to create web pages. You can create your own HTML statements using the HTML view. You can use the WYSIWYG editor in Normal view, or you can use a combination of both. In fact, it's a good idea to view the HTML code as you create and format each part of the page.

Normal view

This view provides you with a full WYSIWYG editor. Text is shown in the defined format and colour, with spelling problems identified. Images are displayed in the actual positions. And if you were designing for your own benefit, there is greater ease of controlling layout and appearance to make the site attractive. Using Normal view saves time, and a great deal of typing.

> **HOT TIP**
>
> *If you don't have access to FrontPage, you can write HTML code in NotePad, and view the pages in your browser. It works just as well, but obviously could take a bit longer to complete each page, especially when you come to more complex objects such as forms and tables. You can also use Word as your text editor, in which case you would save the file as a .htm file, rather than the standard .doc file. There are also other WYSIWYG editors such as Dreamweaver.*

HTML view

FrontPage uses different colours for the text in this view, to differentiate between tag text and content. You should use this view frequently to become familiar with code. FrontPage does not provide a means of checking the syntax of your code, so if you do enter any of your own, you should be especially careful.

Preview

As you build the page you can switch to the built-in Preview window to see the effect, and to check that it works correctly. In this view, you will be able to see any image animations.

Browsers

FrontPage files work with all the popular Internet browsers. It allows you to install many different browsers so that you can check your pages under different conditions.

Publishing

FrontPage can keep files synchronised and manage links when pages are moved or updated. It provides statistical reports to show number of files, links, file sizes and download times. It has facilities to help you upload, publish and manage your web site. Although publishing a web site goes beyond the requirements of the CLAIT Plus course, you may decide that it is an area that you wish to explore.

> **HOT TIP**
>
> *Web pages carry the .htm or .html file extension. There is no real difference between the two, the original operating systems could only handle a three letter file extension, now they can handle more.*

Download files

You can practice downloading files if you visit the In Easy Steps web site and download the exercises for this book. See page 281.

Part of the exercise requirement is to successfully download files from a specified URL (web page address).

1. Create a folder to hold the downloaded files. This will be a working folder to hold the original files. Open Windows Explorer and select the location of the folder.

As you build your web site, copies of the files will be inserted and imported into your web folder. In this way you will keep the original files intact.

2. Select File, New, Folder. Name the folder and press Enter. Close Windows Explorer.

Count how many files are listed and need to be downloaded. When finished check that you have them all.

3. Open your browser and enter the address of the download site. You should see a list of files which will need to be downloaded individually.

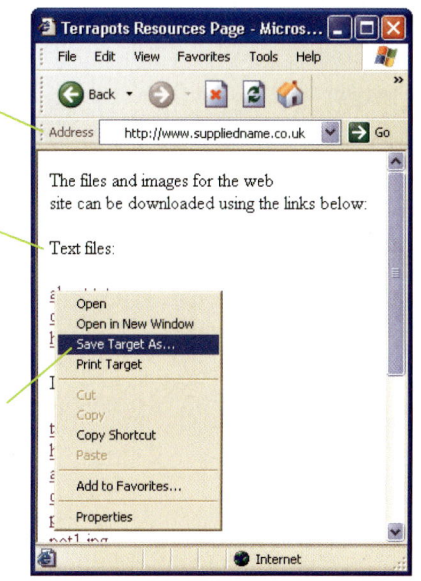

4. Right mouse click the first file and select Save Target As.

5. You will need to navigate the folder structure to locate your new working folder, then select save.

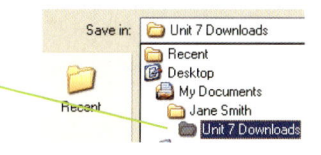

6. The files should be very small and will transfer quickly, you may see them transferring very briefly. Repeat the procedure for each of the files. The system will remember the designated folder, so the process is quite swift. Close the browser when finished.

Create the web folder

The way FrontPage opens can vary and you should check the title bar to see the situation. When you open FrontPage for the very first time, it opens just the program or with a default blank page. It also opens that way if you have previously created a web and closed the web before closing FrontPage. If however, you close FrontPage with the web still open, it will open in that web.

To create a new web folder:

If you select One Page Web, FrontPage takes control of the whole process and will automatically create a new web folder, specifying the folder name. It will also create a blank page named index.htm.

1 Close any open web folders. Select File, New Page or Web. From the Task pane select Empty Web. In the Web Site Template, Empty Web is already highlighted.

FrontPage remembers the previous web and will default to the next number with the same name, eg my webs1, my webs2.

2 Specify the location of the new web. This is a very important step. Click in the location box and check the full folder name and location. You could browse to find your working folder and then specify a web folder inside.

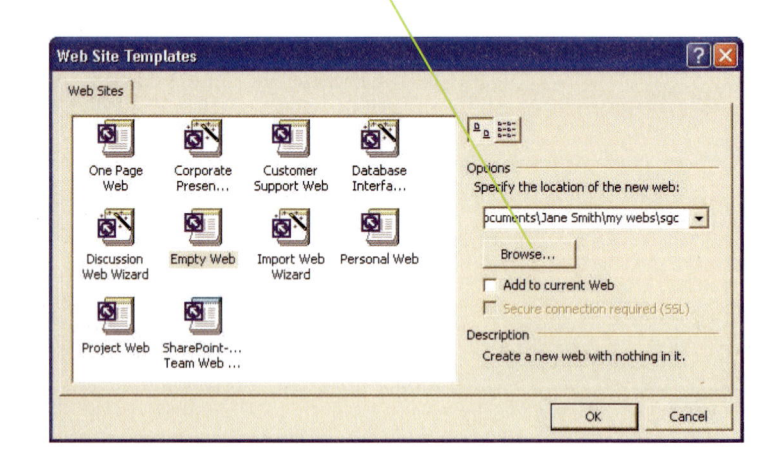

Once you have created your web folder, it will open automatically each time you restart FrontPage. If you visit a different web folder, use File, Open web, or select it from the Recent Webs list.

3 Click OK to confirm and then check the title bar to make sure that it was created correctly.

178 | CLAIT Plus in easy steps

Import the files

Hot Tip: *The text files will be inserted into the pages at a later stage, not imported into the folder. The existing web pages, .htm files, will also be inserted at a later time.*

The supplied files will usually consist of a number of plain .txt text files, a number of images, .jpg or .gif, and one or more .htm or .html files. The files to be imported will be only the image files.

1 Select Folders from the Views bar in FrontPage, and the images folder. On the Menu go to File, Import, and in the Import window select Add.

2 Navigate to the folder where the downloaded files are stored. Select only the image files at this time, using Ctrl+click to select individual files, or Shift and click to select a block. Click Open when all the files have been selected.

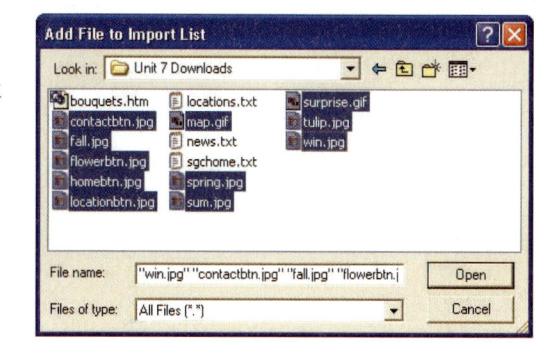

Hot Tip: *If your files end up in the wrong place, they can be dragged and dropped into the correct folder, using FrontPage Folder view, just as in Windows Explorer.*

3 The files will be added to the Import window. Any unwanted files can be selected and removed. This just deletes them from the list, not the original folder.

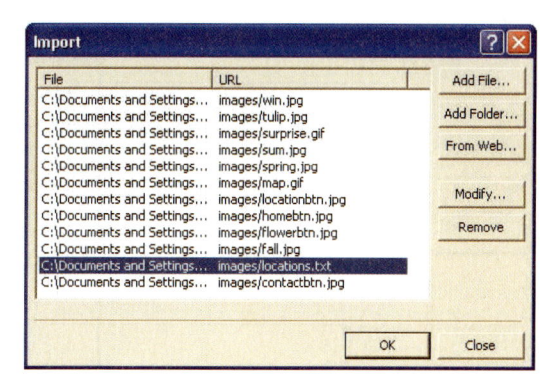

Beware: *Avoid importing Folders as FrontPage will replicate the folder structure.*

4 Folders view in FrontPage will display the files in the Contents pane on the right.

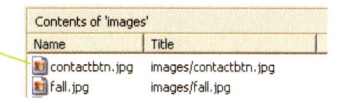

7. Web Pages | 179

Create a template

Using a template is particularly effective in FrontPage. In a business situation, it is likely that your web site would continue to grow or need to be modified on a regular basis. The template would make adding pages so much faster and easier as House styles, colours and standard contents would already be defined.

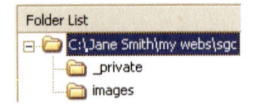

The CLAIT Plus exercise lists standard page properties, text properties, image properties, page contents including a navigation table, and Meta tag details. All these can be included in the template.

When you add a new page to the web, make sure that the main folder is selected in the Folder list, not the images folder.

1. Switch to Page view and select New page. The page will carry the default name of new_page_1.htm. If you were still in Folder view it would create a new page and name it index.htm, but we want to avoid that as we are making a template.

Using the General tab in Page Properties we can insert the Title. However this is different for each page, so is not included in the template page.

2. Right mouse click the page, select Page Properties and the Background tab. On this tab you can set a Background picture, and the colours for Background, Text, Hyperlink, Visited link and Active link.

Tick the box if you want a Background picture and use the Browse button to locate the file. The image will 'tile' the background, and will overlay any background colour selected. The image must be transparent for a background colour to show.

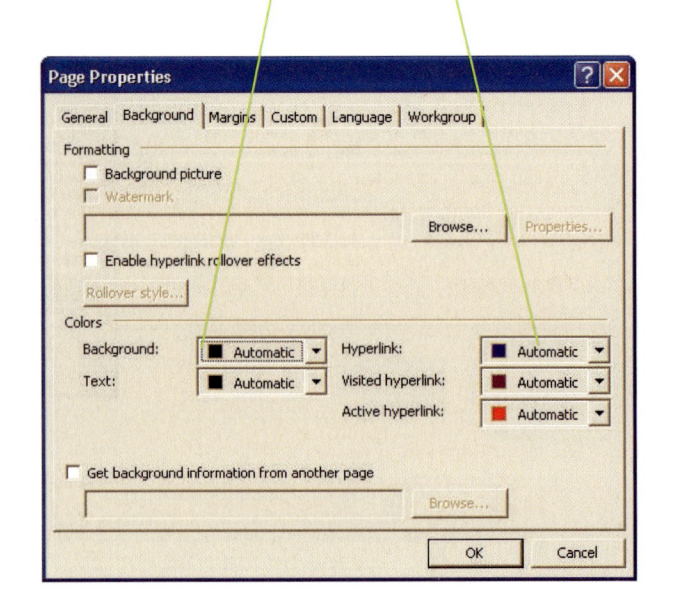

180 | CLAIT Plus in easy steps

...cont'd

3 Click the down arrow on the Background colour and select More Colours.

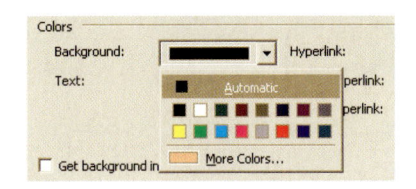

4 Type the hexadecimal value in the Value box and press Enter. FrontPage will create the correct format for you and the new colour will be displayed. Click OK to confirm.

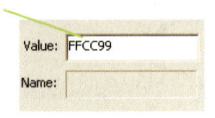

> **HOT TIP**
> Hexadecimal code is based on 0-9, A-F, giving 16 characters in all. You can use either case, but upper case is the standard form.

> **BEWARE**
> You can choose the Custom tab and select from there, but you will need to know the equivalent RGB numbers.

> **HOT TIP**
> If you wanted to try writing some HTML code, the background colour is a good place to start. See page 174. You could also try changing some of the hexadecimal colour code in the HTML view, and switching to Normal view to see the effect.

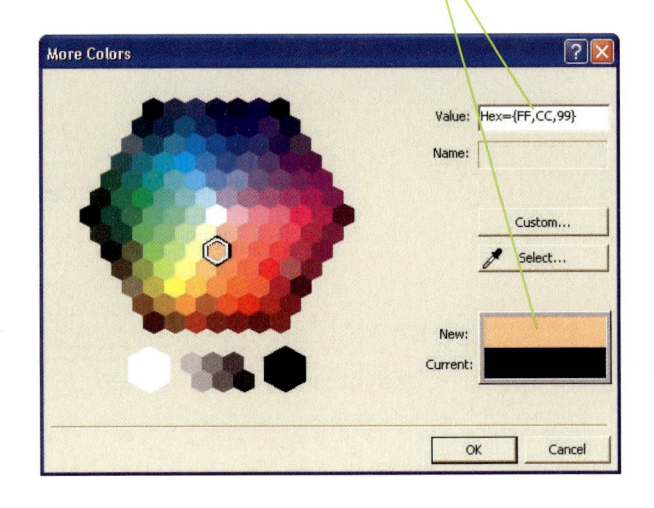

5 Repeat the process to change the Text and Hyperlink colours to those specified. Click OK when finished to see the effect.

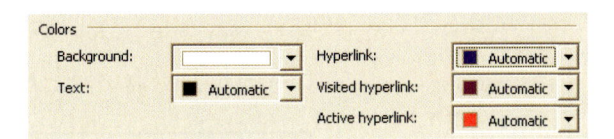

6 Select the HTML view and see how and where the code has been created.

7. Web Pages | 181

Create Meta tags

Meta-variable tags and their purpose were described on page 175.

Of the Meta tags you are required to create, those that will be the same for each page can be included in the template.

1 Right click on the page, select Page Properties and the Custom tab. The top section of the window is for System variables.

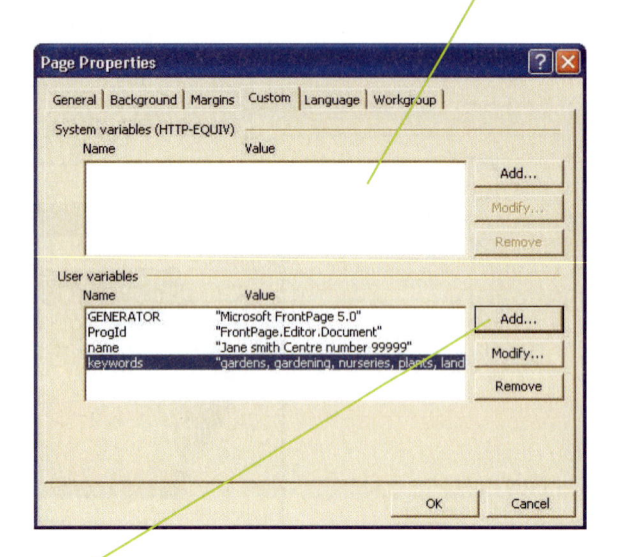

Enter the Meta tag details carefully, following capitalisation and punctuation as specified. You can only see this data in the HTML view where mistakes will not be obvious.

2 Click Add in the User variables section to add the required Meta data, or select Modify to make changes.

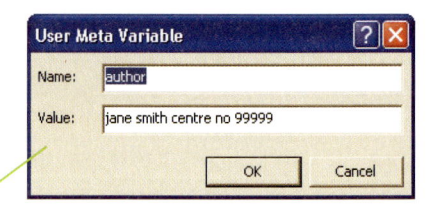

3 Type the name and the value (content) and click OK. Repeat for each Meta tag. When you have added all the Meta tags, they can be viewed in the head section of the HTML code.

Author and keyword Meta tags will usually be the same for each page. You will need to add other Meta tags individually as you create each page.

```
<head>
<meta name="keywords" content="gardens, gardening, nurseries, plants, landscaping,
<meta name="author" content="Jane Smith Centre number 99999">
<meta name="GENERATOR" content="Microsoft FrontPage 5.0">
<meta name="ProgId" content="FrontPage.Editor.Document">
<meta http-equiv="Content-Type" content="text/html; charset=windows-1252">
<title>New Page 1</title>
</head>
```

182 | CLAIT Plus in easy steps

Navigation table

As the navigation table is also to appear on each page, it can be included in the template.

Before you create the table, press Enter to give yourself a blank line. It's much easier then to create a heading above the table, should the need arise.

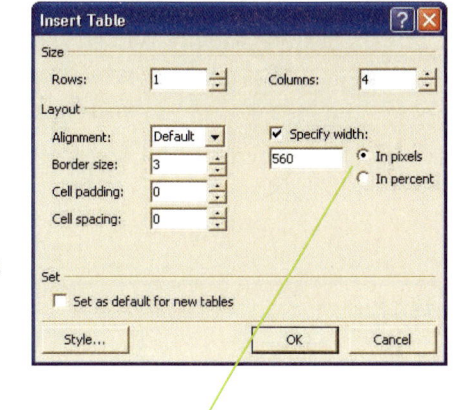

FrontPage provides a sophisticated link bar that can be used to link web site pages together. The link bar can be displayed on each page giving a consistent appearance to the pages and allowing you to move swiftly from one page to another. When FrontPage manages the links bar for you, it will adjust the bar automatically as you add or delete pages.

For CLAIT Plus you will create your own link or navigation bar, using images as buttons and a table to position the images. You are provided with a web site structure diagram with the exercise, which gives you the file names of the various pages, so that you can create links between pages even before they are created. To create the navigation table:

For more information on creating and formatting tables, see page 191.

1. In Normal view, click on the page and select Table, Insert, Table.

2. Select the number of rows and columns, the Border size, Cell padding and Cell spacing. In this initial window you can also specify the width in pixels or percentage, but not the height or other details.

Although you can specify a cell height, it will adjust automatically to accommodate larger contents.

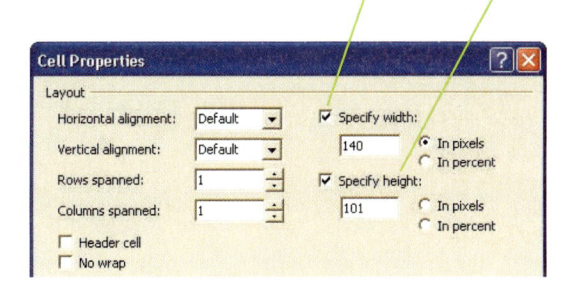

Select Table Properties to specify alignment, or use the standard alignment buttons on the toolbar. The Table Properties window allows you to set the height of the table and any border formatting.

3. With the table now displayed on the page, select all the cells and right click. Choose Cell Properties. Specify the width and height in pixel size. The cell height and width will usually match those of the images to be inserted.

7. Web Pages | 183

...cont'd

Add the image buttons

The images, when inserted, will have an absolute address. This means that they reference your drive and folder path in the complete file name.

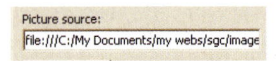

Picture source:
file:///C:/My Documents/my webs/sgc/image

When you save the page, you will have the opportunity to save embedded images. This saves them with a relative address. You must save them with a

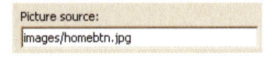

Picture source:
images/homebtn.jpg

relative address, saving with an absolute address will cause a critical error. See page 190.

1. Click in the first cell and select Insert, Picture, From File. You may need to navigate to the images folder, because even though you have imported the images into the image folder, FrontPage will remember any folder used previously.

2. Select and insert the image. Click in the next cell and repeat the process for all the image buttons.

   Each of the images must display Alt text, text which appears and describes the picture, when you hover the mouse over it. You can also create a hyperlink at this point.

3. Right click the first image and select Picture Properties. Choose the General tab. Add the Alt text in the Text box.

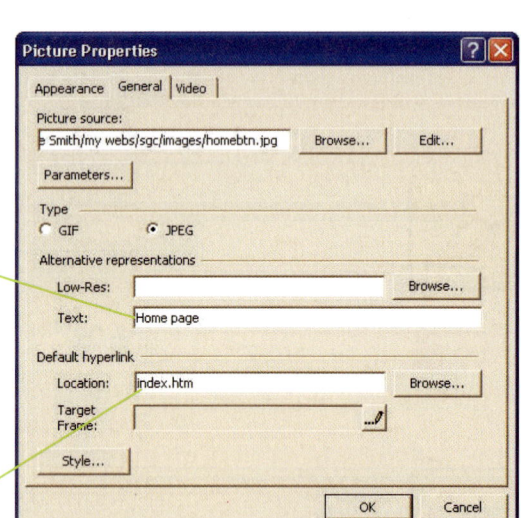

Make sure to follow the Web Site design plan and use the correct file names in the hyperlinks. Check your typing to ensure that the hyperlink address is correct as you will not be able to check it fully until all the pages have been created.

4. Click in the Location box and type the hyperlink address. This must be a relative address, in your web.

5. When you have formatted all the image buttons, switch to Preview and check the Alt text. As the web pages have yet to be created you will be unable at this point to check the hyperlinks.

Font formats and styles

A large number of style formats are already defined in FrontPage, and you could apply these to your text. They can be selected from the Format bar, which shows the font face, size and attributes such as bold. The styles could be applied as you create each page, or when all the pages have been created by using the Format Painter to apply the styles.

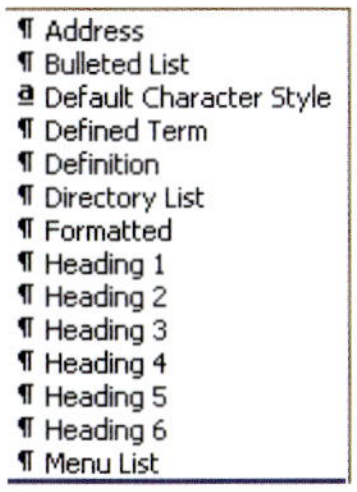

However, the styles may not exactly match those required by the exercise, and you would have to remember to remove bold and change font face. To make it easier, amend the styles in your template.

The built-in styles refer to h1, h2 etc. and in FrontPage/Windows depict a specific font face and attributes. They may be interpreted differently in other systems or Internet browsers, depending on how that system is set up and which fonts it has installed.

1. Select Format, Style. Choose HTML tags. You should now choose an h(level) with the correct font size, as the size should not be changed. For example choose h1.

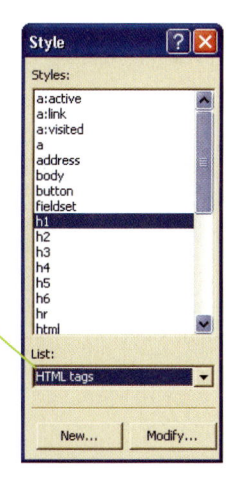

Do not make changes to the font sizes, since your browser will use the HTML default font sizes.

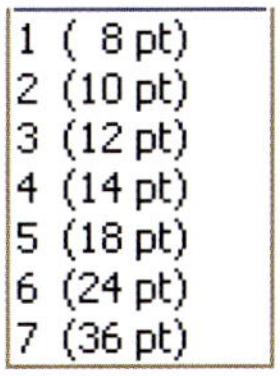

| 1 (8 pt) |
| 2 (10 pt) |
| 3 (12 pt) |
| 4 (14 pt) |
| 5 (18 pt) |
| 6 (24 pt) |
| 7 (36 pt) |

2. Click the Modify button and choose Format and then Font.

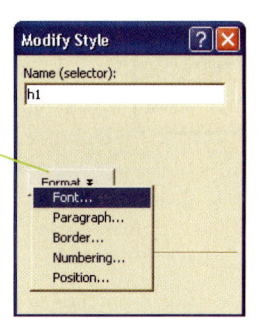

3. Select the font style and attributes, such as bold, from the appropriate areas. Note that you should not change the size.

4. Repeat to amend all the h(level) styles required. They will be listed in the Style box for User-defined styles.

See pages 261-262 for text sizing and management in web pages.

5. The amended h levels can be chosen from the Format toolbar by selecting Heading 1 etc.

7. Web Pages | 185

Save the template

> **HOT TIP:** Include a blank line or two in the template page. This will make it easier to insert text and images in the actual web page.

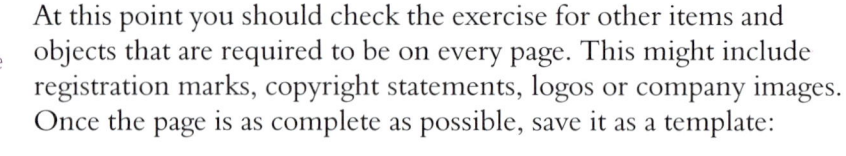

At this point you should check the exercise for other items and objects that are required to be on every page. This might include registration marks, copyright statements, logos or company images. Once the page is as complete as possible, save it as a template:

1 Select file, Save As, and change the file type to a FrontPage template.

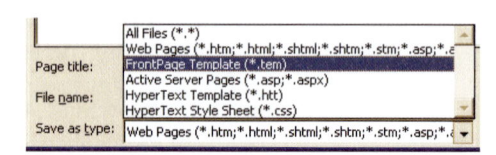

> **HOT TIP:** Inserting a symbol in FrontPage uses the same process as in Word and was covered in Unit 1, see page 37.

2 Supply a name for the template. The file extension changes to .tem and the folder defaults to Pages. You do not need to change the folder location at this time. Click Save.

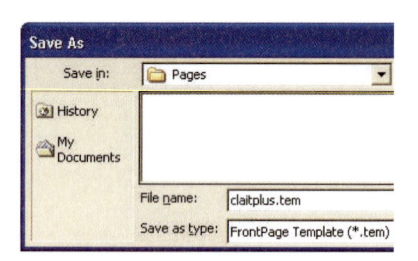

> **HOT TIP:** The template will be stored in a hidden data folder associated with your user name. It is accessible to FrontPage, but only visible in Windows Explorer if you change your system to display hidden folders.

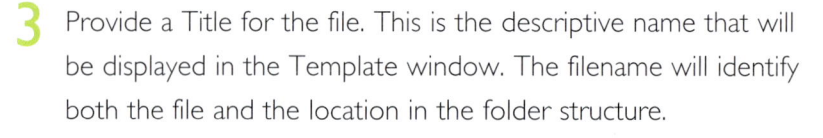

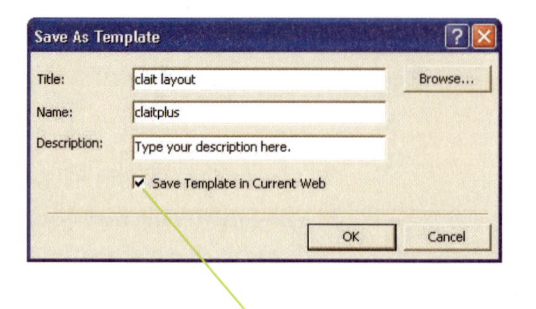

3 Provide a Title for the file. This is the descriptive name that will be displayed in the Template window. The filename will identify both the file and the location in the folder structure.

> **HOT TIP:** If you save the template in the current web, it will be saved along with your web pages and other components, in a hidden web folder.

4 Tick the box to Save Template in Current Web. This is a good idea especially if you are studying the CLAIT Plus course at a college or training centre, but not so essential on your own PC.

...cont'd

5 FrontPage will now recognise that there are embedded images and give you the option to save them.

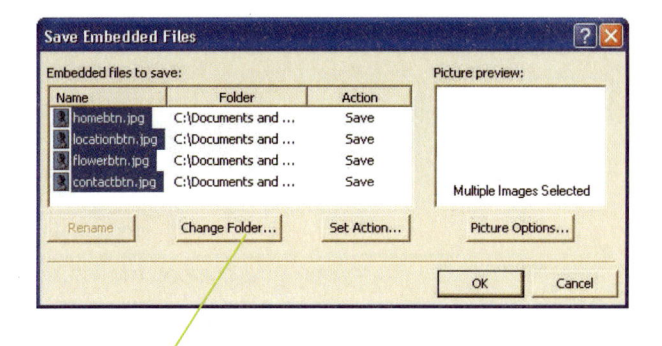

> **HOT TIP** *Each time you save a web page it will prompt you to save embedded images. If the images are identical, then you can use the existing files. Even if you have modified the proportions or size you can still choose Use Existing. It is only the image display that has changed, not the image file. Always check that they are going into the correct folder, usually the images folder.*

6 Click Change Folder, and save them in the images folder in your web. As the files already are located in that folder, the window will now display the action as Overwrite.

7 Select the Set Action button and change to Use Existing.

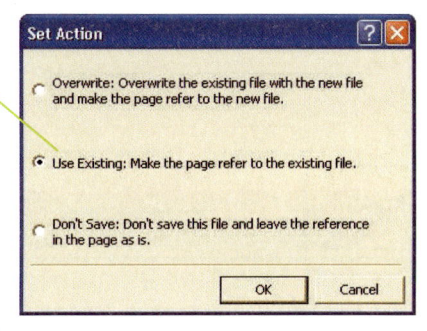

> **HOT TIP** *See page 190 for details on absolute and relative image references.*

8 You must now close the web template, otherwise any further changes will also become part of the template.

9 Select File, New Page or Web. From the Task pane select Page Templates. You may need to scroll down the Templates window to locate your new template. Once you have used the template, it will be listed on the Task pane.

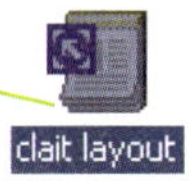

7. Web Pages | 187

Insert text

You can type text into the web page just as you would in a word processor. You will also have text files, in plain text, to insert. These files contain end-of-line markers, which, when inserted into FrontPage, can create problems with applying formats such as bullets or numbering.

1 Select the Show/Hide button to show paragraph marks in your text and go to Insert, File and select the text file.

> **HOT TIP**
> *If you are instructed to create a list, inserting the file with line breaks provides a better idea of the intended layout.*

2 When you choose Normal paragraphs, the body of the text is treated as one line, and has just one paragraph mark at the end.

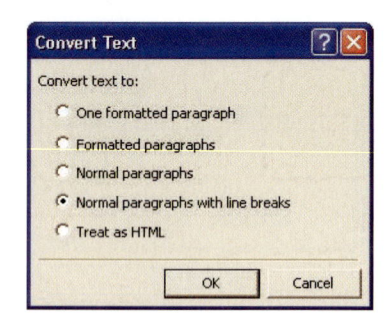

Englemere - Bath Harlequin - Swindon Heronsbrook - Andover Avon - Portsmouth Silver Brook - Reading Rookery - Winchester The Elms - Windsor¶

> **HOT TIP**
> *If you wanted to write some HTML code, creating a bulleted or numbered list is quite easy and effective. It would not matter which of the two methods you used to insert the text.*

3 To apply bullets or create a numbered list with the text in this form, you would have to create your own line breaks by pressing Enter where appropriate.

4 If you select Normal paragraphs with line breaks, the text is more obviously a list. It has end-of-line marks and a paragraph mark. To apply bullets or numbers you would have to replace each end-of-line with a paragraph mark.

Englemere - Bath ↵
Harlequin - Swindon ↵
Heronsbrook - Andover ↵
Avon - Portsmouth ↵
Silver Brook - Reading ↵
Rookery - Winchester ↵
The Elms - Windsor¶

5 Once you have the text correctly displayed, you can then apply bullets or numbering from the Format menu or the Format toolbar.

...cont'd

When you use Insert File, it automatically displays .htm and .html files, so there is no need to change the Files of type box.

Insert an .htm file
You will usually be given an existing .htm file with which to work.

1. Open a new page using the template. Position the cursor where you want the text and select Insert, File. Navigate to the folder where you saved the downloaded files and select the .htm file.

2. You can use the standard alignment buttons to position the text, Apply the font styles and formats from the Style box.

If you are not using a template, you would open the .htm file, apply the required formats and save it to the main web folder.

3. Save the file using the same name as the inserted .htm file. This will not be a problem as they will be saved in different folders.

4. You will be prompted to save any embedded images. Click on Change folder and select your images folder within the web. You can then use the Set Action button and Use Existing as shown on page 187.

Test the hyperlinks as you create each page.

Page Properties
The Title and description are different for each page and so were not included on the template.

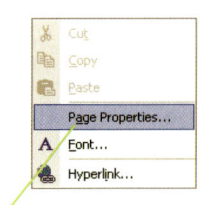

1. Right click each page and select Page Properties. On the General tab, add the Title of the page.

The Title of the page will show on the title bar in your Internet browser. It will also be used when you bookmark the page or Add to Favourites.

2. Select the Custom tab and add the description Meta tag, see page 182 for other Meta tags.

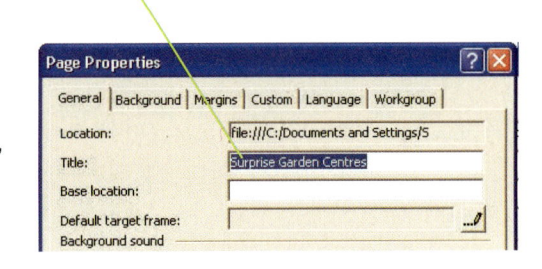

7. Web Pages | 189

Insert and format image

Use the General tab to add the Alt text.

1 Position the cursor and click Insert, Picture, From File. Right click the image and select Picture Properties.

2 Select the alignment. You could also use the alignment buttons on the toolbar. Set the border thickness specified in the exercise.

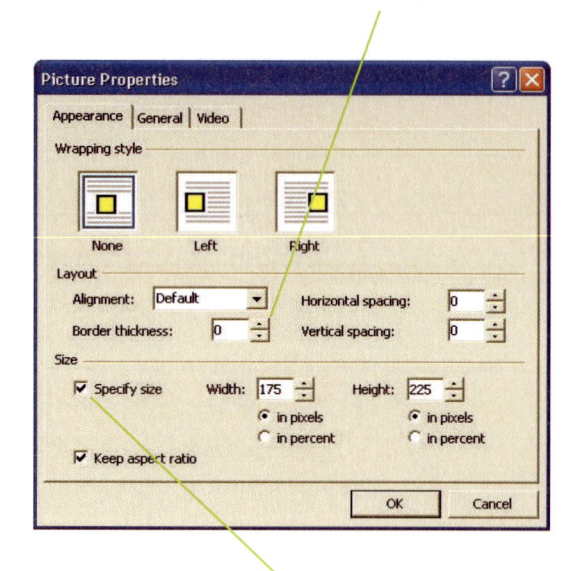

The web page size is very flexible. The screen resolution and the size of your browser window will affect how much of the page can be displayed at one time. Each time you make an adjustment, the objects displayed will move to accommodate the changes.

3 Tick the box to specify image size and adjust the Width and Height. If the exercise requires you to change the picture proportions, you will have to deselect the Keep aspect ratio box.

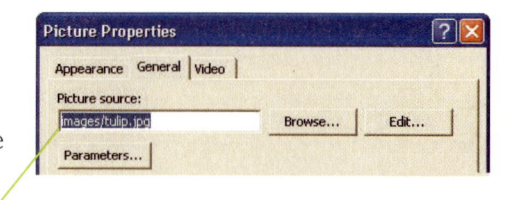

An Absolute reference for the image would specify a drive and full path, such as C:\My documents\My web\image\tulip.jpg. If the web page was viewed on another PC, or over the Internet, the image would not display. Instead you would see a placeholder.

4 Switch to the General tab and look at the Picture source box. The path specified for the image file is in the images folder, and does not reference any drive or other folder. This is a relative reference, and required to enable the image to appear when uploaded to a web. When you Save Embedded Images, they are changed from absolute to relative references.

Tables

Tables in web pages is also covered on page 183 where a table was used to hold images used as navigation buttons.

Table Properties

Width – use pixels when you know the size, specify 100% for full window

Height – usually let it adjust automatically

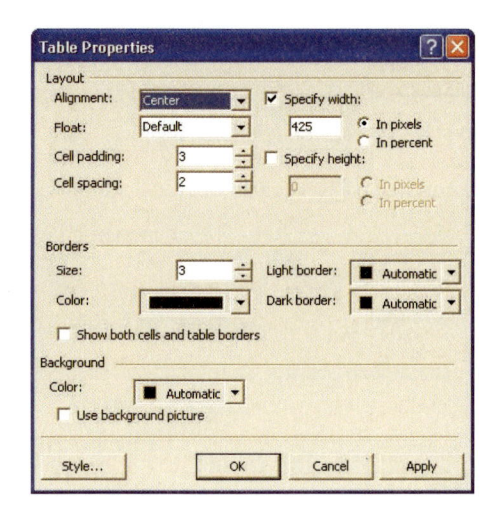

Right click the table and select Table Properties, or select a column or row and then right click and select Cell Properties.

Alignment – sets the position on the page

Float – the position as you resize the window

Cell padding – space within the cell around the contents

The Light border and Dark border can be used in combination to give a 3D effect to the table border.

Cell spacing – space between the cells

Cell Properties

Width – select a column and In percent, specify a proportion of the whole table, eg 50%

When you view the HTML code for a table, you begin to appreciate how easy it is to make a typing error.

Alignment – horizontal and vertical, sets the position within the cell

Rows and Columns spanned – effectively merges cells

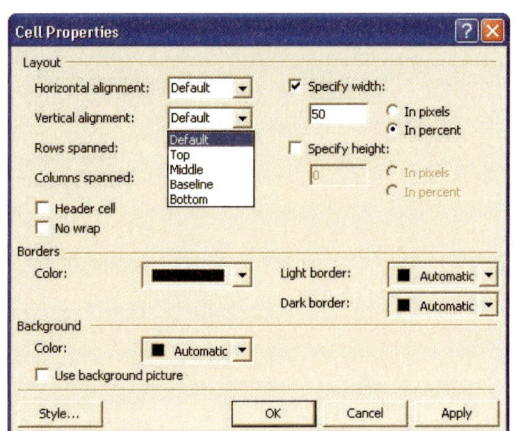

7. Web Pages | 191

Forms

The web page can be made interactive with the use of forms. Some input fields on the form, such as radio buttons, enable the content to be structured and allow for automated collation of the feedback data. Other input methods, such as text boxes, provide an opportunity for comments.

If you have to create the text for the form, position the cursor where you want the form. When the form is inserted it will automatically contain a Submit and a Reset button. Press Enter at the beginning of the line to input text above the buttons.

1. Open a new page from the template and insert the text file with the form content, if provided.

2. Highlight the text to be included in the form. Select Insert, Form, and again Form, and a dashed line will appear around the text.

3. Right click inside the form and select Form Properties.

Common Gateway Interface is a standard for interfacing external programs with information servers.

The Form Properties box allows you to specify the Action and the Method of the form. For the CLAIT Plus exercise, the form handler is CGI, indicated by the URL http://...../cgi-bin/webmail.cgi. Method specifies how the form content will be transferred to the server, as a URL (GET) or in the body of the submission (POST).

4. In the Form Properties box, the default option is to return the information to the private folder in the web folder, on your own computer. We need to send it to a remote server, so select Send to Other, and then click on Options.

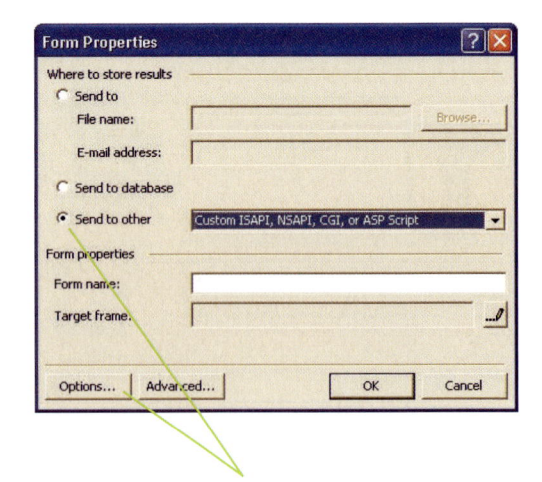

192 | CLAIT Plus in easy steps

...cont'd

HOT TIP: *The Hidden fields contain details that the person completing the form either does not need to see or should not be able to change.*

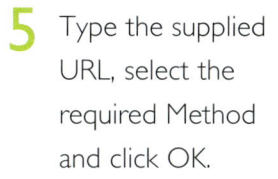

5 Type the supplied URL, select the required Method and click OK.

6 In the Form Properties box again, select the Advanced button. You can now Add the Hidden field.

HOT TIP: *Initially you will enter your own e-mail address in the hidden field, to check that the form really works. The last step in the exercise will be to change that e-mail address to an OCR address.*

The Submit process will send the data to the CGI program which will analyse the data. The CGI program will return an e-mail to the address specified in hidden Name/Value 'recipient'.

Create the form interface

1 Position the cursor where you want the first input box and select Insert, Form, Text box.

2 Double click inside the text box to open the Properties. Enter the required name in the Name box and any Inital value if specified.

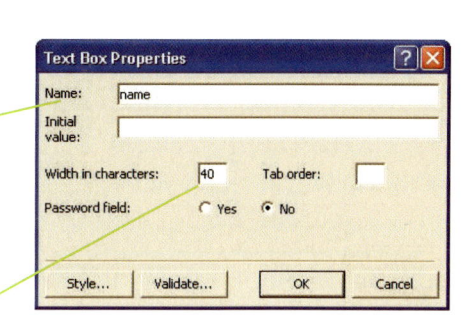

BEWARE: *You should avoid using capital letters when naming fields, and you cannot use any spaces between words in the name fields.*

3 Set the Width in characters, as given in the exercise.

4 For a scrollable text box, select Text Area. Double click in the box to bring up the Properties window and set the dimensions.

7. Web Pages | 193

...cont'd

The Drop Down box will be sized to fit the contents automatically.

5 The Drop Down box style allows you to add a list of predefined options. Double click it and select Add. In the Add Choice window type the first option. Click OK and repeat for each entry.

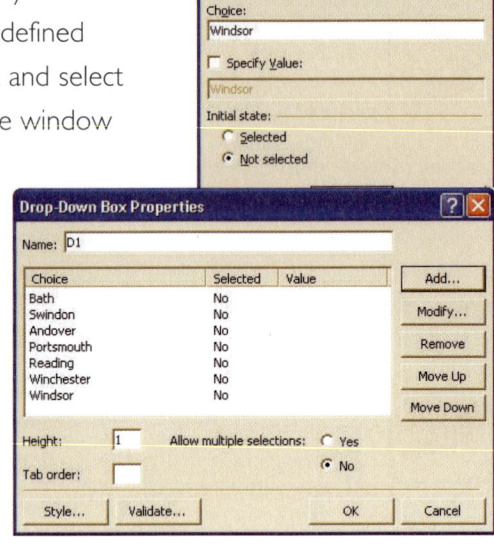

This text box will be sized automatically to fit the contents.

6 You can choose to have an option already visible, allow multiple selections and reorder the list.

If your options are mutually exclusive, such as age groups, you would leave the Group name the same.

7 Radio or Option buttons have a Group name and a Value. To allow multiple selections, each button must have a different Group name, such as R1, R2. The Value should be one text string without spaces, and indicate the contents

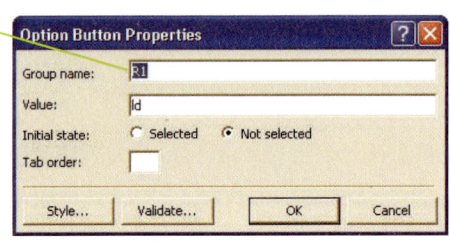

The Submit button sends the input details to the hidden recipient, created in the Form Properties. Submit and Reset are HTML actions.

8 Create Submit and Reset buttons using Push buttons. Double click the Button. Click in Submit or Reset and type the button name in the Value/label box.

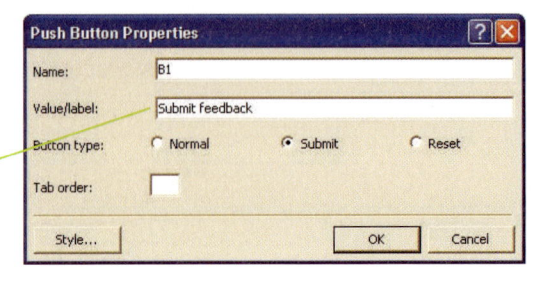

194 | CLAIT Plus in easy steps

Feedback and hyperlinks

Creating and checking hyperlinks was covered in the New CLAIT syllabus.

Save your completed pages, load them into your web browser and check all the hyperlinks. Fill out the form and click the Submit button. If you have completed all the Form Properties correctly, you should receive an immediate acknowledgement from the Webmail company.

If the form does not work correctly, check the Form Properties, Options and the URL you entered. If you do not receive an e-mail, check the address of the hidden recipient field.

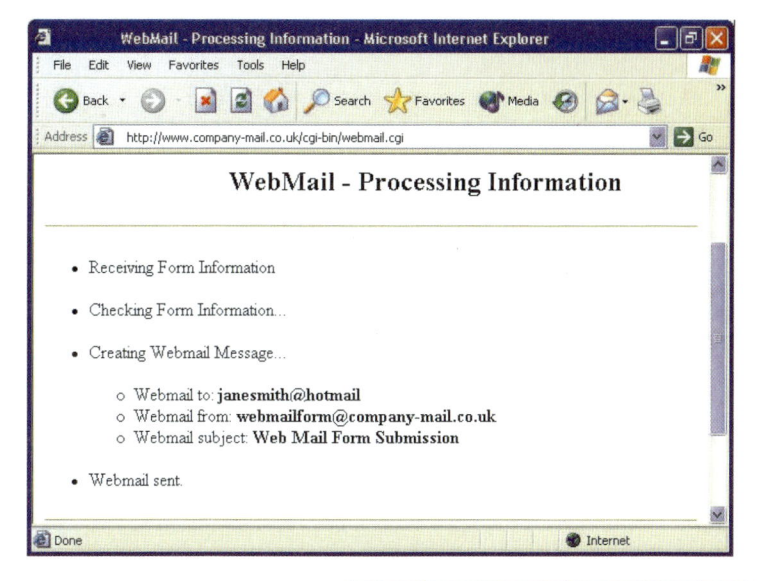

You should also receive an e-mail with the contents of the completed form, showing each field in name and content pairs.

Check hyperlinks

Switch to Hyperlinks on the Views bar and select any of the web pages to see a graphical representation of created and broken hyperlinks.

Select Reports to see an itemised list of broken links. Select Tools, Recalculate Hyperlinks to run a program to validate external links. You need to be online for this.

7. Web Pages | 195

Checklist

You are allowed three hours to complete the OCR CLAIT Plus assessment.

When you have completed the exercise, make sure that you meet all the exercise requirements. Check that you have:

- the correct text and images on each page
- used the required file names
- used the unique title and description for each page
- set author and keywords the same for each page
- created and applied heading and body text styles
- used the correct colours and background

Check your answers against those in the Worked Copy folder, if you followed the downloaded exercise.

- referred to the House Style Guidelines for image properties
- set the correct size and included Alt text for the images
- stored all the image files in the images folder
- checked that links to web pages within the site are relative
- checked that links to images are relative not absolute
- created and checked internal and external hyperlinks
- created and tested the form
- amended the e-mail address for the recipient of the form
- proofread your pages

Marking

You are not allowed any critical errors. The following are considered critical errors:

Check with your tutor for a full list of critical and accuracy errors.

- an inoperative or missing link, hyperlink or e-mail link
- specified text missing in its entirety
- specified image missing
- the form is inoperative
  (incorrectly specified method or action, incorrectly specified hidden field, missing submit button, or button not correctly linked to opening form tag)

Electronic Communications

In this unit you will learn how to use Personal Information Management software to create a contacts list, manage your e-mail, set up and manage a diary, and use notes and a task list.

Covers

Electronic Communications | 198

Microsoft Outlook | 199

The Outlook window | 200

Contacts | 202

Distribution lists | 204

The Calendar | 206

Create appointments | 208

E-mail | 210

Rules | 212

Attachments | 214

Create and send e-mail | 215

Add a signature | 216

Send options | 217

Tasks | 218

Notes and reminders | 219

Print | 220

Checklist | 222

Unit Eight

Electronic Communications

This unit covers all the activities required by an Electronic Communications exercise. The files can be downloaded from the In Easy Steps web site, see page 281. See page 280 for details of e-mail addresses required in this exercise.

Unit Eight overview

This unit covers the following areas:

1 Understanding the concepts of Personal Information Management software and its role in the modern office.

2 Switching between tasks in the same application, and understanding the purpose of each.

3 Creating, and using a Contacts list, and using some of the inbuilt functions to do so efficiently.

4 Managing e-mail, including sending, receiving, filing, adding attachments and creating a mailing list.

See page 275 for the MOS requirements for Electronic Communications.

5 Managing an appointments diary. You will add, amend appointments, set meeting places, lengths and frequencies.

6 Creating notes as reminders, creating lists of tasks with target completion times.

In this unit we will be using Outlook 2002. Any substantial differences between software releases will be highlighted and alternative methods suggested.

7 Controlling printed output to optimise paper use.

Exercise files and documentation

You should have the following items:

- a number of files which will be received as attachments to an e-mail message
- the exercise, which includes details of the company standards for an e-mail signature and printed output

Microsoft Outlook

It's a good idea to have undertaken Unit 3 electronic communications in New CLAIT before starting this unit.

Electronic communications in New CLAIT, Unit 3, could be taken using Outlook Express, a subset or cut-down version of Outlook. Outlook Express is simply an e-mail handler, and as such is well suited to the purpose. It has an address book and filing facility. However, for Electronic communications in CLAIT Plus, it does not offer sufficient function.

If you used Outlook Express previously, you will be able to switch to Outlook very easily. The e-mail element of both programs is almost identical, and when working with e-mail, Outlook can be set up to look just like Outlook Express.

Microsoft Outlook is a Personal Information Management (PIM) application that is designed to co-ordinate and manage all the various categories of data that you deal with. It enables you to control and schedule your tasks, data, e-mail and contacts, using a standard interface. Outlook organises the information by activity.

If you wish to switch from Outlook Express to Outlook as your default e-mail system, Outlook will migrate your existing mail and address book for you.

When you start Outlook you will be presented with the Outlook Shortcuts bar. This displays the full range of functions and allows you to navigate swiftly from one activity to another.

Outlook Today shows an overview of the week, displaying the Calendar, Tasks and Messages, starting with today.

The Inbox is the e-mail handling and storage facility.

Calendar is the diary and appointments facility. It lists daily tasks and can be customised to show one day, one week or a month at a time.

Contacts is the address book facility.

Tasks is a list of to-do items and Notes are simple reminders.

The Outlook bar offers Shortcuts, which include the e-mail folders and it can be customised.

8. Electronic Communications

The Outlook window

When you open Outlook for the first time, it should open with the Inbox displayed, since that is usually where the day's work will begin. However it can be customised to start with any activity, and therefore has multiple display possibilities. Here we will look at the some of the various options so that you will be able to choose and set them for yourself.

The Outlook bar usually shows large icons. Right click the bar and choose Small Icons, to allow for more entries.

1. The Outlook bar was shown and explained on the previous page. If it is not already visible, select View, Outlook Bar.

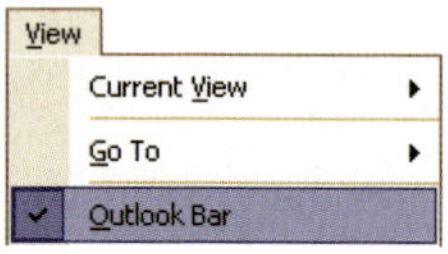

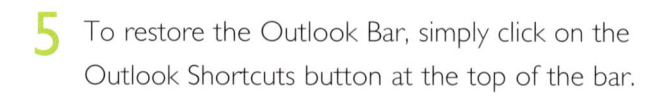

2. The Outlook bar has the heading Outlook Shortcuts. It shows Outlook Today, Inbox etc. See page 199. Click on each of the icons in turn to see the standard screen layout.

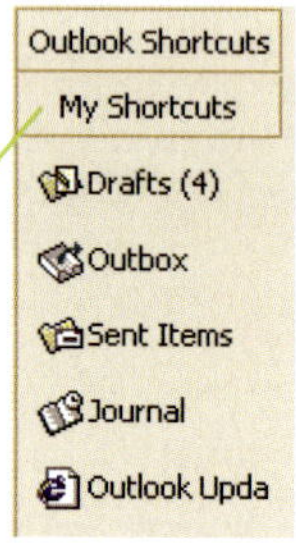

The Journal is not included in the CLAIT Plus syllabus. It can track Office documents and e-mail associated with a contact. Outlook Update is a link to the Microsoft Update site.

3. At the bottom of the Outlook Shortcuts bar is My Shortcuts. When you click on the button the Outlook Shortcuts bar contracts and the new bar opens. It displays e-mail folders (other than Inbox), the Journal and the Outlook Update Internet link.

4. The Other Shortcuts button is opened in a similar fashion and shows shortcuts to the major folders.

Adding entries to the Outlook Shortcut bar is not required in the CLAIT Plus exercise. However, if you begin to use the bar regularly, you might find it a useful facility.

5. To restore the Outlook Bar, simply click on the Outlook Shortcuts button at the top of the bar.

6. To add entries to any of the Shortcut bars, select the bar, right mouse click and select Outlook Bar Shortcut. Select the item you want to add and click OK. You can also create completely new Shortcut bars.

200 | CLAIT Plus in easy steps

...cont'd

The Folder List
The Folder List is another, sometimes simpler, way to navigate around the various activities in Outlook.

> **HOT TIP**
> You can also click on the current activity name, Calendar, Tasks etc in the Navigation bar. This will invoke the Folder list. Click the pin as instructed to have it stay open.

1 Select View, Folder List. If you are accustomed to Outlook Express, the screen may take on a familiar appearance.

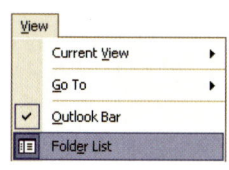

2 The Folder List shows all the Outlook folders. To switch activities, just click on the required folder.

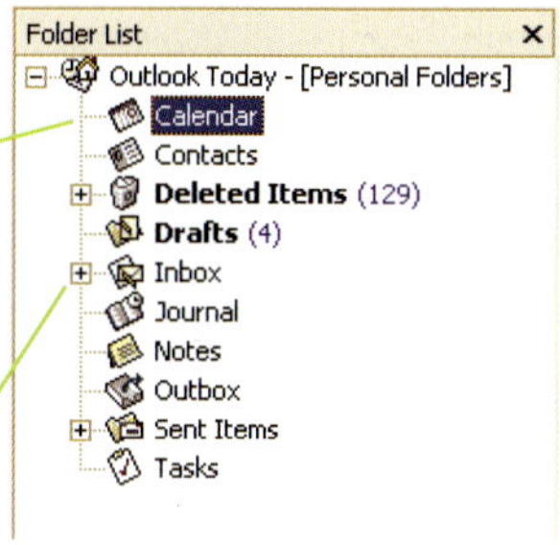

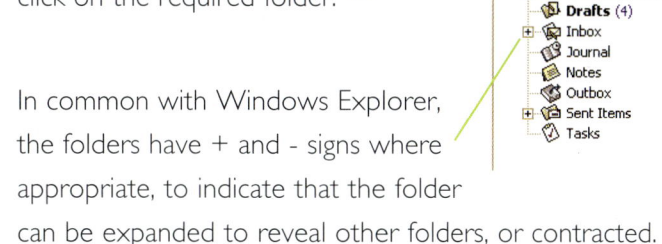

3 In common with Windows Explorer, the folders have + and - signs where appropriate, to indicate that the folder can be expanded to reveal other folders, or contracted.

> **HOT TIP**
> To close the Folder List, click on the Close button on its title bar.

Other View options

1 The options offered in the View list vary according to the current activity such as Calendar, shown here. Some options such as Reminder Window, Outlook Bar and Folder List are always available.

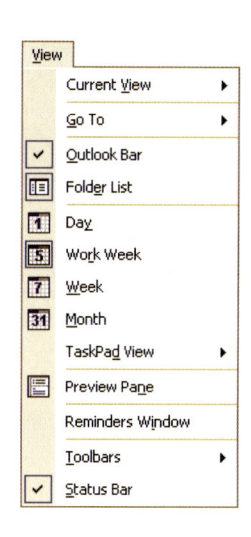

> **HOT TIP**
> It is worth experimenting with the View options, to become familiar with the various windows and ways of accessing the tasks. To avoid confusion, make a note of what you started with!

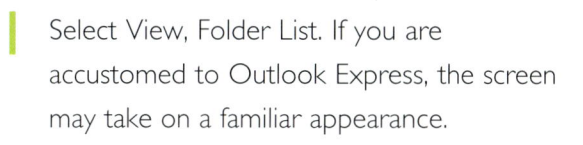

2 Specific customisation of how the data is displayed within an activity, such as number of days per week, is controlled through Current View. These display options will be covered under the individual activities throughout the unit.

8. Electronic Communications | 201

Contacts

If you are undertaking this unit on your own computer, and have an existing contact list, you may wish to keep practice or dummy data in a separate folder.

These steps, 1-5, are purely designed to keep your main Contact list separate, and is not required by the CLAIT Plus syllabus.

1. Select Contacts in the Outlook Shortcut bar, making it the default location for a new folder.

2. Click on File, New, Folder.

3. Type a suitable name in the Create New Folder window, and select Contacts as the location of the new folder. Your new folder will be a subfolder in the Contacts function.

4. You will be prompted to create a shortcut to the new folder in the Outlook Bar. The shortcut will be added to My Shortcuts, not the main Outlook bar.

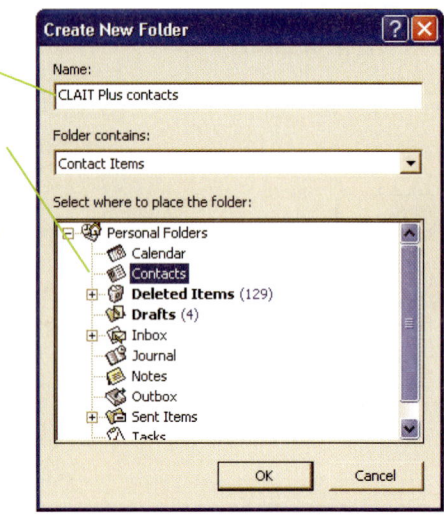

If you decide not to add it to the Shortcut bar, the easiest way to access it is via the Folder List.

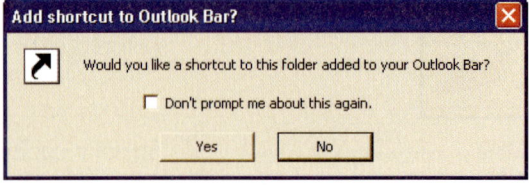

5. When you start to add contacts, make sure that you have the correct folder selected.

...cont'd

Add a contact

> **HOT TIP**
> *When you select an activity, such as Calendar or Tasks, the New Icon changes automatically to reflect the chosen activity.*

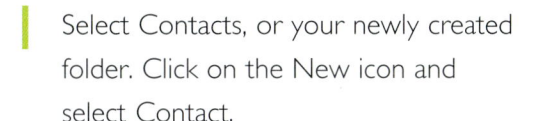

1. Select Contacts, or your newly created folder. Click on the New icon and select Contact.

2. Fill in the details in the correct fields, making sure not to have any typing errors, particularly in the e-mail address.

> **HOT TIP**
> *Outlook will change field labels such as Business address to Home address, and will check phone numbers. Click on the down arrow or the pencil that appears when you fill in details.*

> **HOT TIP**
> *To amend a contact's details, just double click the entry. To delete a contact, select the contact and click on the Delete icon in the toolbar.*

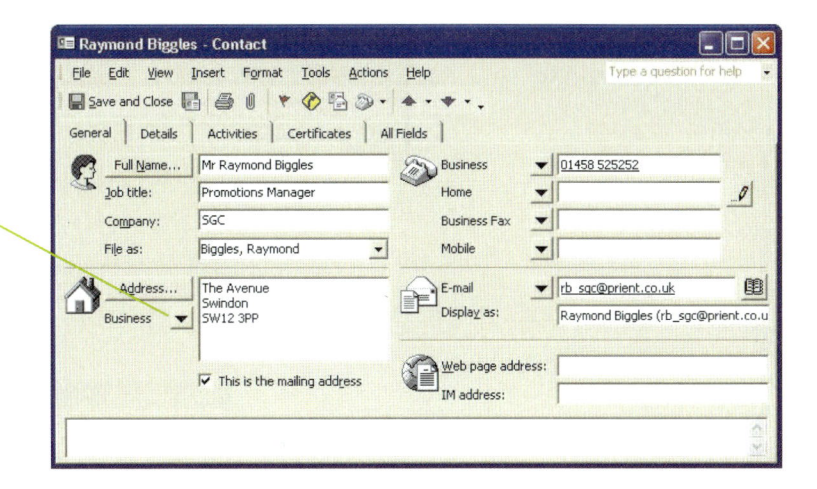

3. If you have only one contact to add, select Save and Close when you are finished.

4. If you have several contacts to add, you can select Save and New, located next to the Save and Close button.

5. To add several contacts from the same company, select Actions, New Contact from the Same Company.
   This will complete fields that may be repeated, such as address.

Distribution lists

The purpose of an e-mail distribution list is to enable you to send the same information to several contacts at one time, by selecting just one name or entry.

1. With the Contacts folder, or your own folder open, select File, New, New Distribution List. Alternatively, right click in the Contacts pane and select from the context menu.

HOT TIP: In common with all Office applications, there are many ways to access or use a facility. It's a good idea to explore some of the Menu entries, icons etc in any of these windows to see what can be done.

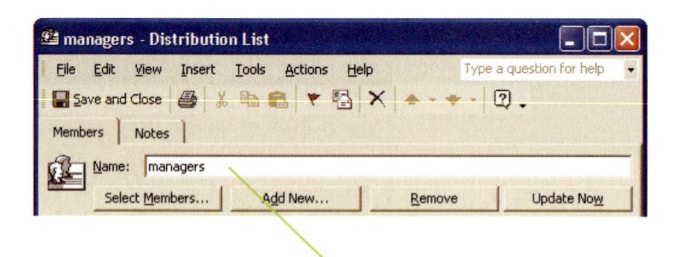

2. Enter the name for the Distribution List and click on Select Members.

3. From this window, first select the folder that contains the contact names, if necessary.

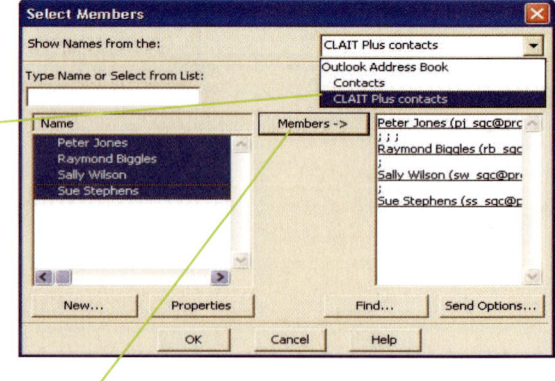

4. Select a name in the left pane and click on the Members button. When choosing several names, you can use Shift + click if they are consecutive entries, or Ctrl + click if they are separated. Click OK when finished.

204 | CLAIT Plus in easy steps

...cont'd

5 The names will be inserted into the Distribution List. You can use this window to Add New, Remove or Update entries. Click on Save and Close when finished.

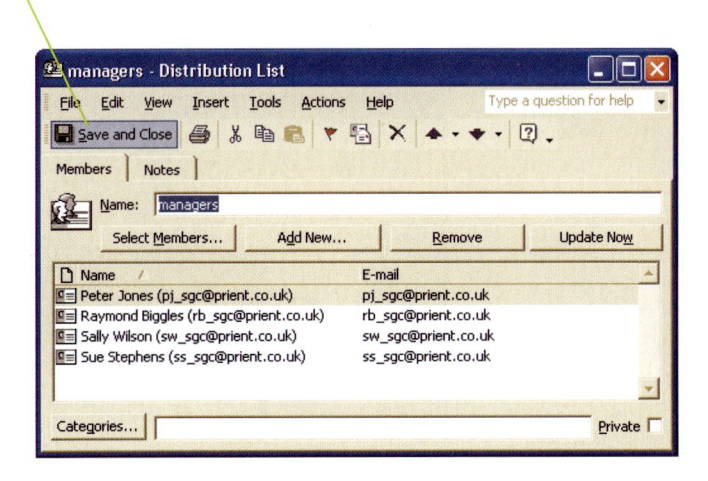

Distribution Lists are identified in the Contacts window with a special icon and bold text.

6 The Distribution List entry will appear in the Contacts, or subfolder, in its correct alphabetical sequence.

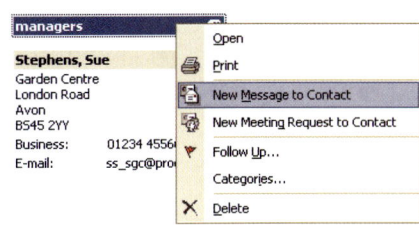

For more information on sending e-mail, see page 215.

7 To use the Distribution list, click on it with the right mouse button and select New Message to Contact. This opens a message window, with the To: field already completed.

8 To send mail to only some names on the Distribution List, you must select them individually from the Contacts list, as you would do normally.

8. Electronic Communications | 205

The Calendar

> **Hot Tip:** *Select View, Current View from the Menu, and try out the different options.* This will be more effective once you have entered some appointments and tasks.

The Calendar window can be customised to display in many different ways. Illustrated below is the Day/Week/month view.

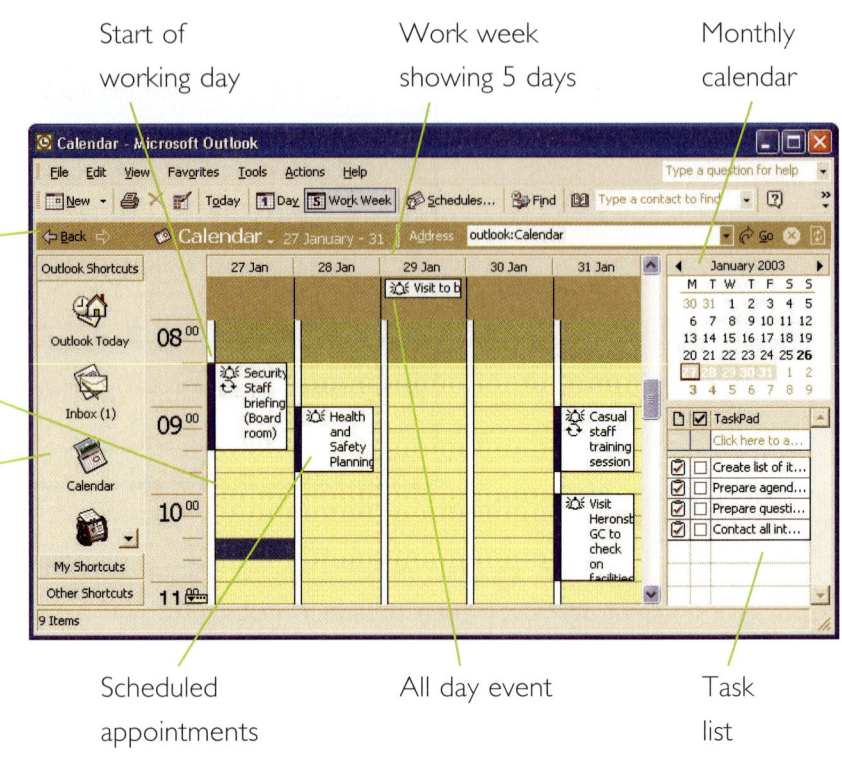

Labels on the screenshot:
- Start of working day
- Work week showing 5 days
- Monthly calendar
- Navigation bar
- Time shown in 15-minute intervals
- Outlook Shortcut bar
- Scheduled appointments
- All day event
- Task list

> **Hot Tip:** *The Calendar can be used to co-ordinate appointments with others. It* can generate invitations and check free time with permitted *contacts.*

The week displayed is the current week. To view the next week, or any particular week, use the forward and back arrows on the monthly calendar to the right. This also indicates in bold, days where appointments have been made.

The working day in the calendar illustrated above, starts at 8.30 am, identified by the change of background colour. Each individual appointment is displayed, and as much of the detail as possible. Each appointment occupies the amount of time allocated. All day events are indicated directly underneath the date.

The Task Pad on the right lists the tasks, again showing as much information as it can. When a Task is ticked to show it is completed, it will be crossed through.

Customise the Calendar

1 To show the 5 day working week, you can select it from the Standard toolbar, or using View from the Menu. To define your own working week, see Step 4 below.

2 To set the Start and End time for each day, select Tools, Options.

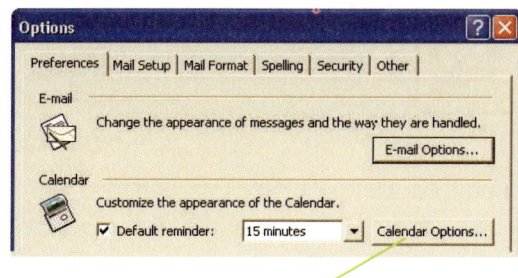

The reminder timer is set to ring 15 minutes before any meeting.

3 On the Preferences tab select Calendar Options.

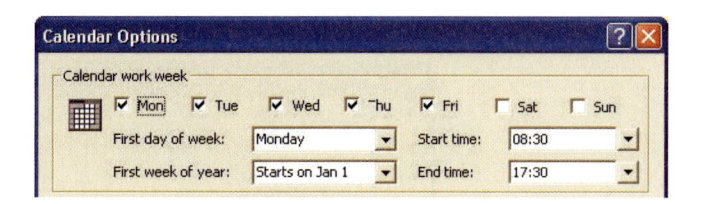

4 Select your work week, first day of the week, start and end time. Click OK to confirm. When you return to the Calendar window, the working day should be shown in a lighter shade of yellow.

5 To set the display intervals for each hour, choose View, Current View, Customise Current View. In the View Summary select Other Settings.

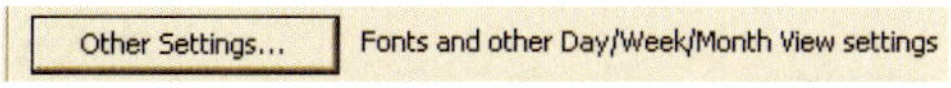

6 Set the Timescale to that required by the exercise.

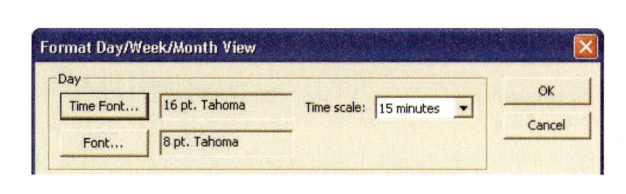

8. Electronic Communications | 207

Create appointments

1 Select Calendar from the Outlook Shortcut bar. If your calendar is set to display a 5 day week, it will show each hour subdivided into your chosen intervals.

> **HOT TIP** *If you have chosen a 7 day week, you can just double click anywhere in the day.*

2 Double click in the day and start time for your appointment. The Appointment window will open. Alternatively, click in the day/time and select New from the toolbar.

> **HOT TIP** *Note that the Reminder box is ticked. A message window will remind you when the meeting is due.*

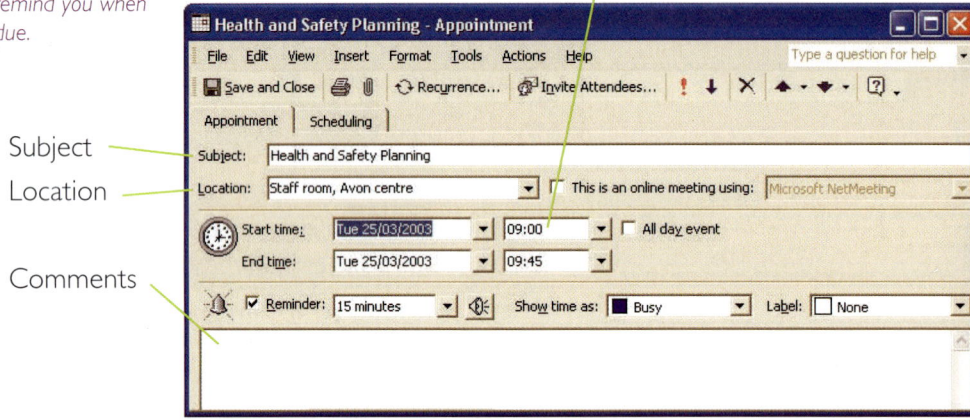

3 Fill in the details using the fields provided. Note that by selecting the correct day/date and Start time, these details are already completed.

Subject
Location

Comments

4 Select the End time, or you can type it in. If you tick the box for an All day event, the End time option disappears.

> **HOT TIP** *When you create an appointment using the 7 day calendar, you will need to deselect the All day event option to reinstate the End time field.*

5 The Location field will remember previous locations, so when you have entered a few you may be able to select from the drop down list.

...cont'd

6   Select Save and Close when you have completed the details.

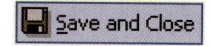

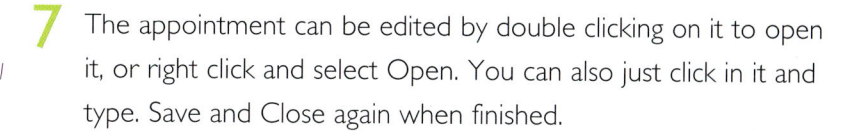

The Monthly Calendar, above the Task Pad, will show in bold days with appointments set.

7   The appointment can be edited by double clicking on it to open it, or right click and select Open. You can also just click in it and type. Save and Close again when finished.

See page 275 for inviting attendees and booking resources.

8   To move the appointment, click, hold and drag with the left mouse button. Alternatively, open the appointment and change the date/time.

Recurring appointments

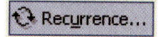

1   In the Appointments window select Recurrence. Completing the details is quite straight forward. Set the Start time and the Duration, the End time will be completed for you.

You can tick any number of days to have the meeting recur several times in a week.

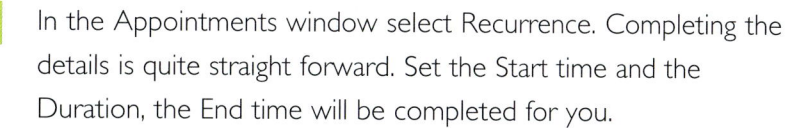

2   Choose the Recurrence pattern and the Start date.

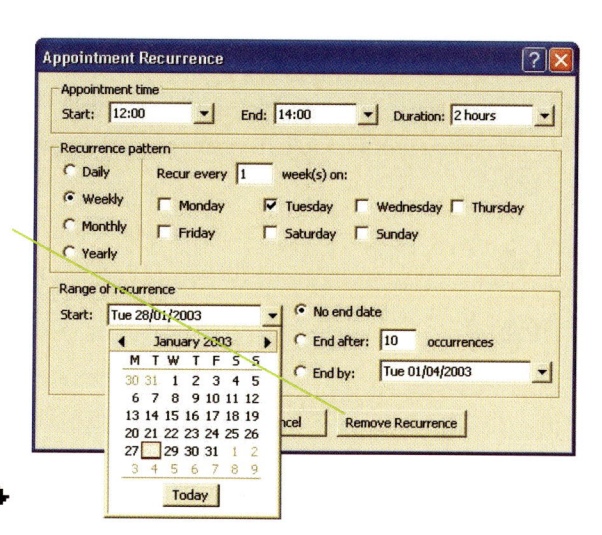

When you amend or move recurring appointments, you will be asked if you wish to open the particular occurrence or all occurrences.

3   To remove the recurrence, click the specific button.

4   Recurring appointments are indicated by a circular symbol.

8. Electronic Communications | 209

E-mail

Outlook organises all its data, Contacts, Calendar, Notes etc into folders. E-mail is treated in the same way. E-mail is received into the Inbox folder. Messages are saved as Drafts in the Draft folder, or sent via the Outbox folder. Copies of sent e-mail are saved in the Sent Items folder.

You can also use the Folder List or Navigation bar to show all the folders at once.

1. The folder contents can be viewed by selecting My Shortcuts from the Outlook Shortcuts bar, see page 199. Then select the particular folder.

The Preview pane is useful, but does in effect open the e-mail. If you are concerned about unwanted mail or viruses, you should avoid using it.

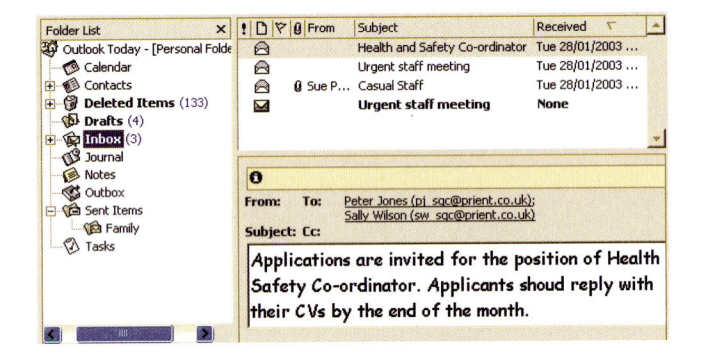

2. Double click an e-mail to open it. You can also select View, Preview pane to see the first few lines of any e-mail.

Outlook and Outlook Express use the same icons to indicate e-mail attributes.

icon	meaning
	unread
	read
	reply
	forward
	high priority
	attachment

3. Occasionally, on opening an e-mail, you will be asked to acknowledge that you have received the message.

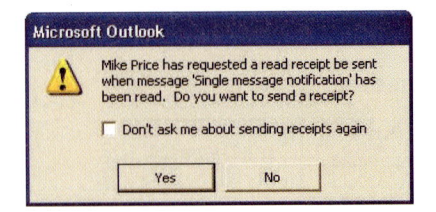

4. To choose this for your own outgoing messages, select Tools, Options, and on the Preferences tab, select E-mail Options, Tracking Options. Request a Read receipt. This is useful if you really want to make sure that the e-mail has been received, but is not a CLAIT Plus requirement.

210 | CLAIT Plus in easy steps

...cont'd

Microsoft has increased security in Outlook 2002, so adding a contact is slightly more restricted than in previous versions.

5 To add the sender to your Contacts folder, open the message and select the sender's name. Right click and choose Add to Contacts. The Contacts form will open with some of the fields, including e-mail address completed.

Organise your e-mail
E-mail will remain in the Inbox until you move it to another folder. This could be Deleted Items, or a specially named folder.

You can use Rules to transfer e-mail directly into specified folders. See page 212.

1 To move mail it is easiest to have the Folder list open, but you can also use the Shortcut bars. Select the e-mail item from the list and drag and drop it in the destination folder. When the folder or Shortcut name turns blue, the mouse is correctly positioned.

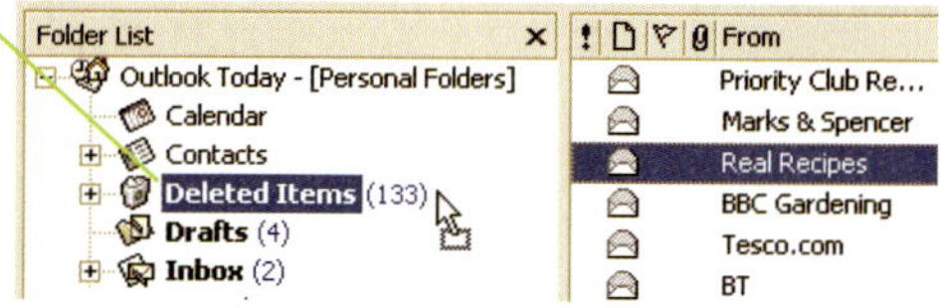

2 To create a named folder for your e-mail, select File, Folder, New Folder and supply an appropriate name. Note that the Folder contains Mail and Post Items.

The procedure to create a folder is the same as that described and illustrated on page 202.

3 On this occasion, select it as a subfolder in the Inbox.

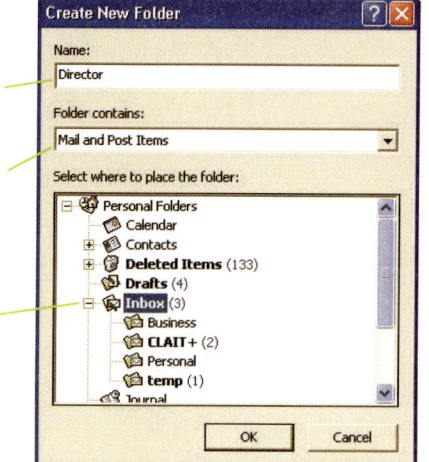

8. Electronic Communications | 211

Rules

Rules and the Junk mail facility are an efficient way of managing messages that arrive in your Inbox. They provide a way of sorting your mail automatically, removing unwanted items and filing those with specified attributes. To create a Rule:

HOT TIP: On the previous page we created a folder, Director, and dragged and dropped specific messages into it. Using Rules we can automate the procedure.

1. Select Tools, Rules Wizard, and click the New button. The rule will be applied to your Inbox by default. The option, Move new messages from someone, is already selected.

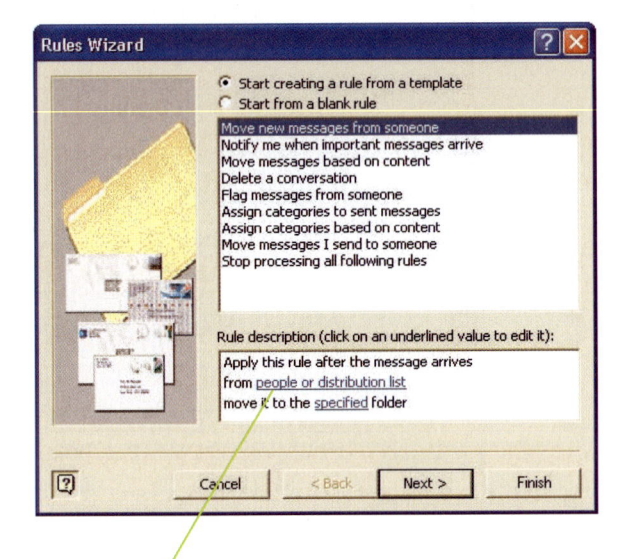

2. Click on the underlined text in the lower pane to specify the sender. Your Contacts list will open.

3. Next choose a folder for the messages. You will see the rule build as you progress through the Wizard.

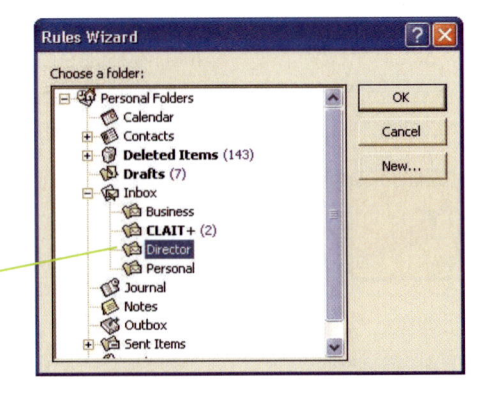

212 | CLAIT Plus in easy steps

...cont'd

4   You can set a condition, such as Where my name is in the Cc box, and on the following step define any exceptions.

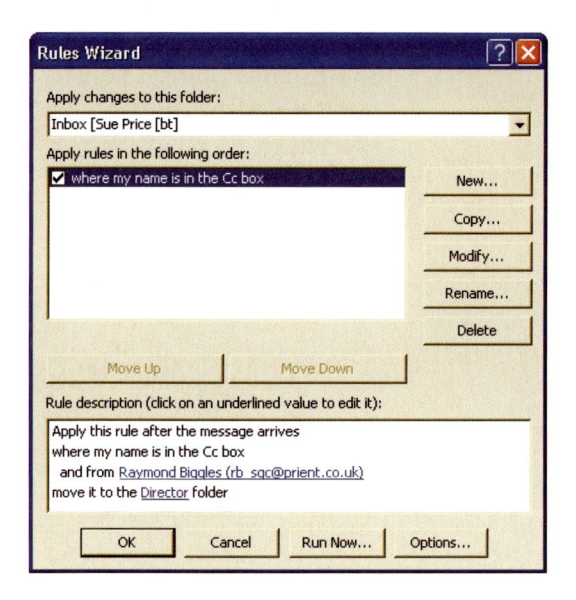

Outlook also offers an Archive function to store older items that are important, but not frequently used. You can set a time interval for items to be archived, when they will be moved into a special Archive folder. The folder structure of the archive will match that of your existing mailbox and you can work with the items in the same way as you do in your main folders.

5   Supply a name for the rule, and select Finish. If you choose to Run Now, it will be applied to the current Inbox and turned on for future mail.

Junk mail

Unfortunately, a great deal of mail is sent indiscriminately and is unsolicited. Outlook can search for common phrases to detect such messages and move them to a junk e-mail or the Deleted Items folder.

Creating Rules and managing junk mail is not a CLAIT Plus requirement, but it's a good idea to understand how to use in-built facilities to control e-mail.

6   Go to Tools, Organise, Junk E-mail. Select the Move action, and the folder, and Turn on checking.

7   The checks will be added as rules and will appear in the list managed by the Rules Wizard.

8. Electronic Communications | 213

Attachments

Outlook 2002 categorises attachment files by security level. Level 1 files, which include .exe (executable or program) files, are completely blocked. Level 2 files, such as .zip, can be saved to disk but not opened from the message.

Attachments will be indicated by the paperclip symbol, and listed in the header area of the message. As in Outlook Express, attachments can be opened, but the recommended procedure, to avoid the risk from viruses, is to save them to disk.

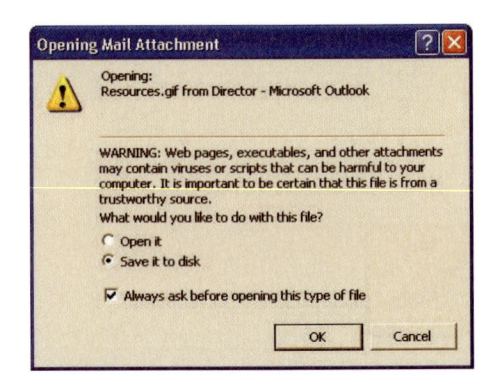

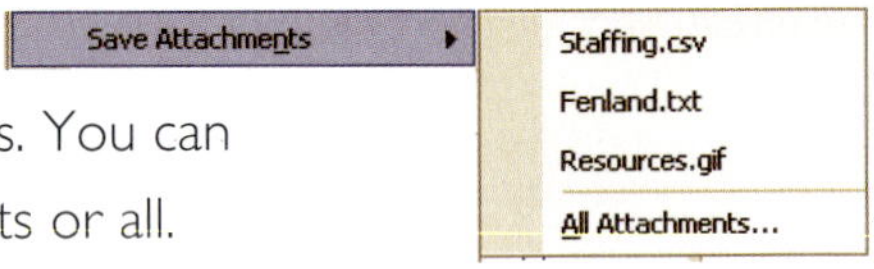

1. Select File, Save Attachments. You can choose individual attachments or all.

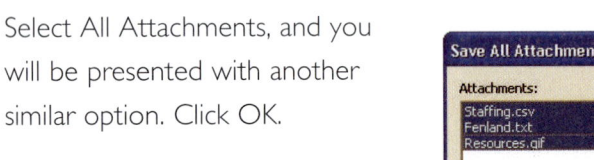

Once you have saved the attachments you can open them with the appropriate application. For example, a .csv file can be opened using Excel.

2. Select All Attachments, and you will be presented with another similar option. Click OK.

3. You must now choose where to save the files. Use the standard navigation window, or use the My Places panel as a shortcut.

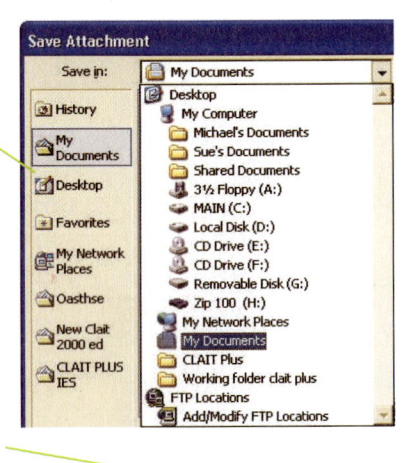

If you forward the attached files, you will also have a copy in the Sent Items folder.

4. Outlook stores a copy of the files in the destination folder, but also keeps the attachments in the Inbox. To remove the file from the Inbox, open the message and click on the attachment names. Right mouse click and select Remove.

214 | CLAIT Plus in easy steps

Create and send e-mail

The basic steps for creating and sending e-mail were covered in New CLAIT.

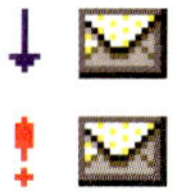

Outlook can use several different editors for its e-mail. The first time you use Outlook, you may find that it defaults to Word. For CLAIT Plus it's better to use the built-in Outlook editor. To enable this editor:

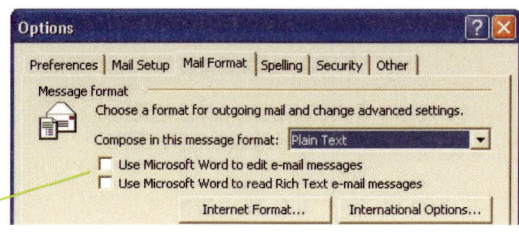

The Outlook editor enables you to print user names on the printouts without having to save the message first, see page 220.

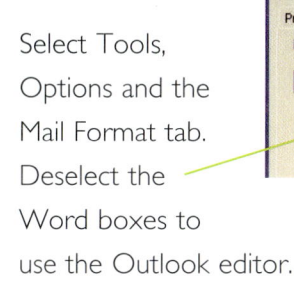

1   Select Tools, Options and the Mail Format tab. Deselect the Word boxes to use the Outlook editor.

2   With either editor, you also have a choice of text format:
   - HTML gives you the fullest function, with stationery effects and backgrounds
   - Rich text allows font selection and formatting, such as bold
   - Plain text is the simplest format.

When you reply to a message, Outlook will automatically select the same format as the originating message. When you send a message to a new recipient, the safest choice is plain text.

Set Priority

Messages are, by default, assigned the Normal level of importance. To view or change the setting for *one* message:

The Flag symbol is for you to use when you want to mark items for your own attention.

1   Click on the High, or Low priority button while the message is open. It will display the symbol when it arrives at the recipient's Inbox. The Priority and Flag fields can be used to sort entries in the message folders.

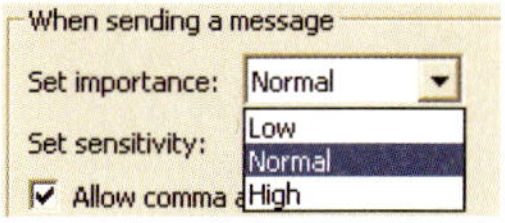

2   To change the priority setting for all messages, select Tools, Options. On the Preferences tab choose E-mail Options, then Advanced E-mail Options. In the Set importance box choose the level.

Low

High

8. Electronic Communications | 215

Add a signature

E-mail signatures can be created for a variety of situations, such as when replying, or forwarding, or when undertaking a different activity. They enable a company or house style, and reduce time spent entering repeated information.

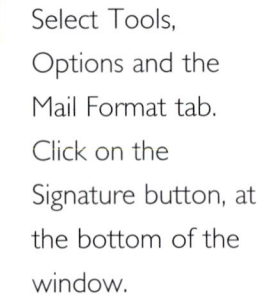

1 Select Tools, Options and the Mail Format tab. Click on the Signature button, at the bottom of the window.

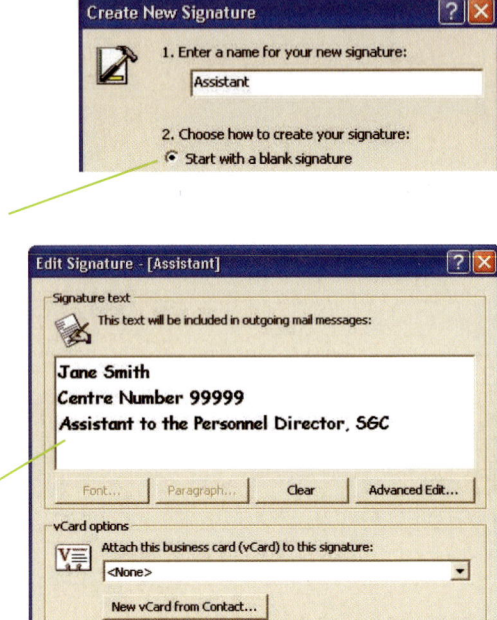

2 With no existing signatures, the default option is to Start with a blank signature. Enter a name and click Next.

If you wished to create a second signature, you could use the existing one as a template.

3 Enter the signature text and click on Finish.

4 The signature can be amended or removed and will be used automatically from this point onwards.

5 To use a different signature, select Insert Signature and select from the list. To change it permanently, or not use any signature, go to Tools, Options and reselect from the Mail Format tab, as shown in Step 1 above.

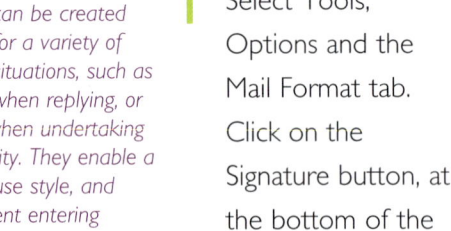

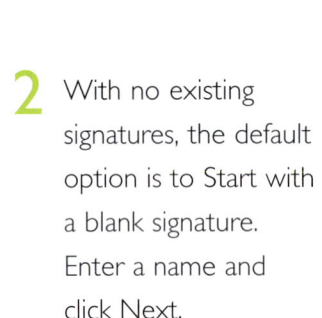

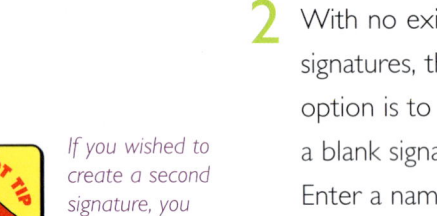

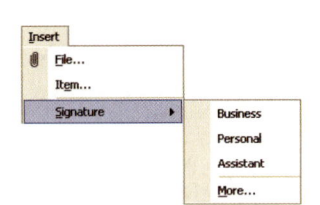

Send options

Send attachments
There are two ways to add an attachment to a message.

1. The first is to use the Paperclip on the toolbar. This opens the My Documents folder, from where you can select or navigate to locate the files.

2. The second is to use Insert. Insert File is the same as using the Paperclip. Insert Item allows you to attach a copy of anything from your Outlook folders – a message, a note, a task description etc.

Select recipients
The differing ways to send e-mail serve particular purposes:

- To: you can select one or several recipients in the To window, each being treated with equal prominence.
- Cc: is carbon or courtesy copy, for information only.
- Bcc: is blind courtesy copy. Unlike carbon copy recipients, their details are not listed on the message, so they remain confidential.

HOT TIP: All recipients can see who is included in Cc mailings. Only the Bcc recipients can see who receives the Bcc mail.

Save copies of e-mail
The CLAIT Plus course requires that you keep a copy of all the e-mail sent. To confirm the setting:

1. Select Tools, Options and the Preferences tab. Select E-mail Options.

2. Ensure that the Save copies of messages box is ticked.

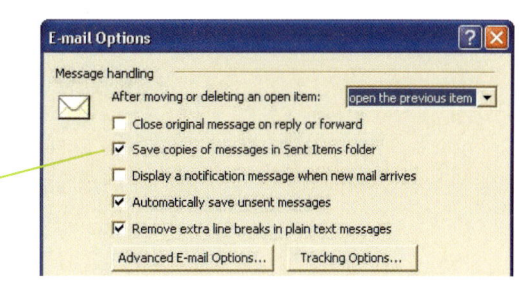

HOT TIP: This dialog box also allows you to save copies of messages while they are being composed.

8. Electronic Communications | 217

Tasks

The Task Pad can be viewed in Outlook Today, Calendar and in the dedicated Tasks window. The Task list indicates items still to be completed, items overdue (in red), and items completed (crossed through).

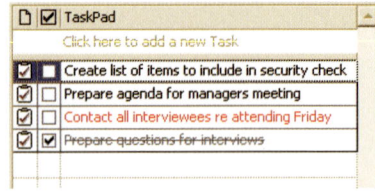

To add a Task:

You can single click in the space at the top of the list and type the task. This does not however utilise the full function offered by Tasks.

1. Select New Task, or double click in the area above the list. A Task window, very similar in form to the Calendar window, will open.

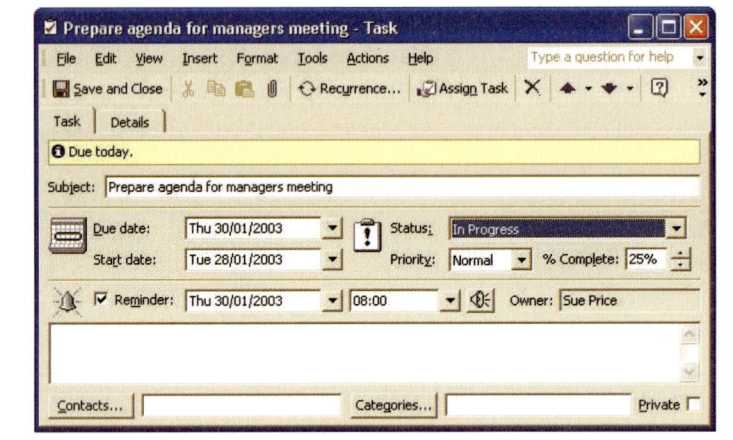

The Tasks form offers a Status report, Priority and % Complete. They can also be made recurring. Tasks can be assigned to others and automatic status reports generated, a feature that takes greater advantage of the integrated approach of Outlook. However, this function is not included in the CLAIT Plus syllabus.

2. Complete the details and select Save and Close when finished.

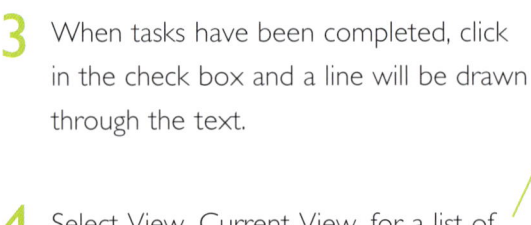

3. When tasks have been completed, click in the check box and a line will be drawn through the text.

4. Select View, Current View, for a list of options for presenting the Task list.

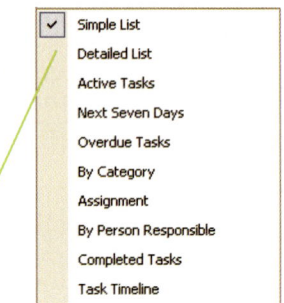

218 | CLAIT Plus in easy steps

Notes and reminders

Outlook Notes are the PC equivalent of the ubiquitous sticky notes, and even come in a variety of colours. Notes are plain text files and can contain names, phone numbers or anything you want to make a point of remembering. To create a note:

1. Select New, Note from the toolbar. The first line of text will be used as the title of the note. It is saved automatically when you close or click elsewhere on the screen.

As part of the CLAIT Plus exercise, you will have to open a text file, usually in NotePad, copy and paste the text into a note.

2. The note will expand as you type, and you can copy and paste text into it as you would in any text editor.

3. Notes, unlike the Task Pad, do not display automatically, you will have to open the folder to view them. However, you can move the note around the screen, dragging its Title bar, and you can also drag them onto the Desktop. This means that they can be seen when you start the computer.

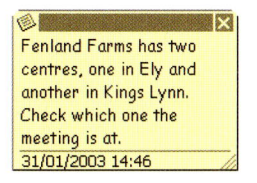

Reminders

When you use the Calendar or the Task Pad, Outlook offers a Reminder facility to alert you when a meeting is imminent or a Task due. You can choose a reminder time in either function. Outlook will sound an alarm and present you with the event. Dismiss will cancel the reminder, select Open Item if you wish to change the starting time.

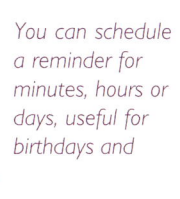

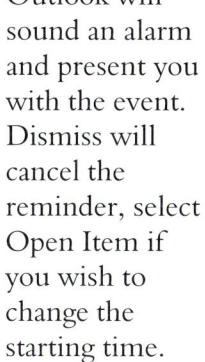

You can schedule a reminder for minutes, hours or days, useful for birthdays and anniversaries.

8. Electronic Communications | 219

Print

Each of the functions in Outlook has its own print layout options so the first step is to choose which item you wish to print.

E-mail
To print the contents of e-mail messages select Memo style in the Page Setup menu.

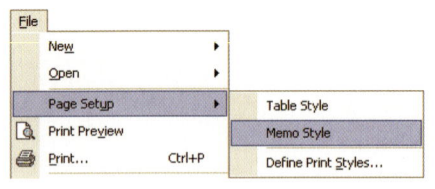

If you are using Word as your e-mail editor, you must save the message before the header information will be included.

1. Compose mode shows the recipients' addresses, including Cc and Bcc, subject, attachments and e-mail text. When you have created the message you can print it immediately or save and print it as a Draft. Use Print Preview to confirm that you have the header details.

2. E-mail that has been sent will also display the From and Sent (date/time) details in the header. Open the Sent Items folder, select the messages and click on Print.

Calendar
Print options in Calendar are for Daily, Weekly, Monthly, Tri-fold or Details Style. Refer to the exercise for the required style.

The CLAIT exercise will require your name and centre number on all printouts. Select File, Print Preview and Page Setup. Select the Header and Footer tab and enter the details. You will need to repeat this procedure for each print style - Memo and Table, and also for other Calendar and Contact styles. You would also be wise to include it in the E-mail prints, even though your signature may be sufficient.

1. Select the Calendar. If you have the correct day or week visible, you could use the Page Setup menu as above. It will offer all the Calendar options.

2. Using the Print menu allows you to select the time period as well, so you can print several weeks at once, using a separate page for each.

...cont'd

When required to print Table style, the options are to print All rows or Only selected rows.

Tasks and Notes

Tasks can be printed Memo style or Table style, Notes only have Memo style.

1. Use Edit, Select All, or use Ctrl+A, to select all entries in the Task or Memo list.

The CLAIT exercise may require you to minimise paper use.

2. Select File, Print. Choose the style for printing. Deselect the option to Start each item on a new page.

Contacts list

The Contact details can be printed Card style, Small or Medium booklet, Memo or Phone directory.

The Contacts print includes an extra page with the full range of contact fields, but no data.

1. You will need to select View, Current View and Detailed Address Cards, to have all the required details in your Contacts print.

2. Then select File, Print, the style of print and All items.

Outlook is the only Office program that enables easy printing of folder contents. If you don't want to print the whole list, use Ctrl+click to select individual items in the list, use Shift and click to select consecutive entries.

Folder contents

To print a list of any e-mail folder contents, choose the folder then select File, Print, Table style. The printed list indicates priority, status (read or unread), attachments, subject and date received or sent. It does not, however, indicate the folder name. To include the whole Outlook folder structure and names you can do a screen print, as described in Unit 1, see page 23.

8. Electronic Communications | 221

Checklist

You are allowed three hours to complete the OCR CLAIT Plus assessment.

When you have completed the exercise, do a final check to ensure that you meet the exercise requirements. Check that you have:

- entered all text, and especially e-mail addresses, correctly, following the capitalisation as shown
- created and used a distribution list
- created and stored an e-mail signature
- configured the calendar as required
- stored attached files outside the mailbox
- assigned a priority level to message(s)
- created a folder for specific messages
- moved the specified messages
- included your name, Centre number and date on all prints
- produced the required number and style of prints
- amended the text as required
- proofread your prints

You can check your printouts against those in the Worked Copy folder for this unit.

Marking

You are not allowed any critical errors. The following are considered critical errors:

- failure to show any files attached to e-mail
- e-mail address missing or incorrect
- calendar entries are incorrect day and/or time
- failure to enter calendar entries or schedule meetings as specified
- failure to set a recurring or repeating appointment or event

Check with your tutor for a full list of critical and accuracy errors.

Graphs and Charts

In this unit you will use Excel to display data in graphical format. You will learn how to modify chart appearance, add trend lines and equations and adjust scales. You will see how graphs can be used to extract information and predict future values.

Covers

Graphs and Charts | 224

Standard and Custom charts | 225

The chart wizard | 226

Chart elements | 228

Chart toolbar | 229

Bar/column chart | 230

Format axes | 231

Stacked vertical bar | 232

XY scatter | 233

Trend line | 234

Exploded pie | 235

XY scatter showing relationship | 236

Line column | 237

Update the data | 238

Print | 239

Checklist | 240

Unit Nine

Graphs and Charts

The supporting exercise and files for this unit can be downloaded from the In Easy Steps web site, see page 281.

Unit Nine overview

This unit covers the following areas:

1. Identifying and selecting data from a worksheet to present in a graphical form.

2. Recognising various graph types and their advantages in displaying data. You will also learn how to emphasise a particular data item.

In this unit we will be using Excel 2002, Any substantial differences between software releases will be highlighted and alternative methods suggested.

3. Using in-built tools to add descriptive annotations, equations and trendlines to the charts.

4. Formatting the graphs and charts to a House style. Amending their display by changing default colours and shading.

5. Controlling scale and measurement units.

6. Understanding how to use the graph information to extrapolate relationships and predict future values.

7. Printing the graphs and charts ensuring that the data is easily identifiable.

The data files will need to be saved in the .xls format. If you open Windows Explorer and double click on them they should open in Excel, just remember to use File, Save As and change the file type. If you have already created the graph when you save, the file type will be changed automatically.

Exercise files and documentation

You should have the following items:

- a number of data files in .csv format to be used as the basis for the charts and graphs
- the exercise, which will include a House Style sheet and specific instructions for each type of chart

Standard and Custom charts

It's a good idea to have taken the New CLAIT Graphs and Charts Unit so that you are familiar with the process.

The CLAIT Plus syllabus lists the chart types that you will be required to use: an exploded pie, a bar/column chart, a line-column chart and an XY scatter graph.

Standard Charts

Excel offers a very wide range of standard chart formats and options. Every standard chart type has two or more sub-types. As you select each sub-type you will get a description of its purpose. Before you start the exercise you should read through the descriptions to familiarise yourself with them. Even though the exercise will specify the chart type to be used, you will need to identify which sub-type is most appropriate for the task.

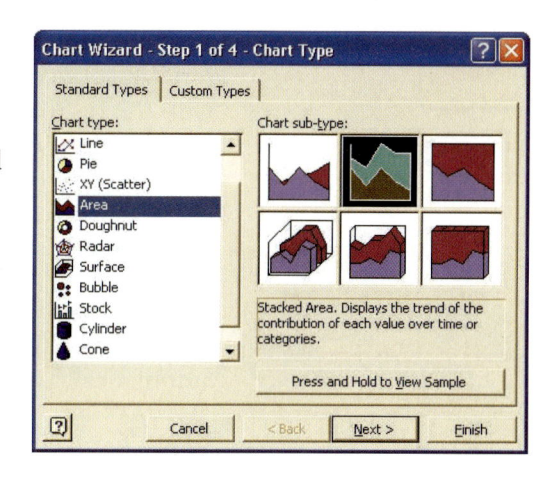

To create a chart very quickly, select your data and press F11. The chart will be created on a separate sheet using the default chart type.

Custom Charts

These are based on the standard charts but include extra information such as data tables, gridlines, or specific formats for on-screen viewing. Included in the custom charts is a black and white pie chart, already formatted to display each segment with a different pattern, suitable for use when you don't have access to a colour printer.

Whichever chart type and options you choose at this point, you can still change them later if necessary.

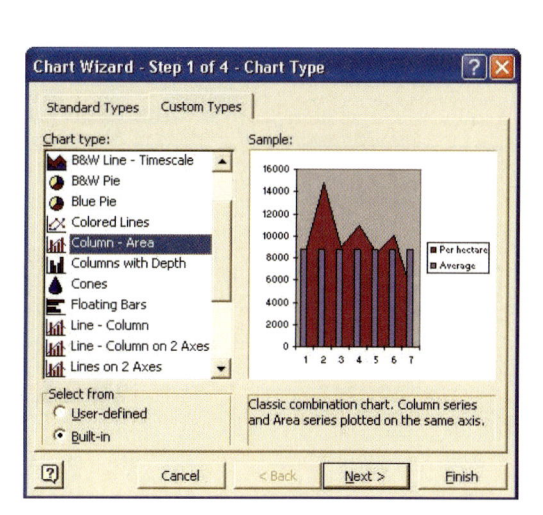

9. Graphs and Charts | 225

The chart wizard

You should be familiar with the Chart wizard from New CLAIT. Here we will just look at the major points for each step.

Step 1

Take advantage of the Press and Hold facility to make sure that you have selected the correct data. In the example shown here, the last data series displayed appears out of line with the rest of the data. In this instance the Total figures have been inadvertently included. It is easier at this point to cancel the wizard and start again.

You can also see that by including the column and row labels, the wizard has automatically created data labels and a legend.

Step 2

In Step 2 check the data range and reselect if needed using the Collapse Dialog button.

Don't worry if the legend or data labels do not display properly. They should be correct when the chart is completed.

The data series is usually displayed in columns. Click in Rows to see the data displayed the alternative way. With the data series in columns, the chart emphasises the comparison between centres.

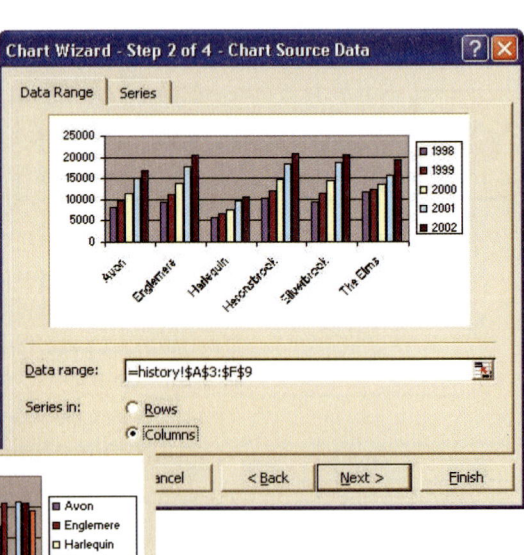

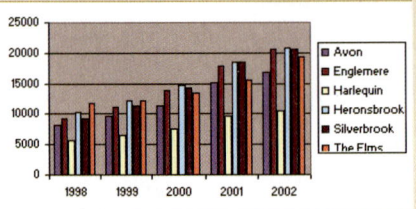

With the data series in rows, the chart emphasises the growth over a period of time.

226 | CLAIT Plus in easy steps

...cont'd

In some exercises you may need to select the Series tab and add or remove a series so that the chart is logical, or displays the data in a meaningful way.

If the Name box is empty, which happens when data labels are not selected, you can use the Collapse Dialog button to minimise the window and select from the spreadsheet. You will also see the legend change from using Series 1, Series 2 etc to the correct names.

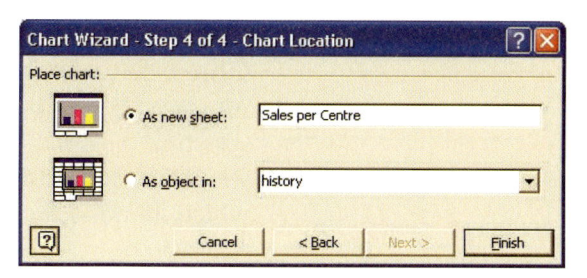

Naming the Chart tab is not a CLAIT Plus requirement, but useful in the working world.

Continue Step 2 by selecting the Series tab. Each Series (column) is listed and for each the source for Name and Values is identified.

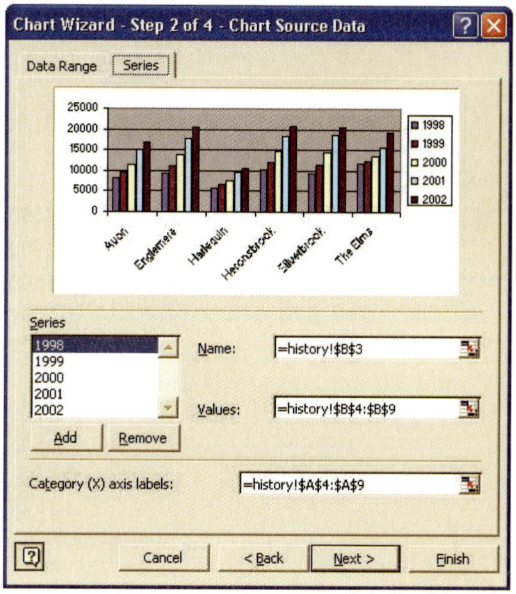

Use the Category (X) axis labels box to add data labels if not already displayed.

Step 3

Use this step to enter the Title, axis labels and to display and position the legend. The scale and grid line settings cannot be specified when using the wizard, but can be set once the chart wizard is completed.

Use the Preview pane to understand the effect of the various options in this step. Select the Data Table tab and tick the box if you need to display the supporting data as part of the chart.

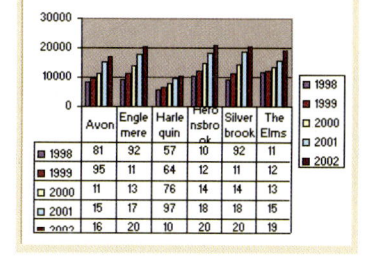

Step 4

In the final stage you should select to save the chart as a separate sheet, and take the opportunity to supply a meaningful name. The supplied name will appear on the chart tab at the bottom of the spreadsheet.

9. Graphs and Charts | 227

Chart elements

HOT TIP: To see the name of each part of the chart appear when you move the mouse over it, select Tools, Options and the Chart tab and tick the box to show Chart Tips.

BEWARE: In this example the Y axis is displayed vertically and the X axis horizontally. The Y axis is the Value axis – it displays the quantity or amount. In some chart types the X and Y axes are transposed.

HOT TIP: Click the title once to select, click again to edit the text. In a column or bar chart, click a column to select the data series, click again to select the individual point. In a line graph, click the line to select the line, click again to select that segment.

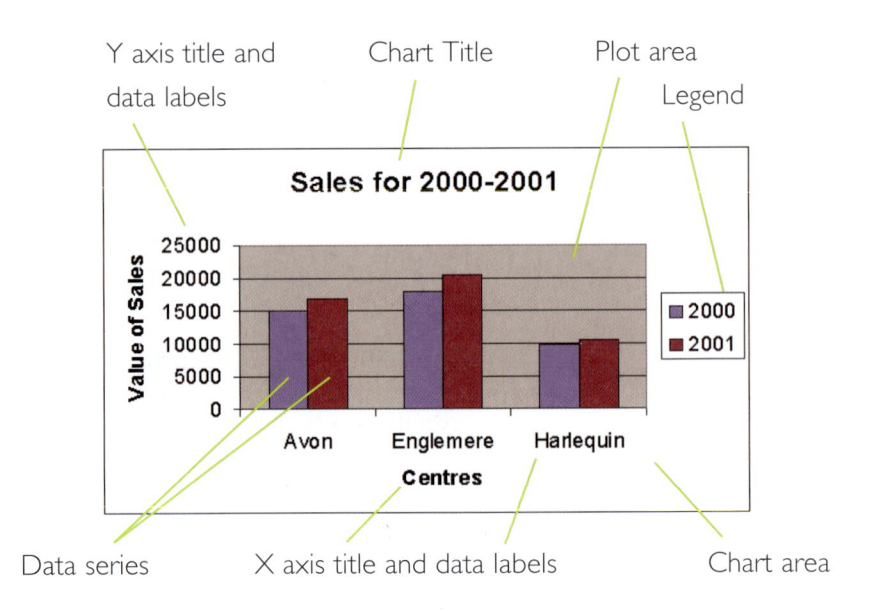

Labels on the chart: Y axis title and data labels · Chart Title · Plot area · Legend · Data series · X axis title and data labels · Chart area

Chart shows "Sales for 2000-2001" with Value of Sales on Y axis (0 to 25000) and Centres on X axis (Avon, Englemere, Harlequin) for years 2000 and 2001.

Each part of the chart is treated as a separate entity. As you move the mouse over the chart you will see the name of each part. To change the display attributes of an element, such as font, fill colour and position:

1. Select the item. For the Title or Legend you will see the framing handles. You can then move, resize or delete it. To select other elements such as an axis, the mouse tool tip should display the name of the object you are selecting

2. With the object selected, right click to open the Context menu and choose the appropriate option.

Chart properties

All chart properties and data can be changed by selecting the Chart menu entry that is available when the chart is displayed. Depending on which item is selected, these chart properties may also be available on the Context menu.

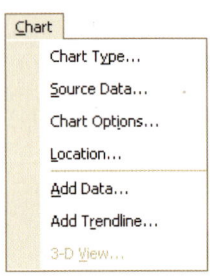

Chart menu options: Chart Type..., Source Data..., Chart Options..., Location..., Add Data..., Add Trendline..., 3-D View...

Chart toolbar

The Chart toolbar provides swift access to many of the required functions. It may be displayed as part of the Standard or Formatting toolbars, or it can be made to float over the chart area.

The angled text, legend, and data table icons, are toggle switches.

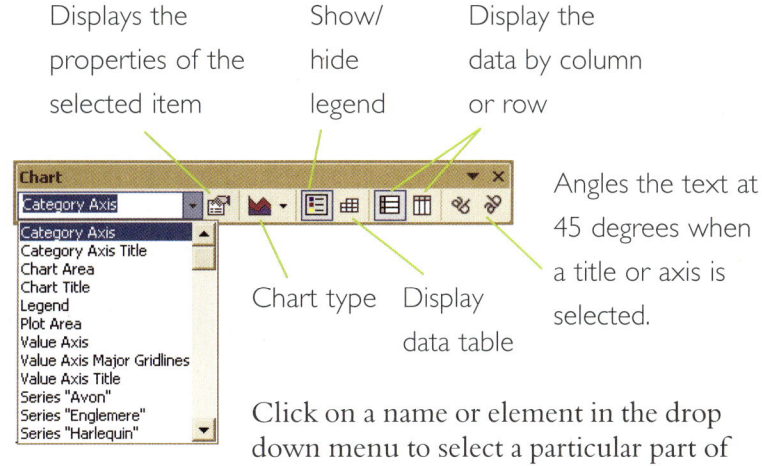

Displays the properties of the selected item

Show/ hide legend

Display the data by column or row

Angles the text at 45 degrees when a title or axis is selected.

Chart type

Display data table

Click on a name or element in the drop down menu to select a particular part of the chart or a data series. The Properties window will automatically display those of the selected item.

House Style

The CLAIT Plus exercise includes a House Style sheet, specifying font style and attributes for the various text areas of the chart.

Unfortunately the Format Painter does not work on text in the chart.

1. Each of the text areas, such as titles, axes titles and axes labels, has to be formatted separately See page 231 for further details.

2. Check the effect of the font and alignment changes. In some instances Excel does not always display all the text., although this problem is more evident in older releases of Excel.

3. Add your name and centre number in the header or footer of all the charts. Even if the charts are created in the same spreadsheet, you will need to specify each chart individually.

Bar/column chart

Before you start each task in the exercise, you should look carefully at the data you have been given for the chart so that you can be sure to select the correct range(s) and include only the required details.

This chart is used to compare values between sets of data. In the exercise it compares sales between different centres. For CLAIT Plus, unless a format is specifically required, the bar and column chart are equally acceptable. To format the chart when created:

This page and the next follow formatting the chart as required in Task 1 in the downloadable exercises for Unit 9. You can also use it as a guide to other CLAIT Plus exercises.

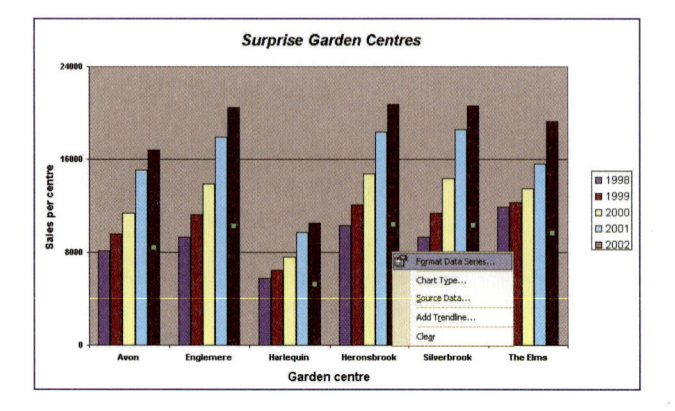

1   Left click on one of the darker colours to select the series. Each column in the series will display an indicator.

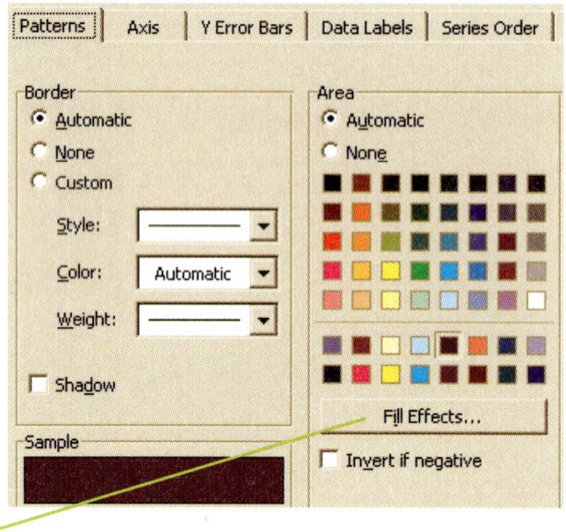

The display colours for some columns would be indistinguishable if a monochrome printer is used.

2   Right click and select Format Data Series.

3   Select Fill Effects and the Pattern tab to fill the series with a more obviously different effect.

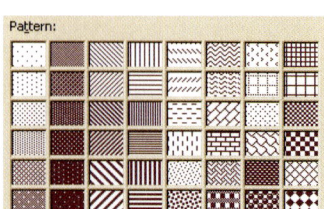

4   To change the background plot area to white, left click the plot area to select it, right click and select Format Plot Area.

Format axes

The X axis

HOT TIP: *When you select an axis make sure that only the axis and not the entire plot area is displaying the selection handles.*

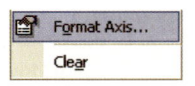

1. Left click the axis to select it and right click to display the Context menu. Select Format Axis.

HOT TIP: *The axis title and axis itself are formatted separately.*

2. Choose the Font tab to set font size, style and attributes. In this window you can also choose superscript or subscript to create a special text effect.

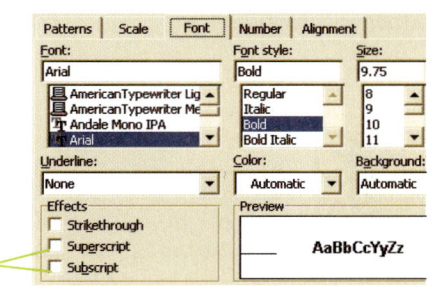

DON'T FORGET: *The X axis is the Category axis; the Y axis is the Value axis.*

3. The Number tab enables you to control the display of decimals, negative numbers, currency and dates.

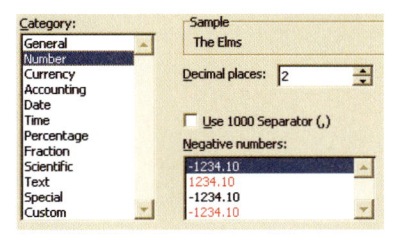

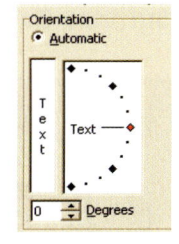

4. Choose Alignment to set the text angle. You can drag the line, set a specific number of plus or minus degrees or select the vertical option.

The Y axis

BEWARE: *The Major unit must be a factor of the difference between the Maximum and Minimum. For example: Minimum = 0, Maximum = 150. Major unit must be 10, 30 or 50. If it isn't, Excel will adjust the maximum and minimum numbers displayed.*

1. The scale on the Y axis is automatically generated with the chart. Deselect Auto and set the required maximum, minimum and major unit.

2. All the other options apply as shown above for the X axis.

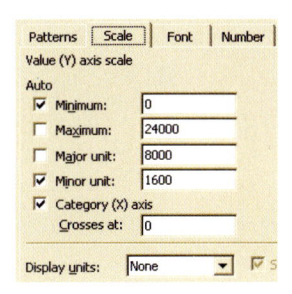

9. Graphs and Charts | 231

Stacked vertical bar

The Stacked Column chart is a percent based comparative chart. However, in OCR exercises you are usually asked to use a comparative bar/column chart. See page 225 for syllabus requirements.

A Stacked Column chart compares the percentage each value contributes to the total.

1 Select the data and start the Chart wizard. Select the Stacked Column sub-type and click Next.

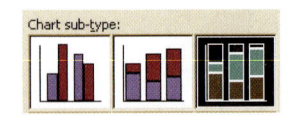

Here we look at some of the steps required to complete Task 2 of the exercise for Unit 9.

2 By default the selected data is displayed in Columns, (category: Centre). For the exercise the displayed category grouping should be by Year, or Row.

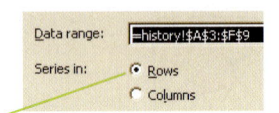

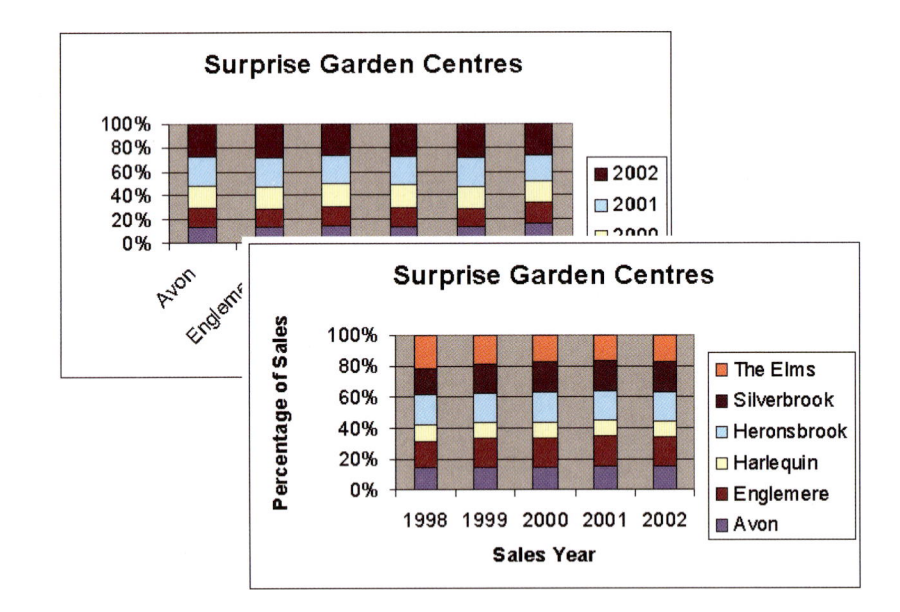

3 Complete the rest of the details using the wizard and check the final chart. Using the Stacked Column chart, the Y axis should automatically show percentages.

4 Adjust the Fill effects using the method shown on page 230.

232 | CLAIT Plus in easy steps

XY scatter

HOT TIP — *Since the data is evenly spaced, year by year, you could have used a Line graph.*

There is a second example of an XY Scatter graph on page 236.

DON'T FORGET — *These two pages follow Task 3 of the exercise for Unit 9.*

HOT TIP — *Although there is no data for 2003, it can be included to allow for a projection.*

However, you should adhere to the specific requirements of the exercise.

HOT TIP — *You could have selected the cell ranges before starting the wizard, even though they are non-consecutive. Select the first range of cells, then press Ctrl and select the second range.*

The XY Scatter graph shows the distribution of one value in relation to a second value, in this example sales over time periods.

1 Select the data as specified in the exercise and start the Chart wizard. Choose the XY Scatter and sub-type that has a line joining the points.

2 In Step 2 of the wizard select the Series tab. The Preview pane currently shows on the X axis the default values generated by Excel. Click the Collapse dialog button to select the X axis values (the years 1998 -2003).

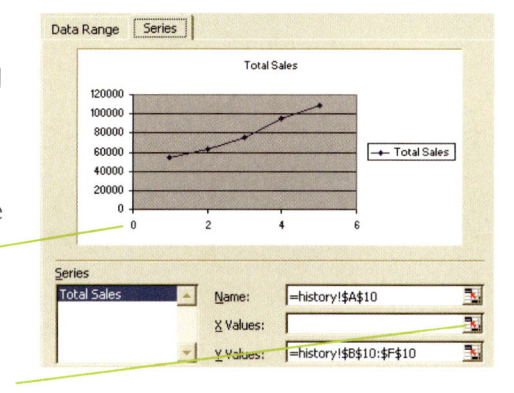

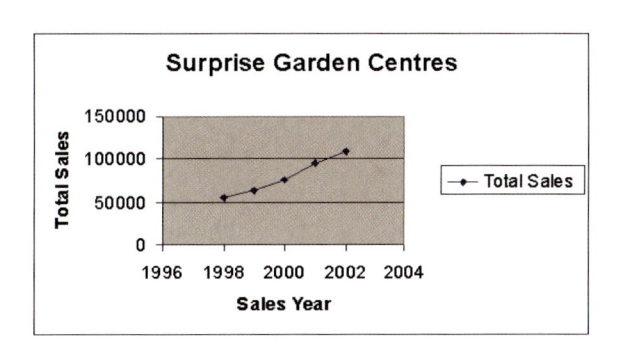

3 Finish the wizard, adding the required details. Check the X axis to ensure that it displays each Year label. To correct if necessary, right click the axis, select the Scale tab and adjust the Major Unit from 2 to 1.

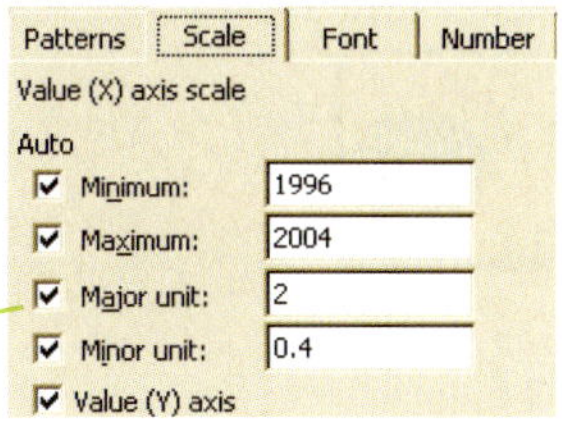

9. Graphs and Charts | 233

Trend line

Trend lines can be added to most types of charts.

1. With the chart selected or the active sheet, click on Chart on the Menu, and Add Trendline.

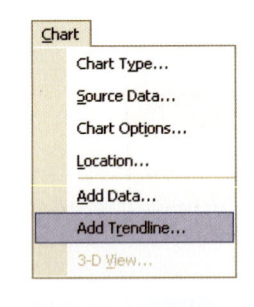

2. Select Linear from the Type options and click OK.

3. To amend the trendline style, colour and weight, select the line, right click and select Format Trendline.

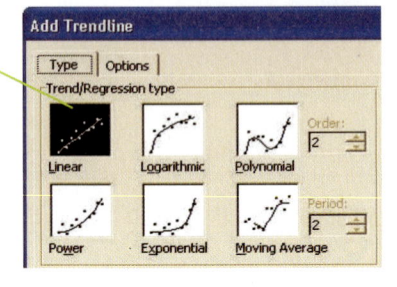

The Trendline equation

1. With the Trendline selected, right click and use Format Trendline. Choose the Options tab and tick to Display equation on chart.

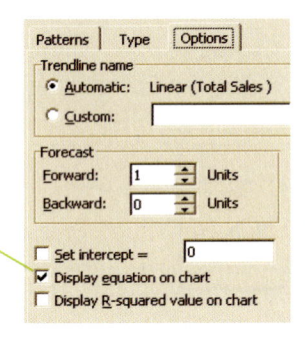

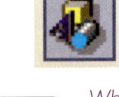

When you want to add comments or other information to a chart, use the standard Office Drawing Tools to create a text box.

2. The equation is contained in a Text frame which can be moved and modified.

Chart annotations

To insert a symbol into an axis title, first insert it into the spreadsheet, then copy and paste it into the destination.

1. Create a text box and type in the text. The font can be formatted in the usual way. You can Insert Symbols if necessary.

2. Right click the text box frame and choose Frame Properties to add a border or fill.

Exploded pie

This page describes some of the steps required to complete Task 4 of the exercise for Unit 9.

The Exploded Pie chart shows the contribution of each part to the whole, whilst emphasising the individual values. In the sample exercise the chart is used to show share of Sales for a year, with particular emphasis on one centre.

1. Create the chart following the wizard. In Step 1 select an Exploded Pie sub-type. In Step 3 add the title and data labels.

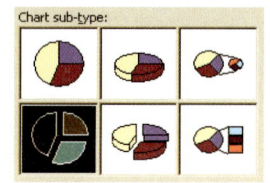

2. Single click the chart to see the selection handles. Click the particular segment once more to select just that segment. Drag it away from the rest of the chart to add further emphasis.

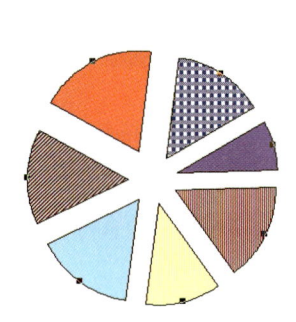

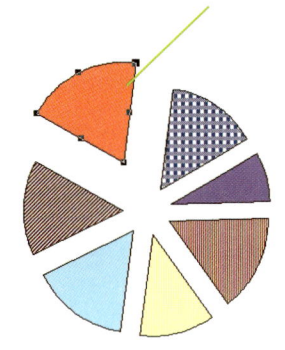

To create a subtitle enter the whole of the title text into the Title box as you create the chart. Once the chart is completed, edit the title pressing Enter to separate title and subtitle text. They can now be formatted individually.

3. To rotate the pie chart to a specific angle, select the whole pie and right click. From the Context menu choose Format Data Series and the Options tab.

4. Use the up and down arrows to set the angle of the first slice to the required number of degrees and view the effect in the Preview Pane.

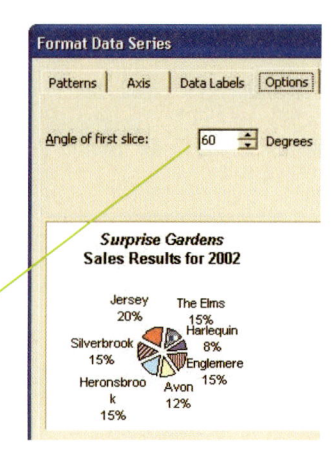

9. Graphs and Charts | 235

XY scatter showing relationship

The data for this chart is in Task 5 of the exercise for Unit 9.

This scatter graph is used to plot Centre Sales against Centre Area to see if there is an obvious relationship.

1. Use the wizard to create the chart, selecting a scatter graph that joins the points with a line. In Step 2 select the Series tab.

Excel has plotted the Area data where it should be used as labels. Whenever you have numbers to be used as labels, such as years and measurements, always check to make sure they have not been plotted as a second series.

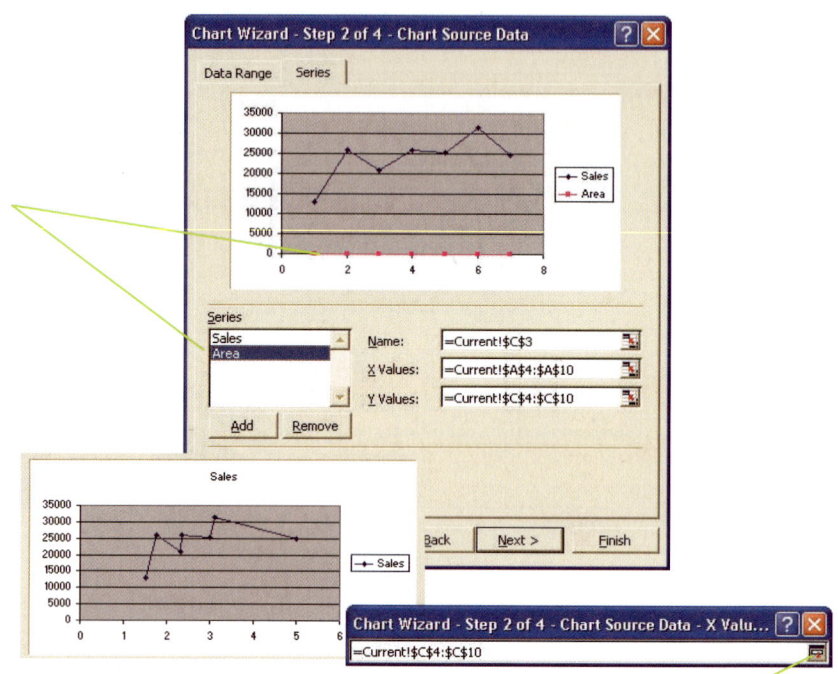

If you select the Options tab, in the Format Data Series window, you can set each marker point to a different colour. Excel will then display a legend identifying the value of each point.

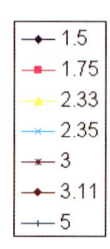

2. Remove the Area Series and use the Collapse Dialog button to reselect the Area data as the X values.

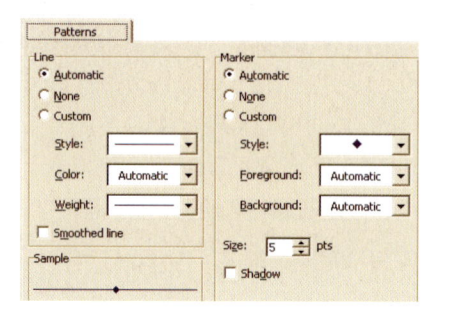

3. With the chart finished select the data line, right click and choose Format Data Series to set the line and marker format.

Line column

The Line column chart is listed on the Custom Type tab.

The Line Column chart is an example of a combination chart. These use two or more chart types to display data. In this example, both the line and the column series are plotted on the same axis. This style of chart is used to emphasise that the chart is displaying different kinds of information.

You can change one of the data series to use a different display format, for example from a line to an area or from columns to a line, without having to start again. Click a data series and choose a new chart type.

The data to create this chart is taken from Task 6 of the Unit 9 exercise.

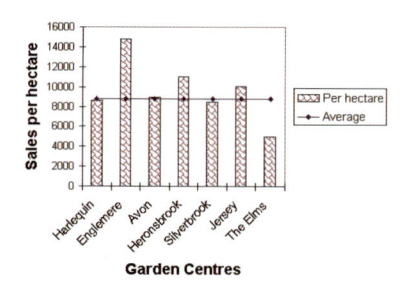

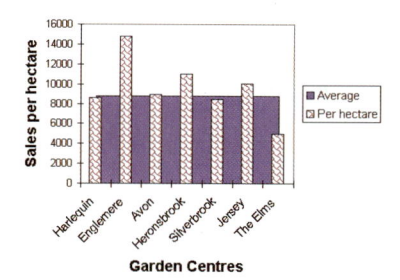

When the range of values for a different data series varies greatly, you can plot the data on a secondary (y) axis.

The Stock chart

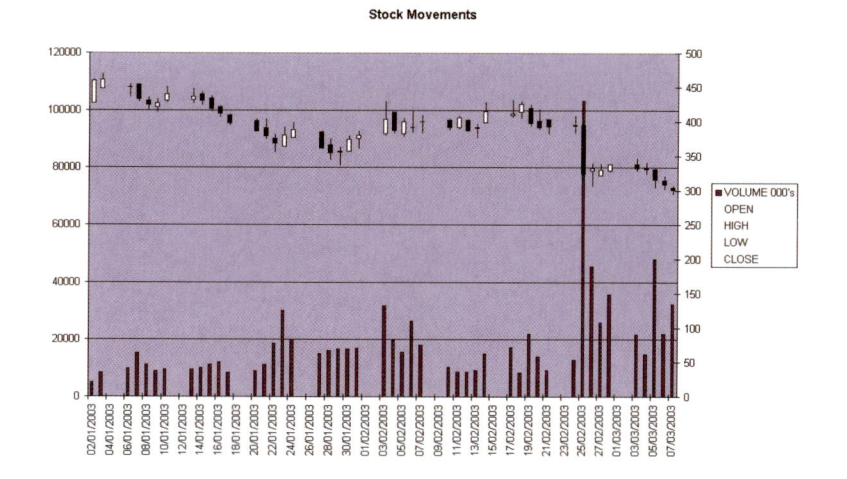

This chart is not included in the CLAIT Plus syllabus.

The Stock Market chart is another example of a combination chart, using a variety of symbols to illustrate the data. This example shows combinations of High and Low, Open and Close Prices vs Volume.

9. Graphs and Charts | 237

Update the data

> **Don't forget:** You do not need to add or amend data for the CLAIT Plus charting exercises. However, in the working environment you are almost certain to need to know how to update any chart.

1. When you amend the underlying spreadsheet data, the chart will automatically adjust to show the new figures, changing the axes scales to accommodate. This does not apply to the axes titles.

2. You can link the main chart title to a spreadsheet cell. As you create the chart put a holding value in the chart Title box, for example an X. When the chart is finished, click in the chart title box to select it and type = in the formula bar. Click the cell that you want and press Enter. The chart title will be now be updated if you make any changes to that cell.

> **Hot tip:** In some instances you could include empty cells in your data area selection, in anticipation. When you add the new data the chart will once again be immediately updated.

3. To extend the chart, select Chart, Add Data. Use the Collapse Dialog button to hide the window and navigate to the spreadsheet. Select the cell(s), using Ctrl+click for non-adjacent cells, eg titles and supporting data.

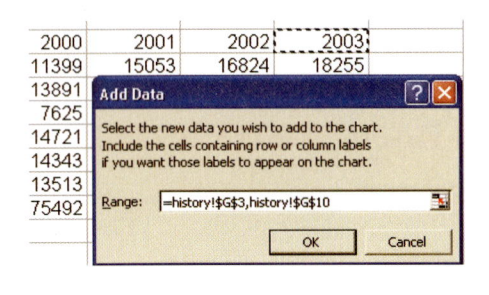

4. You will be offered options in the Paste Special window, but should normally accept the defaults. Click OK for the chart to be updated.

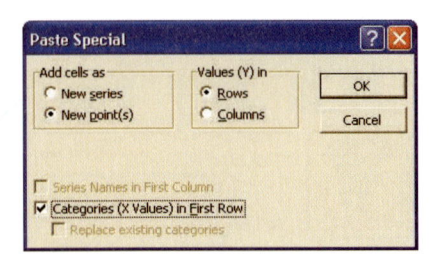

5. To verify that you have correctly selected the cells for any chart, right click the chart and choose Source Data. The Source Data window opens over the spreadsheet with the selected data outlined and the actual address displayed in the Data Range box.

Print

Setting up headers, footers, and page orientation is covered in detail in Unit 2 Spreadsheets on pages 63-65.

1 Select File, Page Setup. Select the Page tab to select between Portrait and Landscape orientation.

2 Choose the Header/Footer tab to enter the required exercise details of name and centre number.

3 Click the Chart tab to view the chart options.

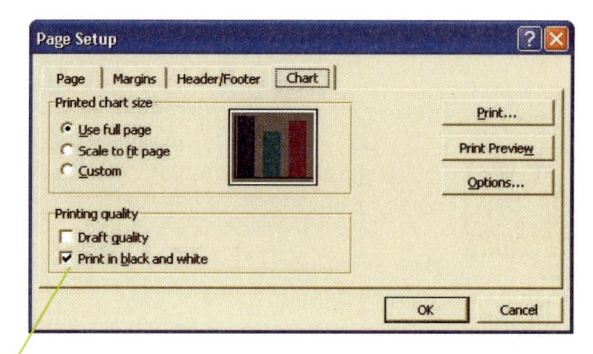

When the chart is created as an object on the spreadsheet, you can print it as part of the spreadsheet. To print it on its own, just click inside it to select it. Check Print Preview before printing.

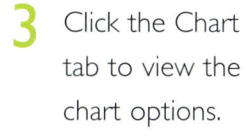

4 If you are using a monochrome printer you can tick the box to print in Black and White. This eliminates having to change each data series individually. Check the effect in Print Preview before proceeding.

Check the printout thoroughly to make sure that the legend clearly identifies each data series or point.

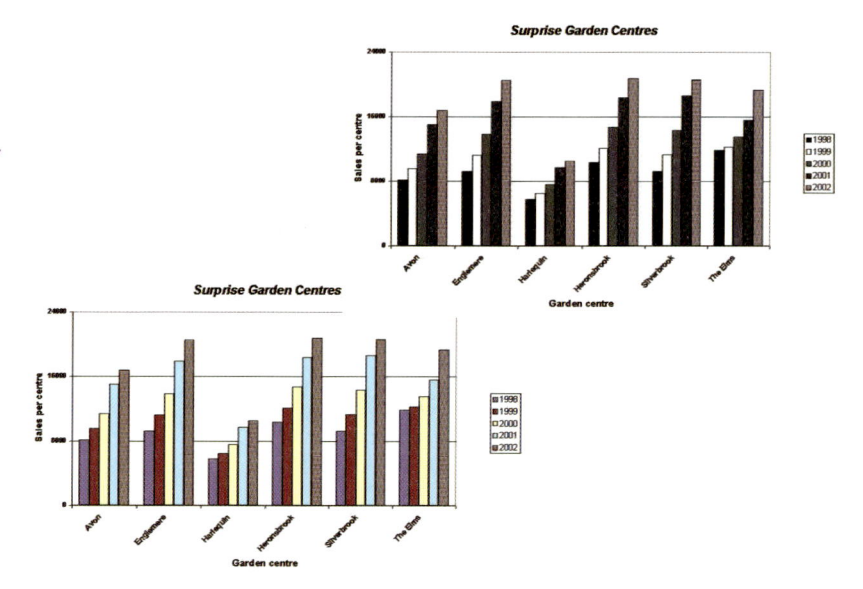

9. Graphs and Charts | 239

Checklist

You are allowed three hours to complete the OCR CLAIT Plus assessment.

When you have completed the exercise, do a final check to ensure that you meet the exercise requirements. Make sure you have:

- created the correct number and styles of chart
- selected the correct data to create the chart
- used the required titles and axis titles
- used the correct labels and scales
- added required details such as trendlines, equations and annotations
- emphasised one segment of the pie chart
- formatted each title, axis title, data labels correctly
- included your name, Centre number and date on all prints
- produced the required number of prints using the correct page orientation
- proofread your prints

Check your answers against those in the Worked Copy folder for this unit.

Marking

You are not allowed any critical errors. The following are considered critical errors:

- failure to select the correct data
- failure to select the specified chart type
- missing or incorrect value on any chart of any type
- unusable legend or labels (ie not distinguishable)
- axis titles missing so that you cannot infer information

Check with your tutor for a full explanation of critical and assessment errors.

CLAIT Plus Solutions

This section discusses the Solutions based units, based on locally devised practical units. It looks at the main differences between these units and the Assignment based units, and reviews topics that will be of interest if you are considering the Solutions route.

Covers

Projects for Solutions | 242

Spreadsheet Solutions | 243

Database Solutions | 245

Desktop Publishing Solutions | 248

Presentation Graphics Solutions | 251

Digital Imaging Solutions | 253

Web Animation Solutions | 256

Web Page Solutions | 260

Units Ten to Sixteen

Projects for Solutions

In the Solutions units, you develop your own solution to meet a specified scenario which could be made up, or based on a real situation.

Units One to Nine are conventional courses which are assessed by final examinations, in the form of assignments set by OCR. To cater for those already in employment and with existing IT skills and experience, CLAIT Plus also offers the Solutions units, which are individual, locally devised, practical projects. There are seven such units, covering the following areas:

- **Spreadsheets**
- **Databases**
- **Desktop Publishing**
- **Presentation Graphics**
- **Digital Imaging**
- **Web Animation**
- **Web Pages**

You may choose up to three Solutions units to count towards your CLAIT Plus qualification. You will of course also require the mandatory Unit One, Create, Manage and Integrate Files. Note that you cannot include more than one unit in the same application area towards your qualification. See page 278 for a table showing the combinations that are allowed.

The Solutions approach allows you to devise a project, based on your own personal or employment experience.

Project tasks

For each solutions unit that you undertake, you'll be required to complete one assessment task that addresses all of the objectives of the unit, in a logical and realistic way. The task and the subtasks that it includes should be practical and should have a clear purpose. Your training centre tutor may suggest outlines of suitable projects, or you may devise your own, based on your personal or employment experience. Review your project proposal with your tutor, to make certain that the task you have defined does satisfy the requirements of the unit, and shows you have knowledge and understanding of the application area.

The work you submit for assessment will not be returned to the centre. If the work does not achieve a Pass, you may re-take the assessment using a different assignment task.

Checklists

The OCR evidence checklist for each solution unit provides concise details of all the objectives. You complete the appropriate checklist and submit it, along with the various printouts and screen prints required, to confirm that your results meet the requirements. See page 279 for an example checklist.

Spreadsheet Solutions

Review contents of Unit Two, Spreadsheets as preparation for this unit. You may also find it useful to practice the exercises for that unit.

Unit Ten overview

This unit measures your skill in using spreadsheets to meet the requirements of a specific task. It includes the objectives and knowledge requirements from Unit Two, Spreadsheets, but it does set some additional objectives, and it requires you to build a larger spreadsheet. This makes the unit more demanding, but it has the advantage that you are working with a situation and with data that you have selected or devised for yourself.

This is not a comprehensive list, see the syllabus and Checklist for the full list of requirements.

Minimum requirements

You will be required to create *two* spreadsheets, taking into account the specified objectives, including:

- The main spreadsheet must have a minimum of *200* cells actually being used

- You must include at least *three* different cell references, and data that is obtained by linking from a second spreadsheet

The format and layout of your second spreadsheet will not be marked.

- Select and use at least *three* suitable cell content formats

- Use at least *two* range functions that produce correct results

- Use at least *four* different display features

- Merge at least *two* cells, include a data sort

This is just a simple, abbreviated example of the type of project you could undertake.

- Make *two* different changes to the existing data on the spreadsheet. You should not add cells

Making changes

Create a spreradsheet that shows one situation, and then adjust some data values, to show the effect of changes. For example:

This spreadsheet calculation shows the total amount paid and the completion date, for a business loan with a specified schedule of repayments.

	A	B
1	Repayment of business loan	
2	Start date of loan	37987
3	Interest rate per annum	0.07
4	Payments per annum	12
5	Annual payment	1200
6	Initial loan	10000
7	Loan reduced to	0
8	Pay in advance?	TRUE
9	Number of payment required	=NPER(B3/B4,-B5/B4,B6,B7,B8)
10	Total repaid	=B9*B5/B4
11	Completion date	=B9*365/B4+B2

10-16. CLAIT Plus Solutions | 243

...cont'd

You must print the spreadsheet highlighting the changes and effect of the changes. The changes may be highlighted by the use of a highlighter pen or by shading (making sure that the data remains visible). Use Tools, Track Changes to get Excel to identify which cells you change.

1. Set the initial value of the loan, the amount of annual repayments and the terminating loan value (this would usually be zero).

2. Set the repayments to monthly in advance, and the interest rate to 7%, and print the results with this schedule.

3. Change the repayments to annually in arrears, and the interest rate to 8%. Select the data cells that you changed, and use Format, Cells, Patterns to choose a background shade colour.

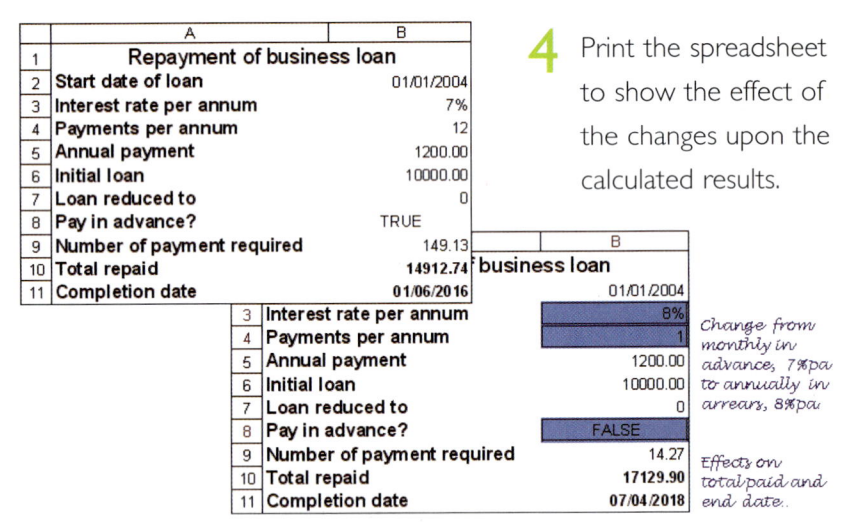

	A	B
1	Repayment of business loan	
2	Start date of loan	01/01/2004
3	Interest rate per annum	7%
4	Payments per annum	12
5	Annual payment	1200.00
6	Initial loan	10000.00
7	Loan reduced to	0
8	Pay in advance?	TRUE
9	Number of payment required	149.13
10	Total repaid	14912.74
11	Completion date	01/06/2016

4. Print the spreadsheet to show the effect of the changes upon the calculated results.

	B
	business loan
	01/01/2004

3	Interest rate per annum	8%
4	Payments per annum	1
5	Annual payment	1200.00
6	Initial loan	10000.00
7	Loan reduced to	0
8	Pay in advance?	FALSE
9	Number of payment required	14.27
10	Total repaid	17129.90
11	Completion date	07/04/2018

Change from monthly in advance, 7%pa to annually in arrears, 8%pa

Effects on total paid and end date.

Evidence

You will be required to complete the spreadsheet checklist identifying where and how the assessment objectives for Spreadsheet Solutions have been met. You must also submit the following printouts

The printouts may be on more than one page.

- Final completed spreadsheet

- Formulae printout (no data must be truncated)

- Linked spreadsheet printout

- Printout highlighting changes and effects

Database Solutions

Review the contents of Unit Three, Databases as preparation for this unit. You will also find it useful to practice the exercises for that unit.

This is not a comprehensive list, see the syllabus and Checklist for the full list of requirements.

For the Date data type, any layout is acceptable, as long as it uses the British day/month format, for example: 01-03-04, 1/3/04, 1 Mar 2004.

Unit Eleven overview

This unit assess your capabilities in creating a database to meet the needs of a specific task, and producing reports based on complex search criteria. It includes the objectives and knowledge requirements from Unit Three, Databases, but incorporates additional objectives, and sets targets for the types and quantities of data fields that must be included.

Minimum requirements

You must create a database that has:

- A minimum of *six* fields
- *Four* different data types, including Date.
- A minimum of *forty* records input.
- A query that uses at least *two* logical operators
- A query with at least *two* range operators.

Use the Analyze wizard

Access will analyse your tables and help you make them more efficient, eg by replacing repeated entries with lookup tables.

The process of analysing the tables to remove redundancies is known as Normalisation. It means that there will be only one place where you have to update information, even though that information is referenced in many records throughout the database. Whilst this process is not required in the Database Solutions, it is used in the MOS unit and is useful when you are creating your own database.

Open your database and select Tools, Analyze, Table. Follow the Wizard prompts and select your table.

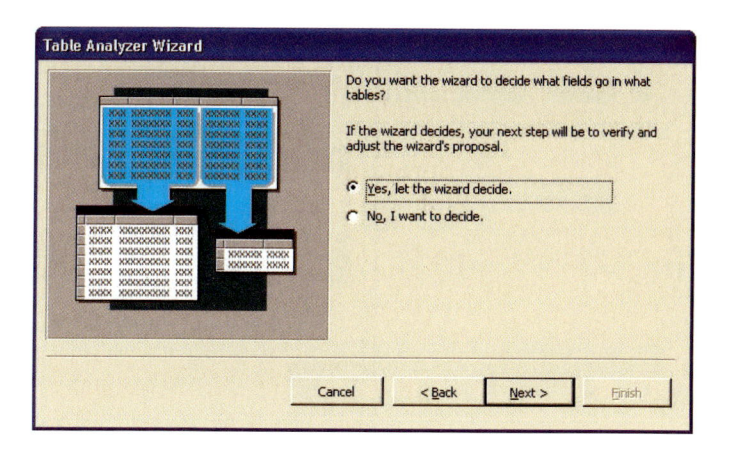

10-16. CLAIT Plus Solutions

...cont'd

2. Let the Wizard decide which fields contain repeated data that should go into a separate table.

3. In the Plants table for example, the Wizard identifies the Colour, Type and Season fields as having repeated entries.

> **Hot Tip:** The Wizard offers to create a separate table for each, and generate a new main table containing references to the other tables. It will create unique IDs for the new tables, but if you know that they already contain unique values, as in the example, this will not be required.

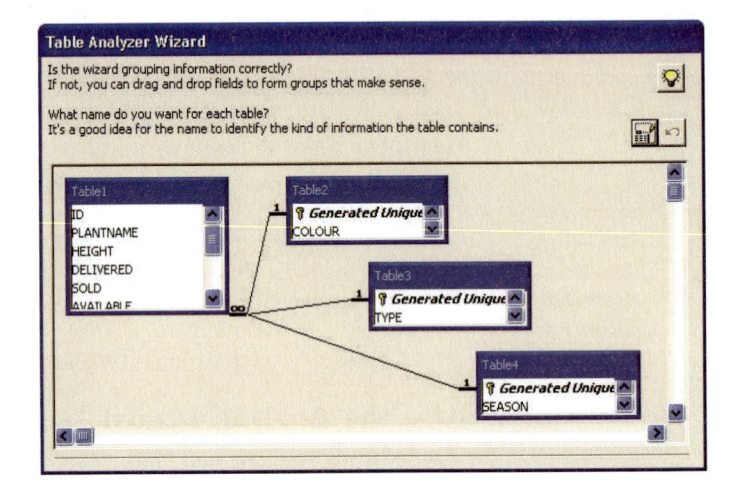

4. Give the tables more meaningful names, and set the fields in the new tables as unique identifiers.

> **Hot Tip:** Double click the title bar on each table in turn, and you'll be able to specify new names for them.

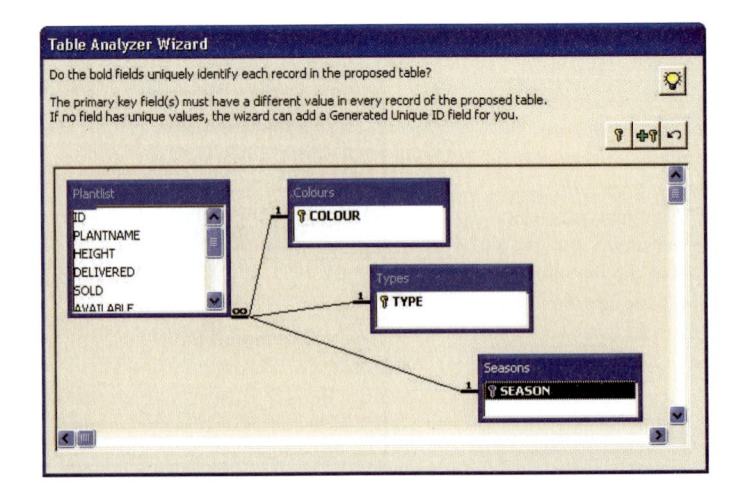

...cont'd

Hot Tip: *The Wizard will generate a query with the same name as your original table. This is helpful if you have already created reports or queries that rely on the old structure.*

5. The Wizard adds the new tables to your database, with the values extracted from the original table.

6. When you add new records to the database, instead of typing an entry, click the down arrow and select one of the existing entries from the lookup tables.

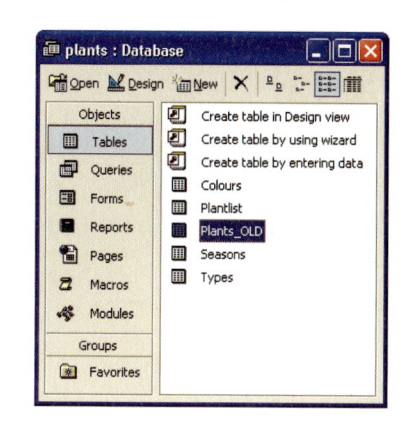

Don't Forget: *If you require new values for the lookup table, for example a new colour or new plant type, open the lookup table and add it there. Then you can select it whenever the new value is required.*

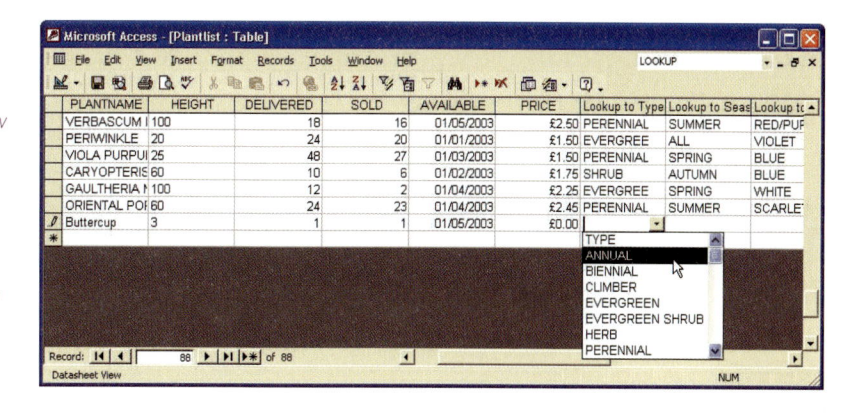

Don't Forget: *One of the reports must include headers and footers. You must also show records/fields sorted in a different order. Remember that all data must be shown in full.*

Evidence

You will be required to complete the checklist identifying where and how the assessment objectives for Database Solutions have been met. You must also submit printouts showing the following:

- A data entry form
- Field types used
- Results of a calculated field
- Results of queries using: 1) logical criteria
  2) range criteria
  3) combined criteria

Desktop Publishing Solutions

Review the contents of Unit Four, Desktop Publishing as preparation for this unit, using its exercises for practice.

This is not a comprehensive list, see the syllabus and Checklist for the full list of requirements.

The styles you use must match the style sheet that you specify for your project. The printout of the publication may be on more than one page.

Your work will be penalised if you type the text straight into the document or there is no evidence of you having imported a text file. If there is no text imported it is a critical error.

Unit Twelve overview:

This unit measures your skill in using Desktop Publishing software to meet the requirements of a specific task by creating a publication which is consistent in style and layout. You must demonstrate a range of Desktop Publishing skills, and the ability to complete a project described in a design brief.

Minimum requirements

You must complete a style sheet and a publication that includes imported text and images that match the style sheet. Each assessment objective must be demonstrated in full at least once, and you must ensure that you have:

- A Master page template and style sheet
- Headers/footers containing at least *two* automatic fields
- Publication with a minimum of *two* pages
- The publication must contain dropped capitals, used appropriately
- Applied at least *three* styles to text
- At least *twenty* words imported
- Image or ClipArt item imported
- A table with at least *three* columns

Irregular text wrap

1 Select the picture and click the Text Wrapping button on the Picture toolbar.

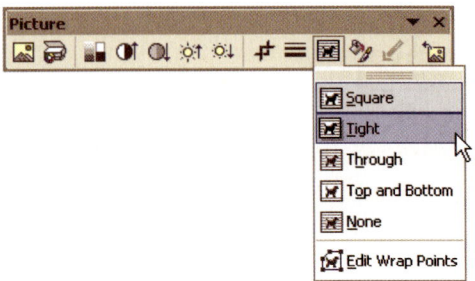

2 Choose the wrapping style Tight.

248 | CLAIT Plus in easy steps

...cont'd

3 To see the details of the irregular outline around the image, click the Text button again, and select Edit Wrap Points.

The text in a table cannot be wrapped around a picture.

> The Christmas tree is one of the most popular and cherished Christmas customs. Each year, many millions of live trees are purchased and decorated. But what is their origin? The first record of an evergreen tree being used and decorated for Christmas is 1521 in the German region of Alsace. The Christmas tree was first introduced into France in 1837 when Princess Helen of Mecklenburg brought it to Paris after her marriage to the Duke of Orléans. The Christmas tree made its royal debut in England when Prince Albert of Saxony, the husband of Queen Victoria, set up a tree in Windsor Castle in 1841. After this it steadily grew in popularity, though in 1850 Charles Dickens was still referring to it as a "new German toy."

Using Tight Wrap may have some unexpected effects on the text surrounding the image, as Publisher tries to fit in all the words. You may have unexpected spacing, wide gaps and awkward hyphenation. Make small adjustments to the positions of the wrap points, to minimise the impact.

4 Position the mouse pointer over the wrap point that you want to move, until the Adjust pointer appears. Drag the wrap point to change the outline of the picture.

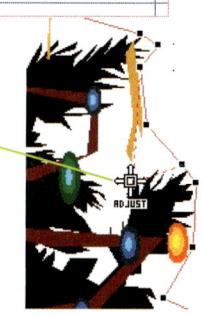

Pack and Go is not required by DTP Solutions. However, it does extend knowledge of Commercial Printing requirements covered in Unit 4.

Pack and Go

To prepare your publication for printing by a commercial printing service, use the Pack and Go Wizard.

1 Select File, Pack and Go then click Take to a Commercial Printing Service.

10-16. CLAIT Plus Solutions | 249

...cont'd

The wizard will span large publications across a number of removable disks, if required.

2 Specify the target drive, when prompted. The default is the A: floppy drive, but for larger publications you might need a ZIP disk or CD-R (writable CD).

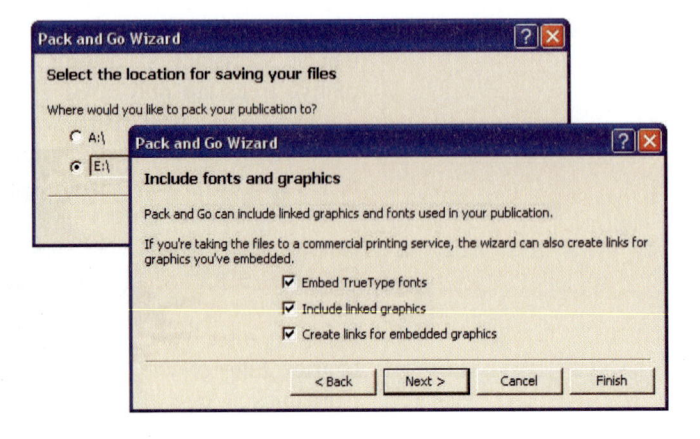

Embedding and linking ensures that your printing service will have the graphics and typefaces you use in your publication.

The wizard will list any fonts that it can't embed and report any problems with linked graphics, so you can correct the errors and re-pack the files.

3 Select to embed TrueType fonts, Include linked graphics and create links for embedded graphics.

4 Click Finish and the publication files are copied to the drive as packed01.puz. Unpack.exe is also added, to unpack the files on arrival at the printers.

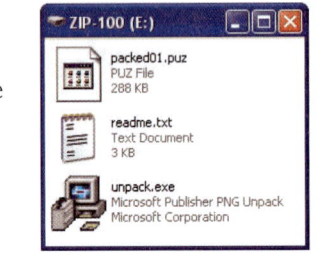

Select Tools, Commercial Printing Tools, Colour Printing to specify that you want process colours or spot colour prints. See page 119-121 in Unit 4 for more details.

The wizard offers you the option to produce a composite print or to create colour separations to send to the printing service.

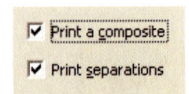

Evidence

When you have completed your project, you will be required to complete the checklist identifying where and how the assessment objectives for Desktop Publishing Solutions have been met. You must also submit printout showing:

- A copy of the publication. A composite print should suffice.

Presentation Graphics Solutions

Review the contents of Unit Five, Presentation Graphics as preparation for this unit, and use the exercises from that unit as practice.

Unit Thirteen overview:

This unit measures your skill in creating a presentation to meet the requirements of a specific task. It includes the objectives and knowledge requirements from Unit Five, Presentation Graphics, and extends those objectives and requires you to build a presentation of reasonable size. It helps that you will be dealing with a topic that you have selected or devised for yourself.

Minimum requirements

See the Checklist and syllabus for the full list of requirements.

You will be required to produce a realistic and professional slide show, demonstrating the assessment objectives, making sure that you:

- Create a master slide as a background for all slides
- Apply at least *three* styles
- Produce a minimum of *eight* slides
- Input at least *twenty* words
- Embed a chart
- Embed an organisation chart
- Apply *two* different transition effects
- Apply *two* different build/animation effects
- Create a hyperlink to access hidden slides

Print at least two individual slide presenter notes to include slide and notes sections.

Set slide show timings

Select all the slides that share a particular timing, using Normal or Slide Sorter view, before choosing Slide Transitions, to amend several slides at the same time.

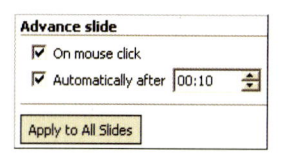

Select Slide Show, Slide Transitions and choose both the On Mouse Click and the Automatically After options, to have the next slide appear automatically after the number of seconds delay specified, or immediately after you click the left mouse button – whichever event comes first.

10-16. CLAIT Plus Solutions | 251

...cont'd

Rehearse timings

To establish the times for the slides in your presentation, let Presentation Manager record them while you practice.

If you know the timing you want for a particular slide, enter it directly in the Slide Time box on the Rehearsal toolbar.

1 Select Slide Show, Rehearse Timings to start the show in the recording mode.

2 Click the Advance button whenever you're ready to go to the next slide.

3 When you reach the end of the slide show, click Yes to accept the timings or No to discard them and start again.

4 Select View, Slide Sorter to see the individual times assigned to each slide. Select an individual slide and use Slide Transitions to adjust any of the timings.

Evidence

You will be required to complete the checklist identifying where and how the assessment objectives for the Presentation Graphics Solutions have been met. You must also submit the following printouts:

It is acceptable for transitions, timings, builds and hyperlink to access hidden slides to be evidenced on the same screen print. This is covered in detail in Unit 5 on pages 143-144.

- Style sheet and Master slide

- All slides (one to a page)

- Audience notes/thumbnails

- Presenter notes

- Screen print(s) showing transitions, builds/effects/timings and hyperlinks to access hidden slides

252 | CLAIT Plus in easy steps

Digital Imaging Solutions

Review the contents of Unit Six, Computer Art as preparation for this unit, and complete the relevant parts of the exercises in this unit (excluding the animation section).

Unit Fourteen overview:

This unit assesses your skills in using photo-editing software and hardware, including scanner and digital camera, to meet the requirements of a specific task. There is no direct equivalent in Units One to Nine, but it shares many of the assessment objectives of Unit Six, Computer Art.

You will gain knowledge and experience in these tasks:

- Acquire images from a scanner and adjust scanning options
- Use a digital camera and transfer images to the computer
- Edit digital images to modify appearance
- Optimise resolution for different outputs
- Convert images between file types
- Save in formats appropriate for the web and print

Minimum requirements

See the Checklist and syllabus for the full list of requirements.

You are required to produce a realistic and professional digital image, that combines text, scanned imagery, and at least one image from a digital camera. The task may be to create a set of images for a web site, or for a printed publication using original photos and scanned material. The task should demonstrate each assessment objective at least once. You should:

You can choose any image to be scanned - it may be coloured or black and white, and you can scan the whole image or part of the image.

- Select scanning mode, resolution and filter options
- Preview and scan an image
- Take at least *two* photographs with a digital camera
- At least *one* photograph must be in colour
- Select flash settings for *each* photograph
- Edit digital images to modify appearance
- Remove unwanted content on at least *one* of the images
- Enter and format text on at least *one* of the images

10-16. CLAIT Plus Solutions | 253

...cont'd

The functions vary depending on the scanner model, but all should offer a method of copying a scanned image to file. Use manual mode so that you can identify and control each step in the process. You may be able to access your scanner directly from the graphics editor or other application, using the Acquire function to copy an image.

Using a scanner

1 Start your scanner software, in manual mode, to copy an image to file.

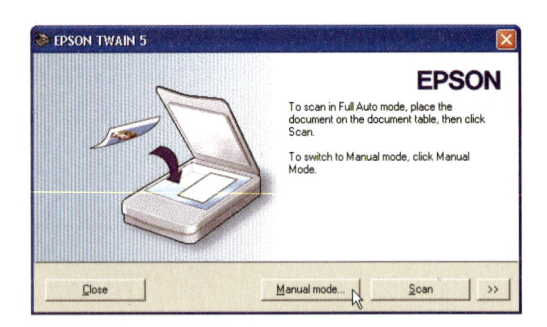

2 Pre-scan the image to select which portion of the image you wish to copy, and apply the settings needed, for example Resolution.

Choose the most suitable file format. The options may be limited, for example it may have uncompressed TIF format only, but you can make your final selection later, using your graphics editor.

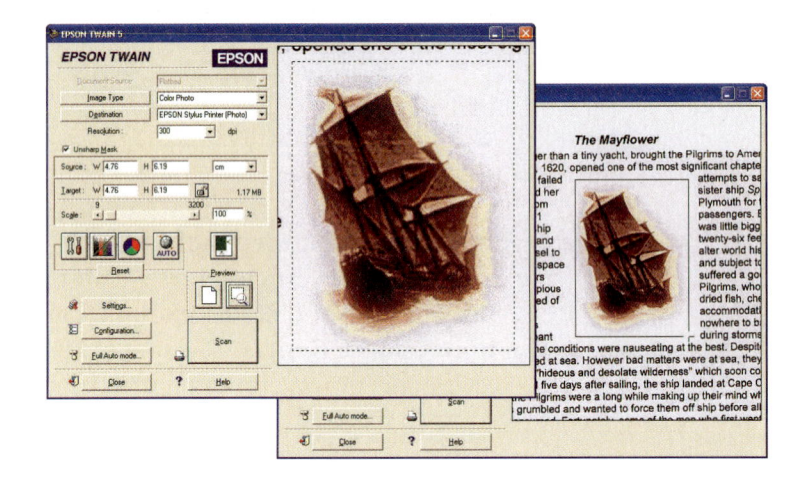

3 Click the Zoom button to Pre-scan the portion of the image that you require and, when you have exactly the right selection, click the Scan button to create the final copy.

Use your graphics or photo editor to make changes and adjustments to the scanned image.

4 Choose the destination folder and the image file type, and save the scanned image to disk.

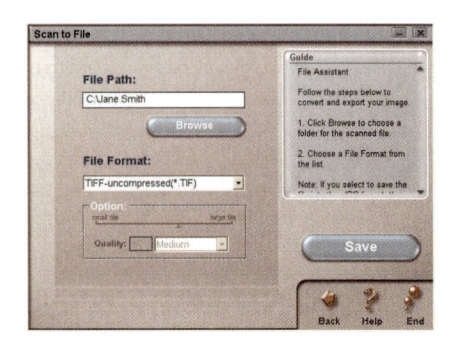

254 | CLAIT Plus in easy steps

...cont'd

> **Hot Tip:** *Some cameras such as Web cameras are directly attached to PCs and use the PC memory and disk to store their pictures, so do not need their own memory.*

Using a digital camera

OCR does not dictate which type of digital camera to use for your photographs, but it would be wise to ensure that it has a flash capability and that it uses some form of memory such as Smart Media or Compact Flash.

You will also need a cable that connects your camera to your PC, or an appropriate memory card reader on your PC.

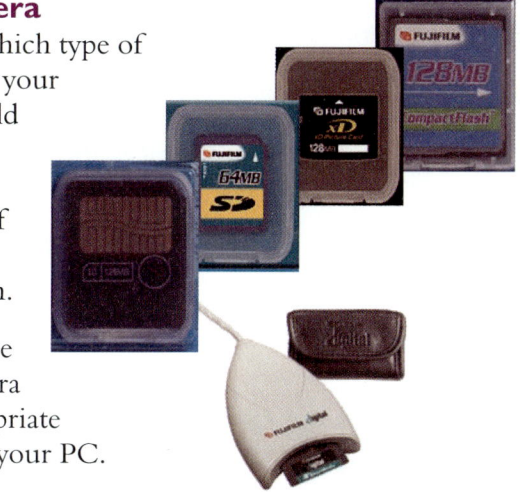

Transferring images

> **Hot Tip:** *Use your photo editor software to crop and rotate the pictures, and to remove unwanted effects such as red eye (see page 158).*

1. If you have a cable, connect the camera to your PC, and read the pictures in using your camera software or photo editor.

2. If you have a memory card reader, insert the memory card from your camera and you will be able to transfer images as if from another disk drive.

Evidence

You will be required to complete the checklist for Digital Imaging Solutions, identifying where and how the assessment objectives have been met. Where necessary, you should include a screen print illustrating the assessment objectives. These can be annotated if the evidence on the screen print is unclear. You must submit the following printouts:

- Original image, plus the specified screen prints
- Two images in different formats
- Image with crop marks

Web Animation Solutions

Review the contents of Unit Six, Computer Art as preparation for this unit, and complete the animation sections of the practice exercises in this unit.

Unit Fifteen overview:

This unit measures your skills in using animation software to develop animations for web media to meet the requirements of a specific task. There is no direct equivalent in Units One to Nine, but it shares many of the assessment objectives of Unit Six, Computer Art.

You will gain knowledge and experience in these tasks:

- Draw and/or paint a graphical image and add text elements to be animated
- Work with library objects, instances and sound
- Create frame-by-frame and tweened animation
- Create and save the animation for the web

Minimum requirements

Your project should be designed to produce a realistic and professional web animation. It should include the following elements:

- Create at least two different graphics shapes
- Set at least two different strokes
- Set at least two different fill effects
- Use at least four different text features
- Select and transform at least one object
- Create frame-by-frame and tweened animation
- Create key frames, and use tweening to animate an object between key frames
- Create an animated sequence frame-by-frame
- Use layers in the creation of the animation
- Create an animation of at least 100 frames
- Create at least 25 key frames in total

This list contains the main tasks, but should not be considered as an exhaustive list of objectives for your web animations project.

Web animation software

OCR doesn't dictate which software you should use for this unit, so you can take advantage of your experience with the product that you use at the office or at home, as long as it is capable of dealing with the minimum requirements for the unit.

One approach is to use a graphics editor such as Photoshop to create frames, and an animator such as Image Ready to assemble the frames into a GIF animation. Browsers have built-in support for this type of animation. However, this method may not satisfy all the unit objectives.

When you visit a web site that requires client software on your PC to support its special features, you are offered the opportunity to download the plug-in if it is not already installed.

Support of more sophisticated animations requires plug-in software to be added to the browsers. This is used to play the animations and movie clips created in a vector graphics based product such as MacroMedia Flash or Adobe LiveMotion.

Macromedia Flash

The Macromedia Flash MX authoring software builds movies that use vector graphics, so they download rapidly and scale properly to fit the viewer's screen size. They may also contain text, bitmap graphics, video and sound. The movies are created as Flash documents (.fla files) and then published as Flash movies (.swf files), so they can be included on web pages, as banners or interactive buttons for example.

Screen prints can be annotated if the evidence on the screen print is unclear.

Visitors to web pages that include Flash movies will be offered the opportunity to download the Flash Player software, if it is not already installed on their system. The Flash movies will then be displayed by the Flash Player on the viewer's PC.

The Flash player, and trial versions of the Flash MX authoring software, can be downloaded from the Macromedia web site at **http://www.macromedia.com/uk/**

...cont'd

Flash animations

Flash MX may be used to create movie strip animations similar to GIF animations such as the one used as the illustration for the second part of Unit Six, Computer Art (see pages 165-169).

Flash components

HOT TIP: You use separate layers for symbols, sounds, actions, frame labels, or frame comments.

BEWARE: Unlike the GIF animations each frame gets the same delay, expressed in frames per second. When the animation plays on the viewer's PC, the actual frame rate is displayed. This may be different from the movie frame rate if the PC cannot keep up with the animation.

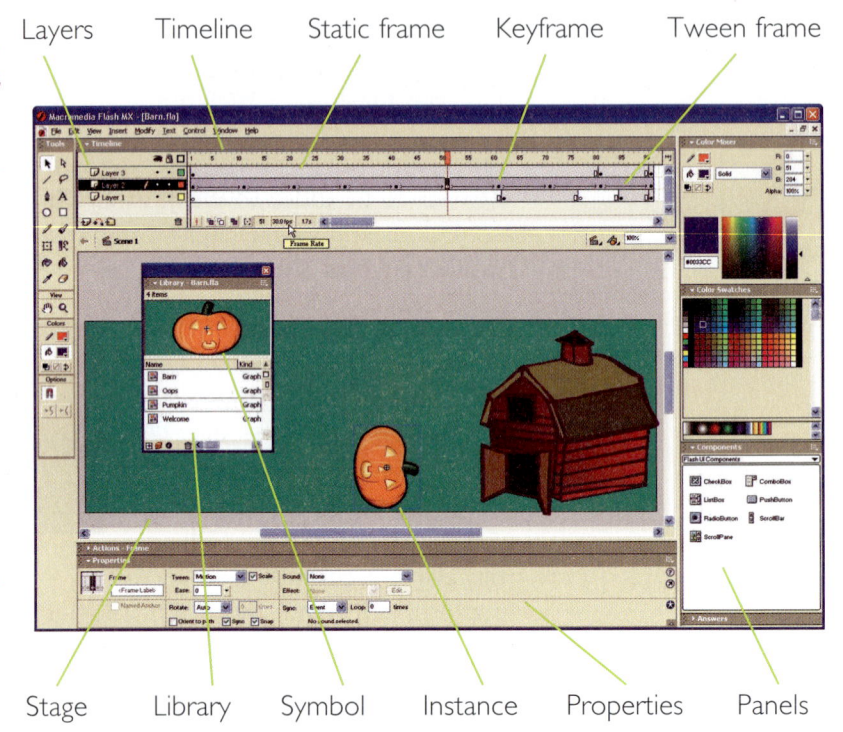

Layers   Timeline   Static frame   Keyframe   Tween frame

Stage   Library   Symbol   Instance   Properties   Panels

Only one copy of each symbol needs to be downloaded. An instance (or copy) of the symbol may be placed on the stage or inside other symbols. The instance may be different in colour, size or function from the original symbol. Editing the symbol updates all of its instances, but applying effects to an instance updates only that copy.

DON'T FORGET: There's also the 400K download for the Flash Player, but this is of course just a one-time requirement.

Using libraries of symbols helps to reduce animation file size and download time. The ten frame GIF animation was 41K. A similar animation in Flash, with ten key frames and 80 tweened frames requires only 16K.

...cont'd

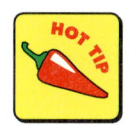

> **HOT TIP**
> There's an enormous variety of ways in which Flash may be used. Visit the Macromedia web site to see examples and find links to other Flash related web sites.

In contrast, the Clock Flash animation, provided as a sample with the application, consists of just one frame, with ten entries in the library and eleven layers. The animation consists of continually updated movements of the hour, minute and second hands.

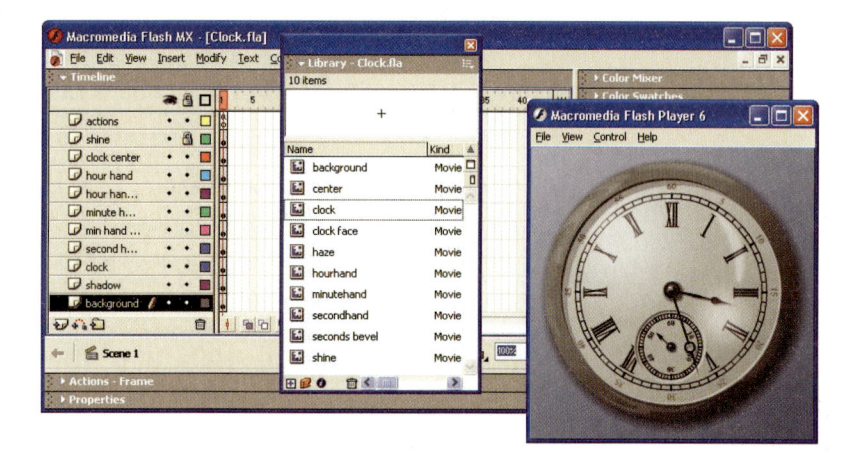

> **HOT TIP**
> In this sample Flash movie, you drag a button around the screen using the mouse, and the readout shows the angle and the XY coordinates.

Flash lets you create interactive movies, in which the viewer uses the keyboard or the mouse to select different parts of the movie, or move objects, or enter information in a form, etc. The ActionScript scripting language is used to specify the actions, operators and objects, and events such as button clicks and key presses, trigger the scripts.

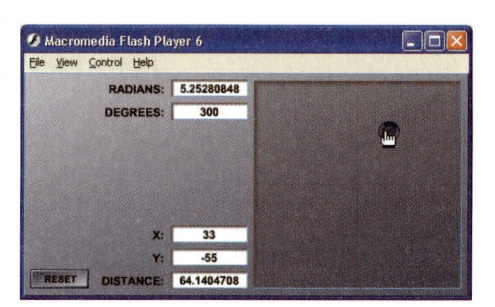

> **DON'T FORGET**
> Screen prints can be annotated if the evidence on the screen print is unclear.

Evidence

You will need to complete the checklist identifying where and how the assessment objectives for Web Animation Solutions have been met. You'll also need to include a screen print illustrating the assessment objectives. You should include the following as a minimum:

- Specified printouts
- Specified screen prints

Web Page Solutions

Review the contents of Unit Seven, Web Page Creation as preparation for this unit, and use the exercises for that unit as practice material. Each printout should be annotated to show where assessment objectives have been met.

Unit Sixteen overview

This unit measures your skill in using software to select, present, manipulate and amend data for the Internet to meet the requirements of a specific task. It includes the objectives and knowledge requirements from Unit Seven, Web Page Creation. You will also need an understanding of common HTML concepts and features, web page formatting and web site structure. A familiarity with raw HTML code is necessary to produce the required evidence.

Minimum requirements

You will be required to complete one assessment task that addresses all of the assessment objectives in a cohesive and realistic way. Your project should be a practical task with a clear purpose, and you should produce a working web site, consisting of four web pages. Make sure that you include the following:

See the Checklist and syllabus for a comprehensive list of requirements.

- A web page house style

- Four web pages

- At least two meta tags to describe page content

- At least two text files and at least five images

- At least three image attributes

- Use text formatting and at least one special character

- Insert table with at least two columns and four rows

- Use at least one example of at least four different input types

- Use at least one image and one piece of text as hyperlinks

- Use at least one hyperlink to an external site

- Use hyperlinks to local pages

All hyperlinks are expected to start with < a href => and close with </a>.

- Use at least one e-mail link

- All links must be relative

- All links must be operative

...cont'd

Hot Tip: The functions that you have available and the way that they operate depend on which particular web page editor you are using.

Software

As usual, OCR allows you to select suitable software. You could for example choose FrontPage, as illustrated in Unit 7, Web Pages Creation, or you might prefer Macromedia Dreamweaver. These products offer broadly similar functions, but you'll find subtle differences in the terminology, and in the ways particular aspects are implemented.

Specifying text sizes

Dreamweaver offers two ways of setting the text size. You can select an absolute HTML size of 1 to 7, or you can specify a relative HTML size of -2 to +4. These adjustments are applied to the default basefont, which is text size 3.

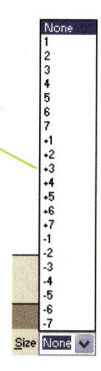

Beware: Relative font size values that are below -2 or above +4 do not cause any further change to text size.

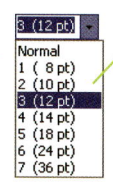

FrontPage also allows you to select absolute HTML sizes 1 to 7, but it does not offer the relative HTML size options.

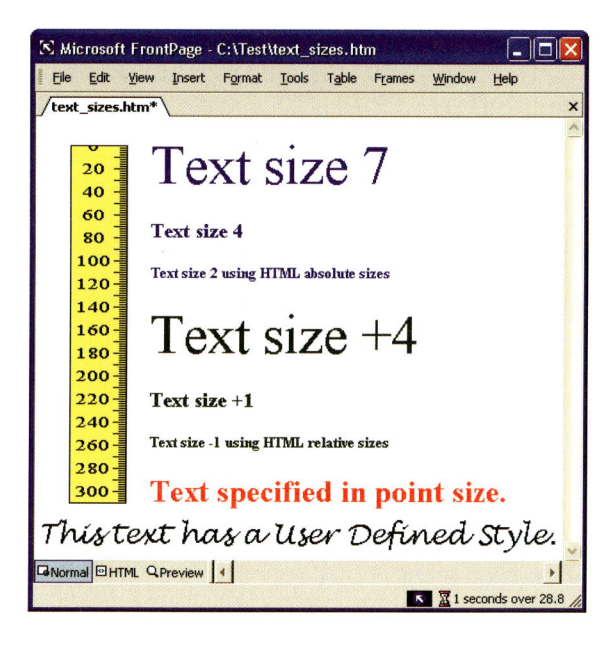

Don't Forget: You can enter the relative values -2 to +4 directly into the HTML, if you wish. FrontPage also allows you to specify text directly in point sizes. However, such text will not be affected when you adjust text sizes in Internet Explorer (see page 262).

```
<p><font size="+4">Text size +4</font></p>
<p><b><font size="+1">Text size +1</font></b></p>
<p><font size="-1"><b>Text size -1 using HTML relative sizes</b></font></p>
<p><font style="font-size: 20pt; font-weight: 700">Text specified in point size.</font></p>
```

10-16. CLAIT Plus Solutions | 261

...cont'd

Hot Tip: *The way your web pages display will depend on which particular browser your site visitors are using so you should make yourself aware of the differences between the main selections.*

Text size in browser

When you preview your page in your browser, the appropriate point size for the HTML size you've chosen will be used.

In the Internet Explorer browser, you can override the default HTML sizes.

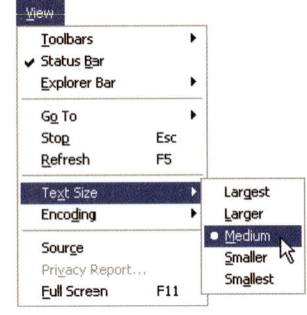

1. Select View, Text Size and choose a different option than Medium.

The text will be enlarged or reduced accordingly. This will not affect text where the size has been specified directly in points, or where the text has a user-defined style.

With the Netscape Navigator browser, the text size options operate differently.

Hot Tip: *When the viewer changes the text size, there will be no change in image sizes or on text displayed as an image (WordArt for example). However, the change in text size could have a significant impact on the page layout.*

2. Select View, Text Zoom, and choose a higher or lower percentage value.

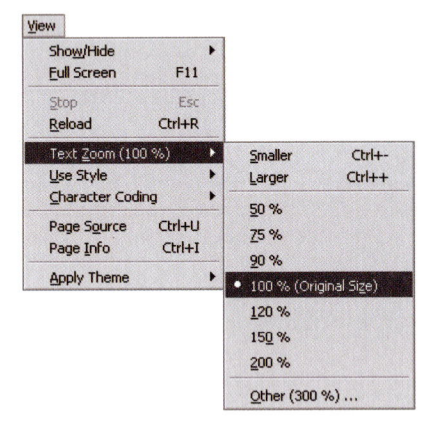

The change will apply to all text, whether defined as HTML sizes, specified in points, or set in a user defined style.

Evidence

You will be required to complete the checklist identifying where and how the assessment objectives for Web Page Solutions have been met. You must submit the following printouts:

- A printout of each web page from the browser with filename clearly visible in header/footer

- A printout of the HTML codes for each web page with filename clearly visible in header/footer

Don't Forget: *Each printout should be annotated to show where assessment objectives have been met. The HTML coding should also be annotated to show where assessment objectives have been met.*

262 | CLAIT Plus in easy steps

Microsoft Office Specialist

This section discusses the units based on exams from the Microsoft Office Specialist (MOS) Core certification, identifying the key differences between these on-line assessed units and the centre assessed CLAIT Plus units.

Covers

OCR and Microsoft certification | 264

Word Processing | 266

Spreadsheets | 269

Databases | 272

Presentation Graphics | 274

Electronic Communications | 275

Exam practice | 276

Units Seventeen to Twenty One

OCR and Microsoft certification

In addition to the nine standard units and the seven solutions units, OCR has provided for five optional units which will be presented and marked on-line. These units are part of the Microsoft Office Specialist (MOS) certification, and they cover the following areas:

- **Word Processing**
- **Spreadsheets**
- **Databases**
- **Presentation Graphics**
- **Electronic Communications**

OCR includes on-line tests for the other levels in the CLAIT suite. New CLAIT has three units from Internet and Computing Core Certification (IC³), while CLAIT Advanced has two MOS Expert units.

You may choose up to three MOS units, but the CLAIT Plus qualification cannot be achieved solely through MOS units. You must also complete the mandatory Unit One. However, for each MOS unit you achieve, you gain Microsoft certification as well as completing part of the requirement for CLAIT Plus.

MOS certification:

Microsoft revised the name of its Microsoft Office Specialist (MOS) certification program, which was formerly known as the Microsoft Office User Specialist (MOUS) program. Some web sites may still include references to MOUS.

The Microsoft Office Specialist programme treats the Office XP suite and the Office 2000 suite separately. Exams passed for one cannot be used towards MOS certification on the other.

There are three levels of certification for the Microsoft Office Specialist qualification. The requirements for these are:

Core: Complete one of the five tests at Core level (the CLAIT Plus MOS units). This will show that you have a comprehensive understanding of a specific Microsoft Office XP or 2000 application.

Microsoft Office 97 certifications are still valid, although they do not count towards CLAIT Plus, and holders are being encouraged to update their certification to Office XP.

Expert: Complete one of the tests at Expert level (the CLAIT Advanced MOS units). This will show that you have a comprehensive understanding of a specific Microsoft Office XP or 2000 application and its many advanced features.

Master: Complete all five of the required tests, including two at Expert level. This will show that you have a comprehensive understanding of Microsoft Office XP or 2000 and many of its advanced features.

...cont'd

MOS Master Instructor (MMI)
IT tutors who have achieved the MOS Master certification, and have the instructional experience required, may apply for certification as a Microsoft Office Specialist Master Instructor for one or other Office suite.

MOS support materials
Centres offering the Microsoft Office Specialist units as part of CLAIT Plus/CLAIT Advanced must use OCR/Microsoft Approved learning support materials and courseware for the delivery of these units. The OCR endorsed publisher for these materials in the UK is IT Services-Feda.

The MOS Exams
The MOS exams are not written exams, but are performance-based, and conducted within a "live" Microsoft Office program. Using the actual program, you will be asked to perform a series of tasks to clearly demonstrate your skills in the application.

There is a pre-exam tutorial, and the exam itself takes about an hour. It uses the actual application software (Office XP or Office 2000 versions). The instructions for each question appear in a separate panel at the bottom of the screen. The question may involve several tasks, each being marked individually. Accidental keystrokes or mouse clicks won't be penalised, as long as you get the correct result in the end.

You can use any method that gives the right result, unless you are instructed to use a particular method. Leave your answer visible on the screen, clear highlighting (unless it's part of the answer) and close toolbars and menus. Make sure you've completed all the tasks and actually entered all the data required, before moving on to the next question. If necessary, you can choose to start the current question over again. However, once you click Next, you won't be able to go back to review previous questions. The test software saves your answers as you complete each question, so if a problem with Windows does arise, the test can be restarted at the point where you left off.

When you've finished all the questions, you will see your score immediately, so you'll know if you were successful.

You used to be able to access Office Help during MOS exams. This facility was discontinued in August 2002, "to ensure a more level playing field for well-prepared examinees."

See page 276 for information on practice examinations. See page 282 for other sources of information.

Word Processing

> **Hot Tip:** *Review the contents of Unit One, Create, Manage and Integrate Files as preparation for this unit, and use the exercises for that unit as practice material.*

Unit Seventeen overview

This unit develops and assesses your skills in using word processing software. It is based on the Word application and covers areas such as:

- Inserting and modifying text
- Creating and modifying paragraphs
- Formatting documents
- Managing documents
- Working with graphics
- Workgroup collaboration

This is the only unit in the Level Two CLAIT Plus that is explicitly Word Processing. However, this unit does include some of the objectives and knowledge requirements from Unit One, Create, Manage and Integrate Files, and it builds on the objectives of the Level One New CLAIT Unit Two, Word Processing.

Paste special

1. Copy text to the Clipboard, then position the typing cursor in your document and select Edit, Paste Special.

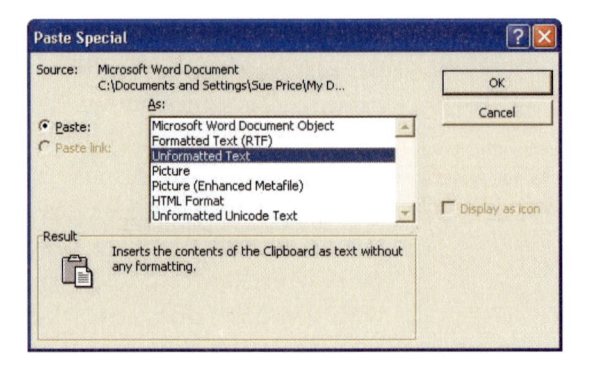

> **Hot Tip:** *Click Paste Link if you want to insert a link to the original source of the text, so that your document gets updated automatically whenever the original text changes.*

2. Choose the type of information you are copying from the clipboard, or choose Unformatted Text to strip off formatting.

...cont'd

> **Hot Tip:** Use Autocorrect to replace any typing errors that you might commonly make. For example, you could replace Teh by The.

Autocorrect

1. Select Tools, and the Autocorrect Options, type an abbreviation, and enter the text to replace it. For example, replace SGC by Surprise Garden Centres.

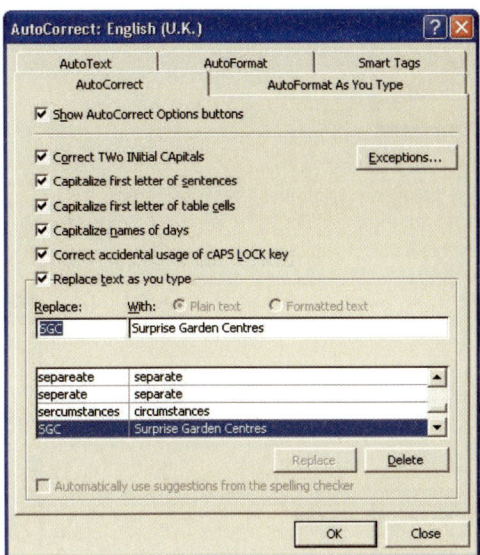

> **Hot Tip:** AutoComplete is another way to save typing. It suggests the complete word or phrase when you type the first four letters of certain items, such as dates or AutoText names. When the suggestion appears, press Enter or F3 to accept the suggestion, or just keep typing to reject it.

2. Hover over the replacement text to display the change indicator and the Smart Tag. Click the down arrow if you want to cancel the auto correction on this particular occasion.

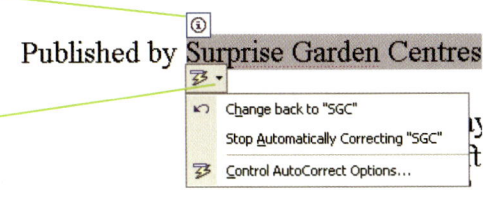

> **Hot Tip:** See page 39 for details of Widow and Orphan control.

Controlling Line and Page breaks

Page breaks occur automatically when the page is full. To keep two paragraphs together:

> **Beware:** Keep with next does not prevent a table being split over pages. You would manually have to manipulate the document (inserting page breaks or changing margins) to prevent splitting the table. If you select Table Properties, and the Row tab, you can prevent a row breaking across pages.

1. Select the paragraphs first. Then choose Format, Paragraph and the Line and Page Breaks tab. Tick the 'Keep with next' box. Use a similar approach to use 'Keep lines together'. Note the option to prevent hyphenation.

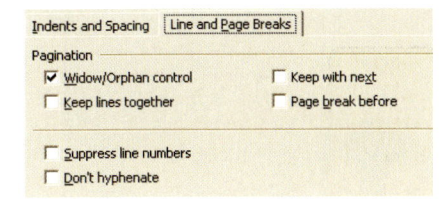

17-21. Microsoft Office Specialist | 267

...cont'd

You can add borders to pages, text, tables and table cells, graphic objects, pictures, and web frames. You can shade paragraphs and text. You can apply coloured or textured fills to your graphic objects.

Borders and shading

Select the picture, table or text, choose Format, Borders and Shading. Select the Borders tab and pick the border and line style to apply to the selected item or text.

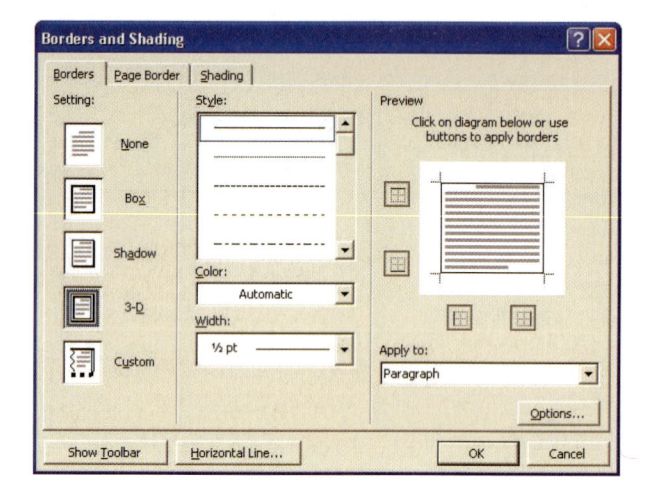

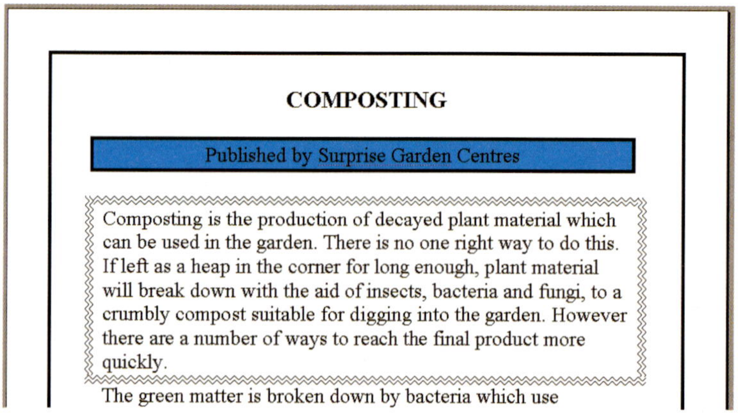

Select the Page Borders tab to apply a border style to the whole page. Select Shading to specify a shading colour.

You'll find details of practice exams on page 276.

Assessment

You will be assessed using the Core level of the Microsoft Office Specialist examination for Word, which is an on-line practical test using Microsoft Word 2000 or 2002.

Spreadsheets

Review the contents of Unit Two, Spreadsheets as preparation for this unit, and use the exercises for that unit as practice material.

Unit Eighteen overview

This unit measures your skills in using Spreadsheet software. It includes the objectives and knowledge requirements from Unit Two, Spreadsheets, but incorporates additional objectives and knowledge requirements based on the Excel application.

Freeze panes

Freezing panes allows you to select data that remains visible when scrolling in a sheet, for example, row and column labels.

1. To freeze both the upper and left panes, click the cell below and to the right of where you want the split to appear.

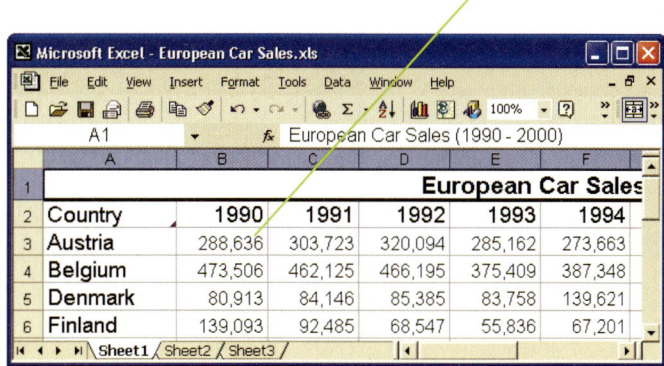

To freeze the top horizontal pane, select the row below where you want the split to appear. To freeze the left vertical pane, select the column to the right of where you want the split to appear.

2. Select Window, Freeze Panes. The lines indicate fixed sections. Scroll vertically or horizontally to see the effects.

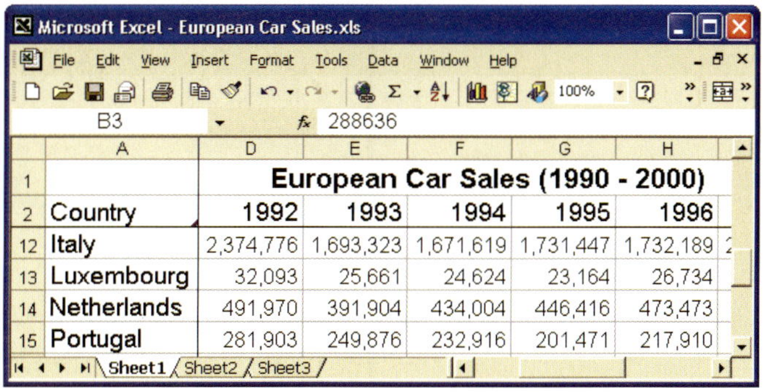

To cancel the effect, select Windows, Unfreeze Panes. There's no need to select any particular cell.

17-21. Microsoft Office Specialist | 269

...cont'd

> You are able to apply filters to only one list on a worksheet at a time.

Filter data

1. Click in the data list you want to filter. Select Data, Filter, AutoFilter.

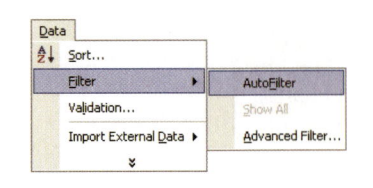

2. To filter the data for values greater than a specified value, click the arrow in the column with the values and choose Custom.

> Excel allows you to filter data lists, selecting for example the smallest or largest value, or a specific value, using wildcards if required:
> ?   Any single character
> *   Any number of characters
> ~   In front of a wildcard code (e.g. ~* to search for *)

> Only the first 1000 unique entries in a list appear when you click the arrow.

> To add another criteria, click And or Or, and repeat the previous step. Click OK to filter the data.

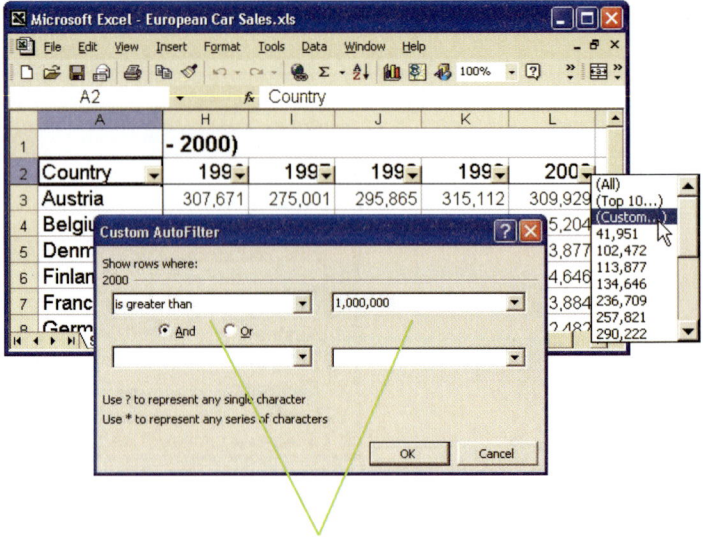

3. On the left, choose one of the criteria, for example Is Greater Than. On the right, enter the value to compare against.

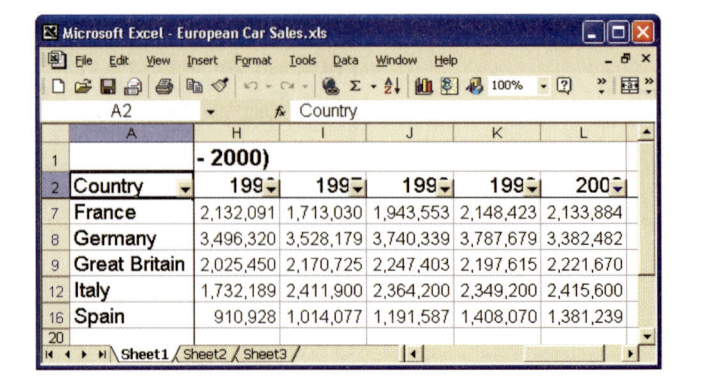

...cont'd

Although it's possible in Excel 2002 to select non-adjacent blocks of data using the Ctrl key, this method does not allow you to generate a consolidated print of the selected data.

Non-adjacent selections

You may be required to print part of a spreadsheet, e.g. showing the data for years 1990 and 2000 only (excluding 1991 to 1999).

1. Highlight the columns that you want to exclude from printing.

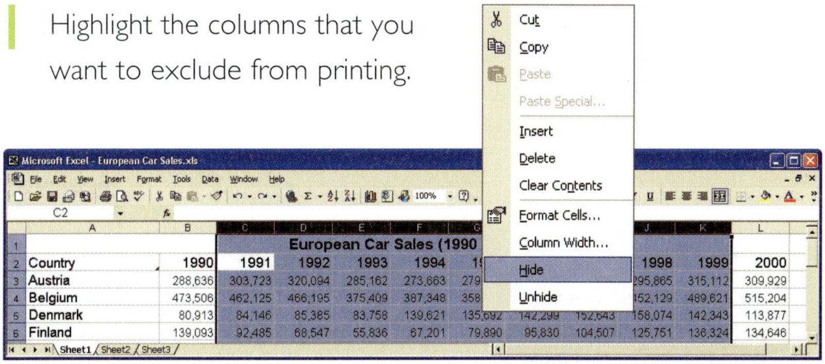

To reveal the columns again, highlight the columns on either side, right click the selection and click Unhide.

2. Right click the selected columns and click Hide.

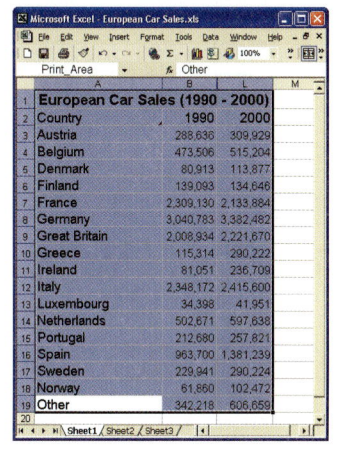

You may need to adjust column widths to ensure that all data and headings display in full.

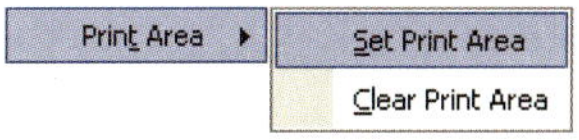

3. Highlight the remaining visible data and then select File, Print Area, Set Print Area.

You will first have to select Clear Print Area to print a different range.

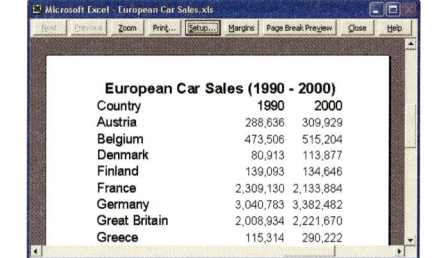

4. Select File, Print Preview to see the effect, or select File, Print to print the required information.

Assessment

You will be assessed using the Core level of the Microsoft Office Specialist examination for Excel, which is an on-line practical test using Microsoft Excel 2000 or 2002.

Databases

> **HOT TIP:** *Review the contents of Unit Three, Databases as preparation for this unit, using its exercises as practice.*

Unit Nineteen overview:

This unit measures your skills in using Database software. It includes the objectives and knowledge requirements from Unit Three, Databases, as well as further objectives and knowledge areas. It is based on the Access application.

Check for duplicates

Use the Find Duplicates Query wizard to see if there are duplicate records in your project database.

1. Open the database, click Queries in the Object bar, and click New.

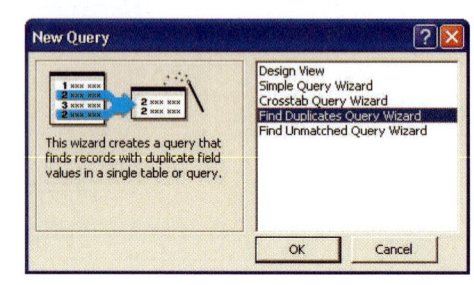

2. Click Find Duplicates Query Wizard, then OK.

> **DON'T FORGET:** *If you don't choose to show extra fields, results will just count the number of records with particular values for the duplicates fields specified.*

3. Following the wizard prompts, select the fields that may contain duplicates, then select other fields to show in addition. Be sure to include the unique identification field.

4. Name the query and click Finish, and the wizard will list all the records that contain duplicated plant names.

> **HOT TIP:** *For example, using the Plant database from Unit Three, Databases, search for duplicate Plant names, and specify ID, Type, Colour and Season as extra fields.*

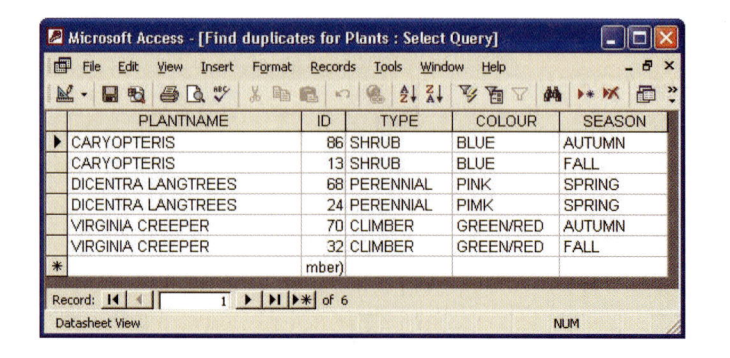

272 | CLAIT Plus in easy steps

...cont'd

Any changes you make to selected fields are applied immediately to the records in the table. If you delete a duplicate, the matching record is removed.

5 Using the extra fields, decide if the records are duplicated. They do not need to be identical – there could be a minor difference between entries, eg putting Fall instead of Autumn, or having a spelling error in one of the copies.

Show relationships

When you have more than one table in your database, you may have relationships between the tables. To view the current relationships:

1 Press F11 to switch to the Database window and click Relationships on the toolbar, or select Tools, Relationships from the menu bar. (If the Relationships entry is greyed, the Relationships window is already open).

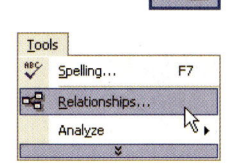

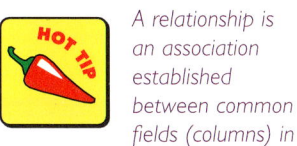

A relationship is an association established between common fields (columns) in two tables. It may be one-to-one, one-to-many, or many-to-many.

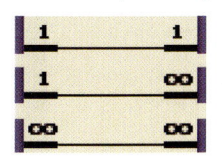

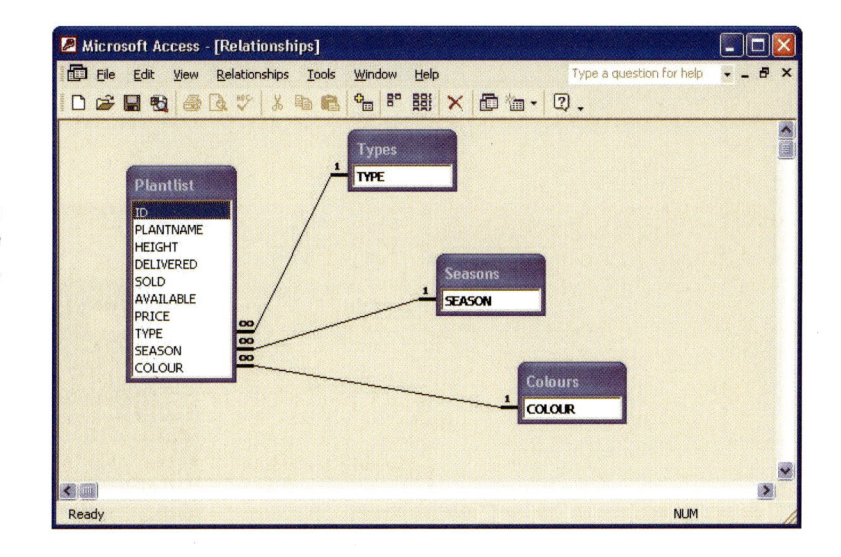

Assessment

You will be assessed using the Core level of the Microsoft Office Specialist examination for Access, which is an on-line practical test using Microsoft Access 2000 or 2002.

Presentation Graphics

Review the contents of Unit Five, Presentation Graphics as preparation for this unit, and use the exercises from that unit as practice material.

Unit Twenty overview:

This unit measures your skills in using Presentation Graphics software. It includes and extends the objectives and knowledge requirements from Unit Five, Presentation Graphics, and is based on the PowerPoint application.

Presentation file formats

PowerPoint slides and presentations can be saved in a number of different formats:

.ppt	Presentation, in normal PowerPoint format
.wmf	Slides, as Windows Metafile graphic
.gif	Slides, as web page graphic
.jpg	Slides, as web page image
.rtf	Presentation, as an outline document
.pot	Presentation, as a design template
.pps	Presentation, as a slide show
.htm	Presentation, as a web page with a files folder
.mht	Presentation, as a single web page including all files

When you save a presentation using one of the image file types, PowerPoint offers to save the current slide only, or to save all the slides as separate files in an image folder, naming them Slide1, Slide2 etc.

1. Select File, Save as Web Page to create an .htm file plus a folder of all the component files. Select File, Save As and choose file type Web Archive, to save everything within the single .mht file.

PowerPoint will supply a default file name and web page title, which you can amend while saving the presentation.

2. Click the links to view the slide show. The transitions and slide animation effects won't be transferred to the web page.

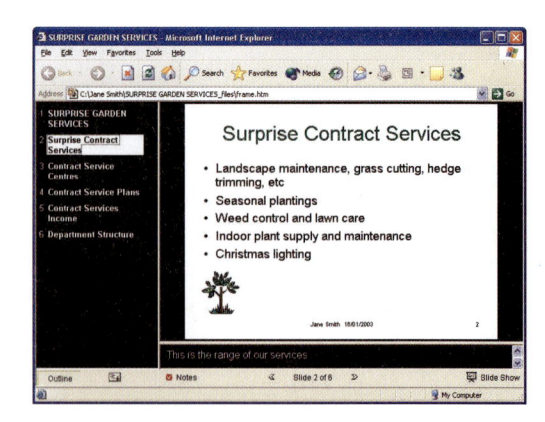

Select File, Web Page Preview, to view your presentation in your browser without having to save it.

Assessment

You will be assessed using the Comprehensive level of the Microsoft Office Specialist examination for PowerPoint, which is an on-line practical test using Microsoft PowerPoint 2000 or 2002.

Electronic Communications

Review the contents of Unit Eight, Electronic Communications as preparation for this unit, and use the exercises for that unit as practice material.

Unit Twenty One overview:

This unit is intended to assess your skills in using e-mail, calendar/scheduling and contact management software. It includes the objectives and knowledge requirements from Unit Eight, Electronic Communications, along with additional areas of knowledge, and it is based on the Outlook application.

Schedule meetings and invite attendees

1. Select Calendar, navigate to the date for the meeting you wish to schedule, and double click the day.

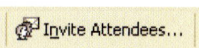

2. Enter details such as Subject, Location, Description, Start time and duration and click Invite Attendees.

Select a Category for the meeting, to help in searching for related messages, notes, contacts and tasks.

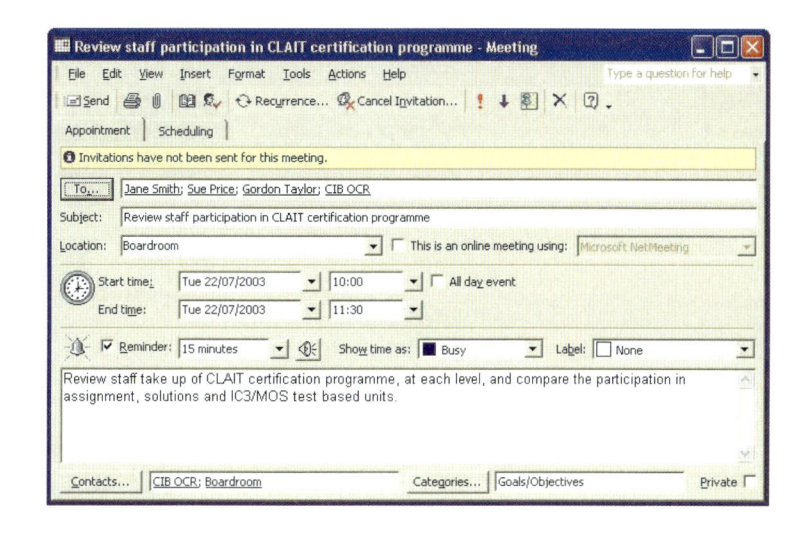

Click Scheduling to find whether the attendees are available at the proposed time. This requires attendees to subscribe to a service such as the Microsoft Office Internet Free/Busy Service.

3. Click To, and select contacts from your address book who are required or optional attendees. You may also schedule resources.

Assessment

You will be assessed using the Core level of the Microsoft Office Specialist examination for Outlook, which is an on-line practical test using Microsoft Outlook 2000 or 2002.

Exam practice

To help decide if the MOS approach will suit you, try one of the sample or demo exams. These are available from a number of Microsoft approved sources, including the following:

Certiport Inc

> **HOT TIP**
> *Each sample test presents three exam questions, or work scenarios, each of which contains three specific tasks. With these demos, only the menu (top bar) commands are functional (i.e. toolbars, shortcuts, or keyboard commands may not be used).*

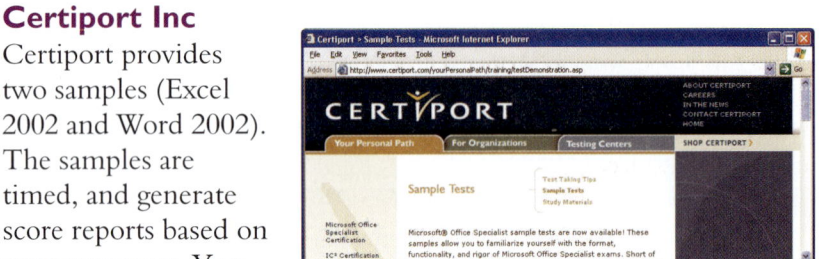

Certiport provides two samples (Excel 2002 and Word 2002). The samples are timed, and generate score reports based on your responses. You need the Macromedia Shockwave Player web browser plug-in to view the sample tests. For details see:

http://www.certiport.com/yourPersonalPath/training/

CCS Ltd

> **HOT TIP**
> *Testing Centres may buy a T-Prep Site licence, which allows unlimited numbers of users and unlimited attempts for that centre's use of the T-Prep product.*

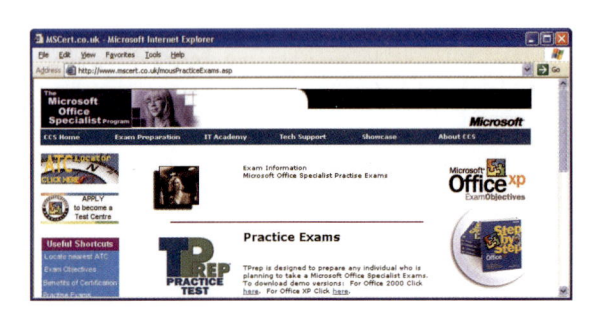

CCS make demo Office 2000 and Office XP versions of their T-Prep practice exams, which simulate the MOS exam environment. The tests may be downloaded from their web site at:

http://www.mscert.co.uk/mousPracticeExams.asp

MeasureUp

> **HOT TIP**
> *To create an account, you just provide some basic details (user name, password, name, job tile and e-mail address).*

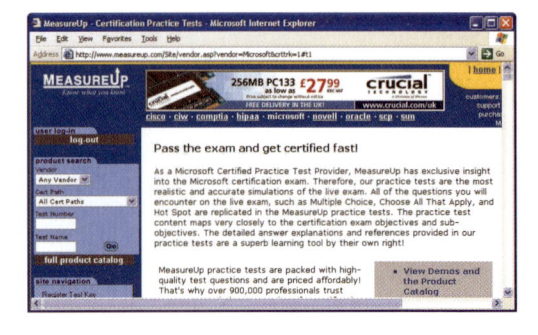

A Microsoft certified practice test provider, MeasureUp offer demo versions of their Office 2000 and Office XP MOS practice tests at their web site, if you register for a free test package account at:

http://www.measureup.com/Site/

Support Material

This section discusses how you might choose which units to include in your qualification, and provides information about support material available from Computer Step and other web sites, including the downloadable exercises and other information sources.

Covers

Selecting units | 278

Practice e-mail | 280

Downloadable exercises | 281

Information sources | 282

Appendix

Selecting units

If you achieve 4 units, including the core unit, you are awarded the CLAIT Plus certificate. Any of the individual units may be achieved separately, and you will receive a Certificate of Unit Achievement. This allows you to broaden your IT user skills, and to satisfy some of the requirements for NVQ qualifications.

You are required to take Unit One: Create, Manage and Integrate Files, but the other twenty units are optional. You could select all your units from one type, or choose mix of Assignment, Solutions and MOS Test units. The only constraint is that you cannot include more than one unit in the same application area as part of the qualification set. The table below shows which units OCR consider to overlap. You should select only one unit from any of the rows, to count towards your CLAIT Plus certification.

Application Area	Assignment	Solutions	MOS Test
Create, Manage, Integrate	1 ★	-	-
Word Processing	-	-	17
Spreadsheets	2	10	18
Database	3	11	19
Desktop Publishing	4	12	-
Presentation Graphics	5	13	20
Computer Art	6	-	-
Digital Imaging	-	14	-
Web Animation	-	15	-
Web Page	7	16	-
Electronic Communications	8	-	21
Graphs and Charts	9	-	-

★ Mandatory Unit

For example, if you want to include Spreadsheets in your qualification, but have only a limited amount of experience with Excel, you might choose Unit Two: Spreadsheets for a more guided learning experience.

Assignment unit

Choose an assignment unit if you are happy working under direction, and where your experience of the application area is limited. You will be able to practice your skills using build up exercises or complete practice assignments such as those included at the In Easy Steps web site (see page 281).

Solutions unit

You could choose Unit Thirteen: Presentation Graphics Solutions, if you have a particular interest in a topic, whether it is a business area such as product marketing, or a personal interest area such as Genealogy.

Choose a solutions unit where you have particular experience of the application area and the subject matter of your chosen project, and where you enjoy the relative freedom of selecting your own ways of satisfying the unit objectives.

You may define your own project scenario, or be provided with an outline by your tutor. In either case, you will provide your own data and action list, using the appropriate evidence checklist to ensure that you meet the unit objectives.

...cont'd

> **HOT TIP**
>
> *This illustrates the evidence checklist for Unit Ten: Spreadsheet Solutions. There are similar checklists available for the other six Solutions units. You must complete a checklist to submit with your project. They provide an excellent way of ensuring you meet the requirements and of assessing the suitability of potential projects.*

EVIDENCE CHECKLIST FOR SPREADSHEET SOLUTIONS UNIT

Candidate Name: Centre Number:

Ensure the following are included as a minimum
Complete boxes with a tick ✓ or required information.

Number of Cells used (must be more than 200)						
Page Orientation	portrait		landscape			
Specify Margins	top		bottom	left		right
Two automatic fields used in headers and footers	filename		page number	date		
Three different cell formats	integer	currency	percentage	fraction	date	time	other
Three of the following cell references in a formula	relative	mixed	absolute	named cell		
Text and number	text	number				
Two mathematical operators	+	-	*	/	indices	
Two range functions	sum	average	max	min	count	other
One logical operator	'IF'	other				
Cell reference of linked spreadsheet						
Four different display features	font	font size	sheet borders	cell borders	italic	bold	others
Two different alignment formats (horizontal/vertical)	wraparound	centre	left	right	bottom	centre across cells	other
Column (A,B,C) /row (1,2,3) headers displayed				Cells merged		
Sort included						
Two changes to data	change 1		change 2			
Printout showing all data in full			Printout(s) with changes highlighted			
Printout showing all formulae in full			Printout of spreadsheet the main spreadsheet is linked to			

Date of completion .... Candidate's signature ....

Microsoft Office Specialist units

These are ideal if you are experienced in using the application, and are comfortable working under time constraints and strict exam conditions.

Availability of courses

> **DON'T FORGET**
>
> *Individual training centres may be restricted by the types of software or hardware components that they have available, or may not have tutors available to cover the more specialised topics.*

You must check that your training centre offers the combination that you would like to follow. Some centres are offering Assignment units only, and even then may list a subset of those units. If the Solutions route is supported, the application areas that are offered may also be restricted, or it may not support the specific software that you need. Centres that offer MOS units may restrict the units for which tuition is available.

Practice e-mail

Exercises for Unit Eight: Electronic Communications require the prepared e-mail message which will normally be sent to you by your tutor. The exercises will also specify the e-mail address from which this message will be sent, and a number of e-mail addresses that may be used during the exercise, to use as targets for sends, copies or forwards. OCR exercises often use addresses related to the made-up company Progress Media and the mail server address progress-media.co.uk.

For the exercise in this book, you will request the initial e-mail message from the author-related web site, by visiting the web page at http://claitplus.prient.co.uk. Enter your e-mail address in the e-mail message box and click Submit.

This web page also offers a link to the In Easy Steps download page.

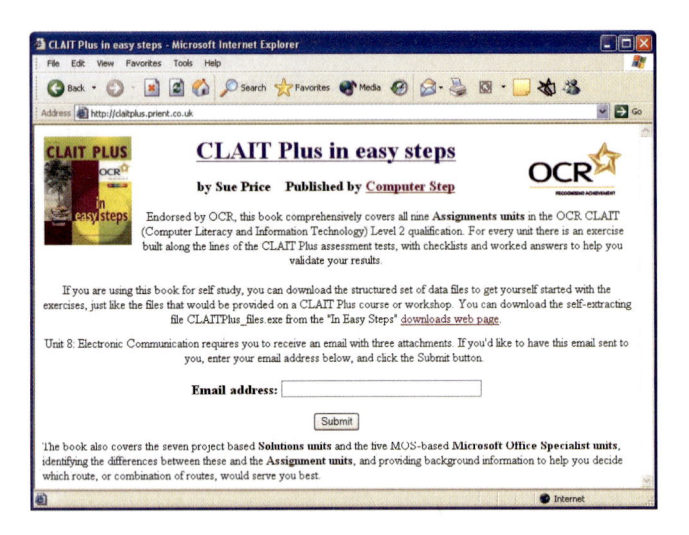

During the example exercise provided in this book, you will be asked to send messages to a specified e-mail address, and when you send the messages, you will receive an acknowledgement from the web site, but no other action will be taken.

In Unit Seven: Web Pages, the exercise will require a form to be completed, and the data sent for processing. OCR provide an e-mail address for you to specify in this form, since this unit will be electronically assessed. No such e-mail is required for the exercise in this book, and you may use your own e-mail address to receive the response from the web site.

Downloadable exercises

For the nine Assignment units, there are complete OCR-style assessment exercises. You'll need an instruction document and a number of data files for each. On a CLAIT Plus course, these would be provided by your tutor. If you are using this book for self study, you can download a full set of the files required, at:
http://www.ineasysteps.com/books/downloads/

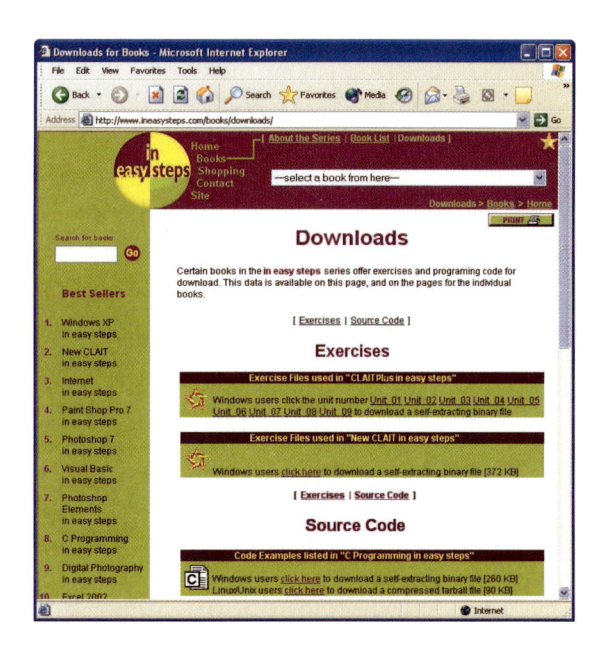

There will be a data folder for each of the nine exercises, each containing the required documents, data files and worked copy folder.

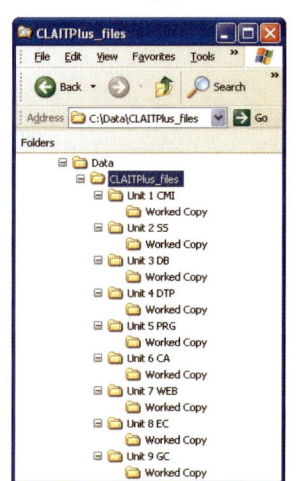

1. Click the Unit number to download the self extracting file for each exercise that you require, e.g. Unit 01 for Unit One.

2. Double click the executable file for the Unit, to start the extract program.

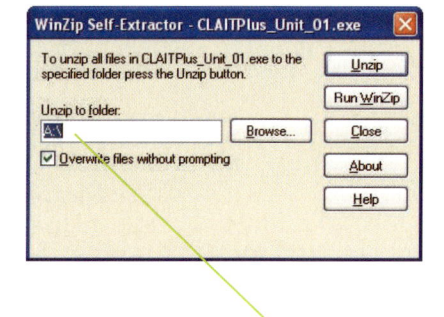

3. The files are within folders in \CLAITPlus_files. By default, this will be created in A:\, but you can specify any drive letter or folder name.

Appendix. Support Material | 281

Information sources

OCR
http://www.newclait.org.uk
OCR is one of the UK awarding bodies, and supports NQF (National Qualification Framework) certifications, including the OCR CLAIT Suite.

Microsoft Training & Certification
http://www.microsoft.com/traincert/default.asp
http://www.microsoft.com/uk/skills/default.asp
These are the USA and UK web sites through which you can access details of Microsoft certifications, including the MOS (Microsoft Office Specialist), the MMI (Microsoft Master Instructor), the MCP (Microsoft Certified Professional), and the MCT (Microsoft Certified Trainer) certifications.

Certiport, Inc
http://www.certiport.com
Certiport is the administrator of the Microsoft Office Specialist program worldwide, responsible for the development, marketing, and administration of certification tests for the Microsoft Office suite. In addition, Certiport offers World Organization of Webmasters (WOW) exams, and the Internet and Computing Core Certification (IC^3) which has been included in New CLAIT.

See page 276 for details of the free sample tests, demo exams and practice tests that organisations such as these make available.

Certified Computer Solutions Ltd (CCS)
http://www.mscert.co.uk
CCS are the UK Master Distributors for Microsoft Office Specialist. Visit the web site to find approved MOS testing centres.

ITS-Feda Ltd
http://www.itservices.org.uk
ITS-Feda is the OCR endorsed publisher for CLAIT Plus and CLAIT Advanced MOS courseware.

MeasureUp
http://www.measureup.com/site/
MeasureUp sells practice tests for many certification programmes, including MOS Access, Excel, PowerPoint and Word, Office 2000 and Office XP.

Index

A

Absolute references   48
Access   10, 70, 245, 272
Active link   180
Alignment   47, 103
Analyze wizard   245
Animation   138, 165, 256, 258
Animation Shop   149, 168
Appointments   208, 275
Assignment Units   10–11, 278
   Computer Art   147–170
   Create, Manage and Integrate files   9–42
   Databases   69–94
   Desktop Publishing   95–122
   Electronic Communications   197–222
   Graphs and Charts   223–240
   Presentation Graphics   123–146
   Spreadsheets   43–68
   Web Pages   171–196
Attachments   214, 217
Autocorrect   267
Autonumber   75
AutoSum   55
Availability of courses   279
Average   56

B

Background colour   128, 152, 180
Bar/column   230
Bleed marks   119
Borders and shading   62, 268
Browsers   176
Bullets and numbering   33, 126, 129

C

Calculated field   84
Calendar   206
Cell references   44, 48
Certification support
   CCS Ltd   276, 282
   Certiport Inc   276, 282
Charts.   *See* Graphs and Charts
CLAIT Advanced   11
CLAIT Plus certificate   278
CLAIT Plus Units   10
CLAIT Suite   10
Colour separated prints   120
Columns   46
Comma separator   79
Composite print   120
Computer Art   147–170
   Animation   165
   Animation frames   167
   Art work   151
   Canvas   152
   Checklist   170
   Colouring tools   156
   Deformation   161
   Exercise   148
   Insert images   153
   Layer Palette   155
   Layers   154
   Marking   170
   Overview   148
   Print   163
   Red Eye effects   158
   Retouch   156
   Run animations   169
   Screen print   169
   Selection   158
   Selection tools   151
   Shapes   160
   Text   159
   Text effects   162
   WordArt   162
Contacts   202
Copyfit   118
Count functions   59
Create, Manage and Integrate Files   9–42
   Bullets and numbering   33
   Checklist   42
   Document management   41
   Folder commands   17
   Footers   25
   Headers   25
   Identify files   18
   Insert a chart   35
   Insert an image   34
   Insert data file   36
   Insert symbol   37
   Locate files   22

Manage files   20
Marking   42
Overview   12
Print folder contents   23
Styles   38
Tabs   32
Templates   40
View folders   14
Criteria   82
Crop marks   119
CSV files   45

D

Data types   72, 76, 80
Databases   69–94
   Amend design   76
   Autoform   85
   Calculated field   84
   Checklist   94
   Comma separator   79
   Create database   71
   Create labels   86
   Create table   73
   Criteria   82
   Data types   72, 76, 80
   Error messages   81
   Evidence   247
   Excel facilities   60
   Exercises   70
   Field names   72
   Forms   85
   Import data   77
   Import Text wizard   78
   Marking   94
   MOS   272–273
   Overview   70
   Primary keys   80
   Queries   82
      And, Or, Not   82
      Range operators   83
      Wild cards   83
   Report controls   92
      Headers and footers   92
      Insert text   92
      Sorting and grouping   93
   Report design   90
   Reports   88
      summary   88
   Save table   75
   Show relationships   273
   Solutions   245–247
   Table design   72
Demo exams   276, 282

Desktop Publishing   95–122
   Alignment   103
   Checklist   122
   Colour separated prints   120
   Composite print   120
   Copyfit   118
   Create styles   102
      Save, apply and modify   105
   Crop marks   119
   Dropped capitals   114
   Font size   103–104
   Gutters   99
   Headers and Footers   100
   Hyphenation   114
   Images   116
   Layering   117
   Line spacing   104
   Link text boxes   110
   Margins   99
   Marking   122
   Master page   100
   Multipage layout   109
   Page numbering   101
   Paper layout   98
   Position text boxes   108
   Print   119
   Reverse text   114
   Solutions   248–250
   Spot colours   121
   Tables   115
   Template   106
   Text box options   112
   Text frame   107
   Useful terms   97
Digital Imaging   10, 253
   Evidence   255
   Overview   253
   Requirements   253
   Transferring images   255
   Using a digital camera   255
   Using a scanner   254
Distribution lists   204
Document editing   12–13, 28
Document management   12, 41, 63
   Headers and Footers   64
   Margins   63
   Orientation   63
Documentation   13
Download files   177, 281
Dreamweaver   261
Dropped capitals   114

E

E-mail   210, 280
Editing symbols   28
Electronic Communications   197–222
   Appointments   208
   Calendar   206
   Checklist   222
   Contacts   202
   Distribution lists   204
   E-mail   210
   E-mail Attachments   214
   E-mail Rules   212
   E-mail signature   216
   Exercise   198
   Folder List   201
   Invite attendees   275
   Marking   222
   MOS   275
   Notes and reminders   219
   Outlook window   200
   Overview   198
   Print   220
      Calendar   220
      Contacts   221
      E-mail   220
      Folder list   221
      Tasks and Notes   221
   Recurring appointments   209
   Schedule meetings   275
   Tasks   218
Evidence checklists   279
Exam practice   276
Excel   10, 36, 61, 224, 243, 269
Exercises   13
   Downloading   280–281
   Expanding files   281

F

Field   72
File formats   12, 18, 274
File management   12, 20
Filter data   270
Fit to page   67
Flash animation   258
Flash player   257
Folders   14
Font size   103

Forms   85, 192
Formula   52
Freeze panes   269
FrontPage   176, 261
Functions   54

G

GIF Animator   150
Graphs and Charts   223–240
   Bar/column chart   230
   Chart elements   228
   Chart toolbar   229
   Chart wizard   226
   Checklist   240
   Custom charts   225
   Exercise   224
   Exploded pie   235
   Format axes   231
   House Style   229
   Marking   240
   Overview   224
   Print   239
   Stacked vertical bar   232
   Standard charts   225
   Trend line   234
   XY scatter   233
Grid lines   31
Gutters   99

H

Headers and footers   25, 64, 92, 100
Hexadecimal   181
Hide columns or rows   66, 271
Hide slides   131
House style   13, 35–36, 42
HTML   173–174
Hyperlinks   132, 195
Hyphenation   114

I

IC³   282
If function   58

Index | 285

Image Ready   150
Images   116
Import data   78
Import files   179
Insert chart   35
Insert data file   36
Insert image   34, 153, 184, 190
Insert symbol   37, 186
Integration   12
Internet Explorer   262
IT Services   282
ITS-Feda Ltd   282

N

Named references   49
Navigation table   183
Netscape Navigator   262
New CLAIT   10
Notes   219

L

Labels   86
Layers   117, 155
Line breaks   267
Line spacing   104
Linked references   50
Linked text boxes   110
LiveMotion   257
Logic operators   82

O

OCR   264, 282
Office 2000   265, 276
Office XP   13, 265, 276
Organisation chart   136
Outline   125, 130
Outlook   10, 199, 275
Outlook Express   199

M

Macromedia Flash   257
Magic Wand   158
Margins   63, 99
Marking   42, 68, 94, 122, 146, 170, 196, 222, 240
MeasureUp   276, 282
Merge and Centre   47
Meta tags   175, 182
Microsoft   264
Microsoft Office Specialist. *See* MOS & MOS Units
Microsoft Training & Certification   282
Mixed references   48
MOS   10-11, 263, 278–279, 282
MOS certification   264
MOS Exams   265
MOS Master Instructor   265
MOS Units   263–276
   Databases   272
   Electronic Communications   275
   Presentation Graphics   274
   Spreadsheets   269
   Word Processing   266

P

Page breaks   41, 267
Page numbers   27, 101
Page orientation   41, 63
Paint Shop Pro   149, 253
Paste Special   266
Percentages   53
Personal Information Management   199
PhotoDraw   150
Photoshop   150
Photoshop Elements   150
Plain text file   45
PowerPoint   10, 124, 251, 274
Practice e-mail IDS   280
Practice tests   282
Presentation Graphics   123–146
   Bullets   129
   Charts   134
   Checklist   146
   Create hyperlinks   132
   Create slides   129
   Exercise   124
   Hide slides   131
   Link slides   131
   Marking   146
   MOS   274

Organisation chart   136
Organise slides   130
Outline   125, 130
Overview   124
Print   145
Print screen   143
Rehearse timings   140
Slide animation effects   138
Slide Master   126
   Image   128
   Styles   126
   Text   127
Slide Show   141
Slide Sorter   130
Slide transitions   137
Solutions   251–252
Speaker notes   142
Tables   133
Timings   140
Print   12, 66, 119, 145, 220, 239
Print folders   23
Print screen   23, 143, 169
Progress Media   280
Projects   279
Publisher   100

Q

Queries   82

R

Range operators   83
Raster layers   154, 161
Red Eye effects   158
Relationships   273
Relative reference   48, 190
Reminders   219
Report controls   92
Reports   88
Rotate text   112
Rules   212

S

Sample tests   282
Scanner   254
Search   22
Selecting units   278
   Constraints   11, 278
Self extracting   281
Shockwave Player   276
Signature   216
Slide Sorter   130
Software   13
Solutions   278–279
Solutions Units   241–262
   Checklists   242
   Databases   245–247
   Desktop Publishing   248–250
   Digital Imaging   253–255
   Evidence   244
   Presentation Graphics   251–252
   Projects   242
   Spreadsheet   243–244
   Web Animation   256–259
   Web Pages   260–262
Spot colours   121
Spreadsheets   43–68
   Borders and shading   62
   Cell references   44, 48
      Absolute   48
      Linked   50
      Mixed   48
      Named   49
      Relative   48
   Checklist   68
   Columns   46
   Delete range   46
   Document management   63
   Filter data   270
   Fit to page   67
   Formula   52
      Percentages   53
      Simple   52
   Freeze panes   269
   Functions   54
      AutoSum   55
      Average   56
      Count, Counta, Countif   59
      Date   57
      If   58
      Maximum   57
      Minimum   57
      Square root   57
      Wizard   54

Making changes   243
Marking   68
Merge and Centre   47
MOS   269–271
Number format   61
Open   45
Overview   44
Print   66
Print formulae   66
Print headings and gridlines   67
Print selection   66
Rows   46
Save   45
Solutions   243
Sort   60
Text alignment   47
Wrap text   47
Styles   38, 40, 102
Apply   39, 105
Create   38
Modify   105
Support Material   277

T

T-Prep practice exams   276
Tables   29, 73, 115, 133, 191
Column width   30
Create   29
Grid lines   31
Navigation   183
Tabs   32, 133
Tasks   218
Template   40, 106, 180
Text frame   107
Text sizes   185, 261
Text wrap   47, 113, 248
Timings   140, 251
Transitions   137
Trend line   234

V

Vector layers   154
Vectors   159, 257
Visited link   180

W

Web Animation
Evidence   259
Flash animations   258
Layers   258
Overview   256
Requirements   256
Solutions   10
Web form   280
Web Pages   171–196
Checklist   196
Create template   180, 186
Create web folder   178
Download files   177
Exercise   172
Font formats   185
Forms   192
FrontPage   172
HTML   173–174
Hyperlinks   195
Import files   179
Insert image   190
Insert text   188
Marking   196
Meta-variables   175, 182
Navigation   183
Overview   172
Publishing   176
Solutions   260–262
Tables   191
Wild cards   83
Windows Explorer   14
Windows XP   13
Word   13, 37, 266
Word Processing
Assessment   268
Autocorrect   267
Borders and shading   268
Line and Page Breaks   267
MOS   10
Overview   266
Paste special   266
WordArt   162
WOW   282